This book is dedicated to You.

George Tsiattalos

ONE WITH LIFE

Insights to Spiritual Enlightenment

AUSTIN MACAULEY PUBLISHERS™

LONDON * CAMBRIDGE * NEW YORK * SHARJAH

Ordering Information
Quantity sales: Special discounts are available on quantity purchases by corporations, associations, and others. For details, contact the publisher at the address below.

Publisher's Cataloging-in-Publication data
Tsiattalos, George
One with Life
www.onewithlifeinsights.com

ISBN 9781649797759 (Paperback)
ISBN 9781649797766 (Hardback)
ISBN 9781649797773 (ePub e-book)

Library of Congress Control Number: 2021912592

www.austinmacauley.com/us

First Published (2021)
Austin Macauley Publishers LLC
40 Wall Street, 33rd Floor, Suite 3302
New York, NY 10005
USA

mail-usa@austinmacauley.com
+1 (646) 5125767

I am deeply thankful to spiritual teacher Eckhart Tolle for his teachings which helped spark a realization I never thought possible. I named this book after his passage, "There are three words that convey the secret of the art of living, the secret of all success and happiness: One with Life. Being one with life is being one with now." With that said, I thank you, Eckhart.

Table of Contents

Preface

Someone once asked me, "How do you know that the present moment is all we have? Show me proof."

I smiled and responded, "Try to get out of it!"

Introduction

Deep down, you know there is more to who you are than who you think you are. Here and now, silence whispers the truth of who you are. These whispers are this book. There is an old Zen story about a Zen teacher's dog who loved to play fetch with his master. The dog would run ahead to fetch a stick, then run back, wag his tail, and wait for the next game. One evening, the teacher invited one of his brightest students to join him. This boy was troubled by the contradictions in Buddhist doctrine. "You must understand," said the teacher. "That words are only guideposts. Never let the words or symbols get in the way of truth. Here, I'll show you." With that, the teacher called his happy dog. "Fetch me the moon," he said to his dog and pointed to the full moon. "Where is my dog looking?" asked the teacher of the bright pupil.

"He's looking at your finger."

"Exactly. Don't be like my dog. Don't confuse the pointing finger with the thing that is being pointed at."

This book is that pointing finger. Spiritual enlightenment is not some future event reserved for Buddhists or lifelong practitioners where you achieve superhuman feats. You don't need books of knowledge or a lifetime of practice. Self-realization takes time, but it can only happen in this moment. It is never out there, only here and now. It is not some achievement after you've gained x, y and z. The only faint knowledge you may need is to understand the workings of the ego, which is your false mind-made self. As the egoic layer peels away, you let go of all you are not and realize what is left. Beyond the knowledge of what you are not is the realization of what you are. Everything this book points to is self-evident. The insights of this book are already yours. Deep down, you already know. This book is simply meant to help you remember, so to speak. As a flower curled up in lifelong hibernation, you must look beyond the finger to bloom in eternal realization.

As you read, don't get too caught up on words or concepts, such as enlightenment, which can be as much a barrier as a bridge. Pay more attention to experiencing what the words are pointing to. Remember this well as you continue reading. The purpose of this book is not to replace your religion or ideology with something new to believe in. This book is neither theory nor fact. This book is a disposable signpost pointing beyond belief to the direct realization of a transcendental reality within. In other words, this book points to your freedom from attachment and identification with thoughts, feelings and emotions. It is not meant to give or add anything to you. It is not meant for philosophical discussion. I speak from direct experience and this book is meant for direct experience.

Particularly in the first few chapters, italicized terms are defined so you are aware of the context they are used throughout the book. The first chapter starts fast and digs beyond understanding. It introduces some of the insights that will be discussed in subsequent chapters. You may find it initially difficult to follow and keep up with. However, everything, including you, will come together. All you have to do is continue reading. Statements that initially sound abstract will reverberate with more reality as you deepen into the book and yourself. Pay close attention to any subtle shifts you feel as you read. This is more important than trying to decipher what you read. This book is not meant to be deciphered in the mind, but felt as a subtle shift of reality. When I capitalize words, such as Being and Self, I am pointing to your intrinsic nature. I sometimes capitalize words to differentiate the defined you with the undefinable You.

Naturally, you may be curious to know a little about me before reading further. You may be thinking, "Are you really writing an introduction without introducing yourself?" Who I am to you spans this book and will come to fruition as the pages turn.

Each chapter speaks through thick layers of human conditioning suspicious of the ego's potential response. For survival purposes, the ego will whisper its best whispers to deter you from finishing this book. Your time-bound sense of self wants the first chapter to be your last chapter. Don't hesitate to pause and direct your attention inward after statements that resonate deeply. At points, you may be wondering, "What in the world is he talking about!" If you come across a statement that does not immediately resonate and seems devoid of understandable substance, just keep on reading. Everything I touch on should be elaborated in a later chapter. This book isn't meant to make much sense in pieces and neither are you. This book truly works best as a whole and so do you.

Chapter 1
Who Am I?

Who am I? This question has perplexed humans for countless ages. The answer to this question is nearer than the breath. You must be willing to question everything, even the questioner. The error in our endless pursuit to answer this question is in the question itself. Instead of asking who you are, ask who you are not. To realize your true self, you must see beyond your assumed self. To see beyond your assumed self, you must let the assumptions go. All assumptions are temporary, ever-changing and will eventually disappear when the mind disappears. The content of the mind is born in the mind and dies in the mind. Are you really that content? Have you allowed complete silence into the mind to feel your own presence beyond content? Can you sense the lack of content that allows content? Can you sense the awareness behind what happens and know that in it, you are enough? Or is your mind stuck in a torrent of thinking that you can barely break from the moment you wake to the moment you sleep? Perhaps you have it all figured out already by knowing your name, age, occupation, social status, memories woven into your identity, etc. I too had it all figured out until one day I realized the epic illusion I was living. What felt like a colorless flash of long-forgotten familiarity deepened as a universal understanding coming back to me. Transparency abounded. Everything started blending. I no longer felt things were happening to me, but rather within me.

Growing up, I would rarely question who I was. Why should I? The answer seemed so obvious and everyone had it. My mind was heavily conditioned to believe, "I am what this thought says. I am what that thought says. I am the actions I take. I am what he or she said. I am what my birth certificate says. I am my past. I am my expectations, attachments and so on." Why bother questioning what we all apparently know? It never occurred to me to truly investigate this question. Like most humans, I would assume the answer and ignore the question. After all, everything else seemed far more important and entertaining. It seems most of society is designed to pull us away from such questions by training us to assume the answer. For 30 years, I settled for "George" as my answer. Of course, what George meant changed all day depending on the instability of what happened. I was stuck in a prison-like story called "my life" and suffered intensely as a result. I sought many ways out, but only found short-lived pleasures and further entanglement in what happens.

The answer to who you are must not be a distant goal for the future. Nothing ever happens in the future because the future is always just a thought you have now that can only manifest now. In time, your realization of the timeless grows until its appointed hour, which can only be now. Like all things, Self-realization can only happen in the present moment. *Self-realization* is a more precise, down to earth term for enlightenment. The word enlightenment is not bad or wrong, just usually inflated as some glorified status. I use both terms interchangeably.

Who you think you are is constantly changing, subject to time and inherently unstable. Your thought-made self is shaped by what happens, which is the most unstable thing in the universe. When I use the term *what happens*, I point to everything that transpires on the level of mind, body, and universe. This is where we look to assign ourselves an answer to who we are. We look to what happened, what is happening or what is expected to happen. In other words, we look to our thoughts. This means you are susceptible to anything and anyone at any moment as you meander through a world that plays tug of war with who you are. Why do we rely on unreliability for meaning and fulfillment? Because we are not in conscious connection with who we are. Who you are is not something to believe in, it is an underlying reality to realize. Do not take my word for it. Use this book as a bridge to be left behind and directly experience what I'm pointing to. This passing reality of human experience is interconnected with an underlying reality of spiritual consciousness. To be enlightened is to realize this omnipresent intersection. When I use the word *consciousness*, I point to the formless fabric of life. Consciousness is the space in which everything resides, the silence in which all sound comes from and the stillness in which all motion is born.

When you're fully present in the moment, you don't derive a sense of identity from an evanescent world. Being fully present in the moment doesn't mean you lose peripheral vision of future goals and past lessons. It means your feet are grounded in the here and now as your arms reach back and forth. Your home is nowhere else, only here and now. After all, there is nothing else. This allows you to be far more effective at what you do and think because you are fully present in the moment doing and thinking. Would you rather worry about the future or accept what is expected, then fully plan for and be at peace with it now? Would you rather suffer from the past or accept what has happened, then fully learn from and be at peace with it now? Both past and future are always mere thoughts you have in the present. They are tools to use, not places to live. Learn from the past and plan for the future, but don't make them your illusory home or identity. You only have one true home and that is in this moment you are reading this word.

If you consider yourself just human, then you will suffer. Convinced you are just flesh, bone and thought, you will continue living your life at the mercy of what happens. When you are fully here and now, rooted in reality, there is no suffering. Realize you are not just human and you get to redefine what it means to be human. When I use the word *suffering*, I point toward mental suffering, not physical pain. Everything that happens instantly becomes a memory of a previous appearance of this moment that is remembered in this moment. Everything that is expected to happen is just a thought you have in this moment that may eventually happen in this moment, which is ever-changing its appearance. Although life seems like a series of moments, it is always this one, ever-changing moment. When you stop regularly worrying about the future and suffering from the past, all that's left is possibility to be as you choose to be in the only moment that is real – this moment.

Contrary to popular belief, you can never find yourself in thoughts, things, people or places, just illusions destined to fail you. A false sense of self is created through attachment to thoughts about who you are. Thoughts cannot describe who you are, but you are misled by the ego to believe they can. To feel an *attachment* is to lack space between a thought you have and who you are. To lack space around thoughts is to be identified with thoughts. Much of the time, we don't have a choice in what to do or how to be because there is no space between an event and our response. Thus, the event chooses for us. Free from attachments, you have a choice to act from or rest in wholeness. When I use the word *whole* or *wholeness*, I point to the essence of who you are that cannot grow or shrink with what happens. You are already whole, which you will realize as your egoic conditioning diminishes. As a reminder, *ego or egoic* points to your false mind-made self.

As the ocean, most of us only know the waves. We believe we are separate waves. "I am this wave and you are that wave," says the ego. How long does it take for a wave to realize it is the ocean from which all waves arise and cease? How far does a wave need to travel to remember it is the ocean? No time. No distance. Like thoughts, waves are passing outer expressions of a lasting inner silence. Fleeting waves cannot describe the enduring depths of an ocean just as fleeting thoughts cannot describe the enduring depths of who you are. The conceptualized you is no more than changing thoughts merging memories and expectations. It is no different than walking around attached to a fictitious hologram of who you take yourself to be. When I use the word *hologram*, I point to the mental image you create of yourself that represents who you are. Exposed to the elements of judgment, you and others add to and take away from this image based on the most unstable thing in the universe: what happens. When two people interact, it is usually the holograms of what each person takes themselves to be interacting. Each hologram then creates its own hologram of other people. This is not wrong or right, it is simply the normal reality for most humans on the planet. We only know ourselves as isolated holograms at the mercy of what happens. This is not to say that we should avoid the roles and functions in our lives. All roles and functions can be far more peaceful, joyful and effective given we lose our attachments to how they should or shouldn't be and don't seek ourselves in them.

We all have the seed of enlightenment within. This seed is unveiled in the absence of thinking and grows the longer you ease into this absence. Any attempt to define yourself is ultimately adding to your fragile hologram that changes with the seasons of your mood and volatile moods of the world. Such definitions are passing experiences of a passing reality on the outskirts of this ever-lasting moment. By letting go of who you think you are, what is left is a watchful presence – a silent awareness – containing all that comes and goes. Declarations of who you are ultimately have nothing to do with who you are. Become aware of thoughts as they pass, not automatically and conditionally attached to them. Use thoughts, but don't let them use you. The moment you try thinking your way into knowing who you are, you fail. Any answer you come up with will eventually reveal itself as insufficient. Everything in the mind passes. The answer you seek doesn't pass. You cannot use the mind to reveal what contains the mind. You must go beyond the mind by allowing silence into the mind. The egoic whispers in your head continuously define who you are because without those definitions, the ego wouldn't exist. And, like all entities, what does the ego – or who you think you are – want most? Survival. This is why I said, "The ego will whisper its best whispers to deter you from finishing this book."

To realize who you are, do not look to the mind for help. You will only hear what you've always heard. Even if it tells you otherwise, the message, like all thinking, was born in the mind and will eventually die in the mind. You have to go beyond the mind and realize what was never born and will never die. How to do that? Allow your thoughts to subside and unveil what remains through a silent mind. How to do this? By not turning it into something to do. You must be, not do. Be. Here. Now. Consciously be the space containing the appearance of this moment, not an object in it. Although it is not ultimately necessary, meditation certainly helps, especially if you do not sit as a means to an end or carry any expectations. As thoughts arise, do not judge your mind for doing what it is supposed to do. That is just adding more unnecessary commentary. Gently watch your thoughts and in your watching, they will pass until all that is left is a watchful presence. Like holding in your breath underwater, this cannot be done under the weight of thoughts waiting to come crashing down. A moment of complete inner silence is all you need for a glimpse.

Are you the thoughts you have about yourself? Are you the thoughts others have of you? Are you a combination of both? When you become anchored in the present moment and free of thinking, you are still there. If you are defined by thinking, then who are you in the absence of thinking? How are you still alive if you cease to think since thoughts are all you know yourself to be? Shouldn't you just be an inanimate bundle of flesh by now? Did you, as a thought-made entity, die and resurrect yourself a few seconds later when you started thinking again? Was this identity ever real to begin with? Or, are you the subtle void between thoughts? Are you the empty space in which thoughts come and go? Are you the silence beneath all sound? Are you the stillness beneath all motion? This indescribable, formless and timeless presence is beyond perception, but it can be realized. This is your leftover essence when you unravel all you are not. This is pure consciousness containing time and form, yet untouched by time and form. Underneath all you do and think, this awareness allows and watches all your doing and thinking. When you are not what happens, all that is left is the awareness behind what happens. Let go of all you think you are and it will be here waiting for you, for it is You.

Chapter 2
The Cause Behind Everything

Waking up on a beautiful Sunday morning in the middle of Spring, I felt the warmth of the sun creeping in through the blinds as I slowly opened my eyes. I could hear the soft white noise from a nearby humidifier amidst a backdrop of beautiful songbirds. I began to slowly stretch my legs and arms as I gently turned over to lay on my back. Being slightly sore from the day before, I scanned my body for signs of distress and felt only radiant aliveness emanating from each cell in my body. As my eyes continued to open, I felt each eyelash begin to separate from the crust that had bound them. Suddenly, there was great distress passing through my mind and body. I could not open my eyes. My eye crust was imbued with super glue or so it seemed. I tried using my fingers to help, but it became a tug of war between the crust and my eyelashes. My eyelashes were losing. After having laser eye surgery, my eyes were granted better vision, but at the cost of frequent dryness. I forgot to put in my eye drops the previous day. My forgetfulness was to blame! I was the perpetrator! I even accused my wife Alexis as an accomplice for not reminding me. I had figured out the cause behind my temporary blindness – or did I? If we were in a courtroom, the judge would have slammed the gavel by now and this seemingly simple case would be closed with a definitive answer. Question is, how simple is this case really? What is the true cause of my crust-induced, temporary blindness?

The day before my eyes woke to a prison of super-crust and torn lashes, I spent the day kayaking down a river with Alexis and friends. We arrived home late, exhausted and ready for bed. Perhaps our busy day, which led to me forgetting, is the true cause?

When I first met my father-in-law, he reached into his chest pocket with a smile and gave me a boyfriend application sheet he printed from the internet.

The questions were absurd, but I answered them with complete honesty and somehow passed the test. Perhaps my passing this boyfriend application sheet, which led to marriage and kayaking, is the true cause?

Before I met my wife, I signed up to online dating websites. I tried them for a few months and realized it was not working for me. I cancelled them all, but still had three days left on one of the sites before the cancellation went into effect. I received a wink and so I responded. We exchanged information right before my month was over and that is how we met. Perhaps her wink or my response is the true cause?

After pondering the idea of life without contacts or glasses, I made the decision to start a two-year payment plan and improve my vision with laser eye surgery. Perhaps it was my decision to go ahead with the surgery that is the true cause?

During the invention of laser eye surgery, no one found a way to prevent the risk of dry eyes following the procedure. Perhaps the surgery is the true cause?

About 66 million years ago, the asteroid believed to have killed the dinosaurs wiped out most life on Earth and allowed the blossoming of new life. If it weren't for this event, would we even be here right now? Perhaps it is this asteroid that is the true cause?

About 300 million years ago, the only landmass on Earth was one massive continent called Pangea. Perhaps if this landmass didn't break up into seven continents, the world wouldn't be as it is and I would never have made the decision to get laser eye surgery. Perhaps it is the separation of Pangea that is the true cause?

The moon was formed some 4.5 billion years ago when a celestial body crashed into the Earth helping create the moon. If this celestial body never hit the Earth, would I have been on any dating websites? Perhaps this collision is the true cause?

Over 13.8 billion years ago, the universe is said to have begun as a singularity and expanded rapidly with the Big Bang. Some say it never began and it will never end. Many say God created the universe. If the universe was never created by God or formed by the initial singularity, would I have been able to sleep long enough for an intense amount of crust to bind my eyelids shut? Perhaps the formation of the universe is the true cause?

This is turning into a very long court case. If it weren't for the formation of the universe 13.8 billion years ago, which led to the formation of the moon 4.5 billion years ago; which led to the breakup of Pangea 300 million years ago; which preceded the major asteroid impact 66 million years ago; which led to the evolution of humanity; which led to dating websites and laser eye surgery; which led to my father-in-law giving me a passing grade for my boyfriend application sheet; which led to marriage, kayaking, exhaustion and forgetfulness; which led to the beautiful morning of my crusty awakening, I would never have asked for a warm washcloth to end the war between crust and lash and reclaim my eyelids!

Nothing that happens has a single or simple cause. Everything is infinitely connected and therefore has numberless causes. The seemingly simple and impossibly complicated all stem from billions of years of evolution, mystery and innumerable causes. Seeking out an underlying cause to what happens is a diversion of the mind to shrink the immeasurable to a single event. Whatever happens already happened and instantly becomes a fact of life. Everything is as it is because the universe is as it is. When you struggle against the present moment, you deny the reality of the infinite reasons that led up to the present moment. You cannot pinpoint a single cause behind what happens because every cause has its own endless causes. Any attempt to isolate a single cause to blame will still have within it the accumulation of untold causes and therefore can never truly be isolated. You can only try and figure out the latest causes. This is most useful for acceptance of what is and not for practical use of what can be. If you light a match, you will make a fire. If you press on the brake pedal, you will slow down. Ultimately, even these causes have within them incalculable causes, but this serves little use in practical terms. The power here is in disciplining your acceptance of what is and realizing that complaining is a pastime of the ego built on a resistance to what is. To resist what happens is futile because it already happened. You don't need to resist what happens to do something about what happens. Inner acceptance doesn't necessarily mean an outer acceptance. It means you are aligned with reality and ready to choose how to proceed without limiting your potential or suffering in the process.

For billions of years, all of creation has led up to this very moment. This moment is the face of all who came before you. This precise moment is perfect just the way it is because it already is and everything has led up to it. Once you see this moment through a thick lens of memory and expectation, there is imperfection everywhere. When I say this moment is perfect, I do not mean it in the traditional sense. This doesn't mean life is the way you would like it to be or if a loved one is suffering, you should say, "Hunny, don't worry! Everything is perfect!" The purpose here is to fuel your acceptance of what is by seeing the universe behind what is. This vision allows inner control, connection and clarity. You still have a peripheral vision of good and bad, but you aren't attached to how things should be, you are aligned with how things are. This is your starting space for what you do next. Rather than be at the mercy of the voice in your head screaming good and bad, you are rooted in possibility. Although you may be able to change something after it's happened, you cannot change that it already happened. You can't reverse the bottomless events layered deep within each passing event. This helps you accept all apparent imperfections as perfections in the sense of there being absolutely no mistakes. Again, this doesn't mean you must go along with what happens. Prior to any action, you can resist or accept what already is. With resistance, you have little to no space between the event and your reaction. In this fragmented world, you conditionally attach to your reactive thoughts, which are fueled by a threatened false sense of identity and reality. People and events determine who and how you are. With acceptance, you open up a clear space of powerful possibility surrounding the event. You endow yourself with true choice to act or peacefully observe the moment unfolding. Be wary that partial acceptance of what is means you are on the precipice of the ego taking full control of your mental state. Complete acceptance implies a home fully secured with your watchful presence.

What happens is merely one link in a never-ending chain of causation. Everything that happens is a fact that has been in the making for billions of years. Resisting what is by blaming a fragmented cause from an eternal whole is no different than yelling at the sky for being as it is. It is you versus the universe. Misaligned with what happens, you will always experience some form of suffering or limitation because you cannot change that something already happened and everything that's led up to it. What you can do is accept what happens and allow yourself choice to take action, reflect clearly or continue observing as a valley of presence. Learn to consciously accept what happens rather than unconsciously resist what happens. This is your innermost strength where true choice is possible and true peace is unstoppable. This is where you rise above the world, yet remain inextricably connected to all that is of the world. This is how you use the mind and stop being used by the mind.

When I use the word *unconscious*, I refer to your identity consisting primarily of thoughts wherein you only know yourself by what you do and think. Reduced to the mercy of thoughts you define yourself by, your entire reality is founded on a misleading sense of identity and separateness. When I use the word *conscious*, I refer to being fully present in the moment as the awareness behind what happens.

All suffering is due to an inner resistance to what you think, feel and perceive now. When you resist what already is, you split reality into conflicting, unequal halves of "me" and "this or that." First, you need to accept what is because it already is and there's no use in denying a fact of life. From there, take action if necessary, without self-imposed limitations. Inner mastery starts with inner acceptance. Accept what happens because it already happened, not because it is good or bad. This allows rationality and choice in how to proceed without possession by external situations. With acceptance, you open up clear space around your thoughts for true choice. With resistance, you have limited space around your thoughts with limited choice. True choice is born of saying an inner yes to what happens and is free of worry over deceptive ideas of who you take yourself to be. An inner yes doesn't necessarily mean an outer yes. Saying yes to what happens doesn't mean you will always be happy or go along, but you will be at peace, clear-minded and self-controlled. It means you are anchored in wholeness and who you are cannot be taken away from or added to.

From the perspective of the mind, things seem to happen too early or too late. Unless it's an event one enjoys or expects, the mind quickly asserts, "This shouldn't be happening!" This assertion has been the accepted norm for thousands of years. Within this assertion is a resistance to a fact of life and one of the greatest strongholds the mind builds. The mental stronghold of inner resistance is the source of unending human suffering. In the throne room of this conceptualized stronghold sits the thought "I" infused with personal history, weapons, armor, deception, fear and insufficiency. Unlike other strongholds throughout history that were broken down with catapults and other weaponry, you cannot go to war with mind-made strongholds. To "overcome" them, you must simply see them. This seeing takes place outside the resistance and frees you from the resistance. This is a very subtle battlefield in which your direction of attention determines your reality. Always keep at least a portion of your attention on the field in which everything happens. Stay watchful of your conditioned mind and its habitual, automated ways. The more watchful you remain of mind activity, the more free you become from it to use it.

What happens when we resist reality and rely on the instability of what happens for stability, fulfillment and identity? Read a history book or go online and browse the news. Take a moment to reflect on all the suffering you and others have endured. Look at the degradation of the natural world, the crimes committed, the extinction rates, the wars we create and how fragmented this world has become. Despite all the beauty of humanity, this is a legacy of dominance the mind has over who we are. This is all an outer reflection of an inner fragmentation; an outer abuse born of an inner abuse. What is at the core of this madness? The ego. A false thought about who we are creates separation and suffering whereas a realization of all we are not creates the strong possibility of awakening. When I use the word *awake* or *awakening*, I point toward a spiritual awakening, not rolling out of bed. As you awaken, there is a natural emergence of unity, peace, love, joy and inner control. This is not some future utopia. This is a present-moment emanation of Self-realization. This is all that's left when you realize your intrinsic nature. This doesn't mean you are perfect, just that you are whole. The ego is not bad, just unconscious. We need unconsciousness before we can be fully conscious human beings. The question is: how long will we remain in this dream-like state? It is time to wake up. Amid all the environmental destruction and suffering we create, the way out is in.

I tune into the news once in a while and see the endless seduction of the human mind fooling its countless hosts into mistaking its whispers for reality. For example, "I am white and you are black," says the mind. "I am better than you," says the mind. It cuts up reality into bits and pieces and judges each piece from an apparently superior mental position. It always has a justification for its insane actions. If left unchecked, the insanity of the human mind will lead to the demise of the human race and most life on Earth. As technology advances so does our capability for destruction. Without a profound transformation in our level of oneness, the wonder and beauty of the human race will be destroyed by its false sense of separation and insufficiency.

The answers are within each and every one of us. We must ease into this moment and realize our inherent, uncaused source of joy, peace, love and unity so we no longer rely on the instability of what happens for it. This way, we become lights unto ourselves and beacons of peace. The awakening of one human being has a profound impact on the collective energy field of humanity and the presence of such a person naturally and effortlessly waters the seeds of awakening in others.

Keep in mind the ego reads this book alongside you. If you defend yourself by saying, "I did what I did because the universe is as it is," or, "I decided to steal the mannequin from the store because I can't find myself a girlfriend since the universe is as it is," then the ego is speaking through you with reverse psychology as its strategy. When you are aligned with what happens, the ego retreats as a faint whisper to a distant shore. It is no longer a megaphone to your ear.

Chapter 3
The Hologram

My palms were sweaty, my heart rate was hasty, my thoughts were fearful, my chest was tight with suspense and all I could see was more than a thousand people judging me. In the end, I was more judgmental to myself than anyone in the crowd. In the summer of 2016, I had been preparing for weeks to give a powerful speech at the Electric Factory in Philadelphia to close out a major work event at Tesla. What I had not prepared for was the weight of anxiety crashing down on me while speaking. This fear would regularly accompany me while speaking to large groups, but it was usually manageable. Walking up the stairs to the stage right after the Vice President gave me a glorious introduction, I felt confident and my anxiety and fear were mostly at bay. A minute into my grand speech, all was well until I lost my train of thought for a quick second. A second later, I had become completely paralyzed. My ever-patient ego, waiting in the dark armed with fear and anxiety, seized the moment and unleashed a grip so tight that it was hard to breathe, let alone think. I stood there awkwardly silent and still, looking straight into the crowd. I had a few supportive cheers, but I still could not think or move. About ten painful seconds had passed until I finally spoke and what came out was completely irrelevant, but surprisingly relieving! I did not plan to say this, I just knew I had to say something; so, I somehow settled for, "I love you guys!" The laughter helped me get back on my feet to at least finish the speech. I emailed the leaders of my company, who were relying on me for a memorable closing, an apology and took off the next day to grieve. This had weighed me down for months as I carried it forward beating myself up every time I looked in the mirror. What happened?

The ego is born of attachment to thoughts as the untamed narrator in your head. The ego is neither good nor bad, just unconscious, conditioned and limited. Your attachment to the stream of thought fuels the ego which creates the hologram called "me" that you spend your entire life concerning over. This deceptive hat trick is the root cause of all your fear, suffering and separation. Humans have been ensnared in the tight grip of the ego for thousands of years. Even when liberated of your false mind-made self, the ego will maintain a sickly existence of its own in dark corners of your mind waiting for pockets of renewal. It becomes a faint whisper on a distant shore, but with a ready ship capable of sailing straight to the forefront of your mind and body. Unattached to thoughts, you are free to use or watch them instead of becoming them. You tame the narrator in your head by controlling knowledge and relinquishing the control knowledge has over you.

A hologram's survival requires you to have a relationship with yourself. When you have a relationship with yourself, you split yourself in two pieces called "I" and "myself." "I" is the apparently superior judge that judges the apparently inferior criminal called "myself." "I" is the perfect innocence and "myself" is the imperfect culprit. Some days, the "I" piece likes the "myself" piece. Other days, the "I" piece dislikes the "myself" piece. Either way, you remain stuck in a hallucinatory relationship with your imagined self on a roller coaster ride in a divided world. When you have a relationship with yourself, you're having a relationship with your made-up hologram. As a reminder, when I use the word *hologram*, I point to the mental image you create of yourself that represents who you are. The hologram becomes your mental boyfriend or girlfriend where love can quickly turn to hate. Whether love or hate, all self-relationships limit your potential as you endlessly chase desires to keep your self-love or earn your self-love. You must free yourself from dating yourself by not attaching to judgments about yourself. The ego thrives on approval because it lives in fear.

It is a natural human tendency to try and love oneself. We may spend our entire lives trying to create or maintain a love for ourselves, depending on what happens. My self-love was always dependent on how proud my father was and how I saw myself through the eyes of others. Practically everything I did was to satisfy these conditions so I can love myself. This conditional self-love was an uncontrollable rollercoaster ride I was stuck on for decades. Loving yourself is loving a phantom identity. You are already whole and cannot truly be split into pieces to love. This realization is love. The mind tricks you into self-division because it needs you split into multiple pieces of seeming existence. This is one of its many strategies to preserve its control over your sense of self and reality. Realize exactly what it is that you are trying to love. Is it not just a thought that changes with time? Who is left to love in the absence of that thought? Pay attention to what factors your self-love depends on and why they exist to begin with. Investigate the apparent reality of proclaiming, "I love myself." Eckhart Tolle explained this investigation in his book, *The Power of Now*, by saying, "'I cannot live with myself any longer.' This was the thought that kept repeating itself in my mind. Then suddenly, I became aware of what a peculiar thought it was. 'Am I one or two? If I cannot live with myself, there must be two of me: the 'I' and the 'self' that 'I' cannot live with.' *Maybe,* I thought, *only one of them is real.*"

"I" and "myself" can't be the same since "I" seems to be the perfect judge and "myself" is constantly changing depending on what "I" thinks and what the world says. True love doesn't need chasing or condition. True love is your leftover quality in the absence of inequality. "You will not stop me from loving myself," says the ego as the voice of a threatened hologram. No, I cannot and will not. All I can do is point to the emergence of true love beyond your imagined self and relationship with this creation. True love doesn't contradict itself and isn't acquired. We work so hard to create a hologram that is lovable. Stop trying to love yourself, realize you can't be split in two and true love will be here and now, waiting. Every time we use the word "I" and mistake it to be who we truly are, we are bound to suffer. Use it, but don't become it. Don't let your immeasurability shrink to some fleeting word, sound or thought. Stay immeasurable by being the here and now instead of in the here and now as some isolated fragment.

It is one thing to learn from what you do or don't do and another to have a dreamlike relationship with yourself. You don't need to split yourself in two to reflect, improve and learn. You can learn, act and reflect more effectively without the clutter of personal judgment in the process. You can say, "I did not do a great job with this, let me think about how I can do it better," without saying, "I didn't do a great job here, I'm so mad at myself! I can't believe I did this!" Look in the mirror long enough until the incessant voice in your head subsides and you will have the clearest view. The ego tricks you into having a relationship with yourself because it wants to thrive at the center of the universe. Apparently, the universe has many centers. As a survival mechanism, it wants to split the present moment into a collection of judgments against yourself and others. There is never truly a separate you to have a relationship with. To be One with Life, you must be one with what happens, not two with yourself.

We spend entire lifetimes stuck in a judgmental self-relationship while inviting the world to an open house of adding and subtracting from who we are. Even if you have a good relationship with yourself, which is better than having a bad one, you are still split in two with a separate "you" to have a relationship with. It is still limiting, conditional and illusory. Drop it and you will be free to love without fear of maintaining your self-love. Drop it and all other relationships will bloom without unnecessary worry about a loss of self. When you date yourself, an incredible amount of energy is spent on maintaining a polished image of a loveable you. This perfect you becomes your life goal. You plan on meeting this perfect you at some point in the future. If the meeting comes, you'll enjoy it momentarily until you have to continue keeping this perfect you perfect. Drop this goal and you are free to be without attachment to who you "should be." Accept how you are, then choose how you may want to become; however, do not let how you are absolutely define who you are. This allows you to strive from a space of completeness, not lack. Already complete, you are free to accomplish, improve and learn without a sense of neediness or self-love to endlessly keep up with.

Your sacred alliance with what happens is the most important bond of your life because it contains your life. As a reminder, when I use the term *what happens*, I point to everything that transpires on the level of mind, body and universe. With the ego in control, resistance abounds and choices in your life are automatically made for you. Your faulty relationship with what happens causes separation and dysfunction within and without. When you accept what happens, you have true choice at your disposal. It can no longer bend you to its will.

Let's say you're shopping at the grocery store when all of a sudden, a passing man's dreadlocks get caught on your jar of taco sauce which falls, breaks and spills. What do you do? Perhaps you will laugh or the ego may tell you to respond with defensiveness, pin blame on the man's dreads and tell him to get a haircut. If that voice comes, acknowledge its presence and become aware of it as the voice of your ego. To be aware, and not attached, means there is space between who you are and what happens. The egoic voice will pass quickly in the light of your awareness. This doesn't mean if the man with dreads tells the manager it was your fault and you have to pay for it that you have to go along. It means you first accept that it spilled and that he blamed it on you. That's something you cannot change because it already happened. Accept it and don't make it a personal problem. This prevents the grip of unruly emotions creating and guiding conditioned actions. See the reality of the moment, then make a choice to act without attachment to a desired outcome. Aligned with what happens, no energy is expended on a civil war with what is. You have a clear mind to empower your actions. This is how you allow yourself true choice in situations instead of being at the mercy of situations as an automated reaction. It's simple, yet incredibly profound the difference this makes. Be wary to have an intention for a desired outcome, but not become attached to one. The power of choice you just had may no longer be there if you're attached to an outcome you never get.

The ego endures by knowing who you are, which is born of an ancient fear of being no one. When you no longer carry this fear, you are free to use thoughts powerfully instead of trying to find yourself in them desperately. Once you claim to know the unknown, you split yourself in two and continue fueling the egoic voice in your head. This voice relentlessly breathes imaginary life into your hologram and you now have an identity to protect, cherish, defend, harass, fulfill, add and subtract from. Your hologram is your imagined answer to a question you cannot truly answer: Who am I? Your hologram is a fragile, ever-changing mental model of who you take yourself to be. It's created by you, carved by others and endlessly finalized by how you see yourself through the eyes of others. Fueled by the ego, your hologram accompanies you everywhere you go as an invisible persona of "me." Your hologram is completely susceptible to the turbulent, unpredictable atmosphere of your mind and is thoroughly shaped by the most unstable thing in the universe: what happens. When life goes your way, your hologram is radiant with power and pride. When life doesn't go your way, your hologram is threatened with death and decay.

You are walking around attached to a fictitious creation of who you are that acts as a warped lens to the world. Instead of seeing the world as is, you see the world how you see yourself. If you see yourself as fragile, you will see the world as scary. If you see yourself as better than someone, you will feel your hologram has been diminished when that person outperforms you or reinforced if you outperform them. If you see yourself as someone who needs this or that to fulfill your identity, you will feel incomplete if you don't get this or that and react accordingly. If you see yourself as an excellent English teacher and you make a mistake presenting English, you will feel that your hologram is less than it was just a moment ago. If you see yourself as a successful businesswoman and you end up losing your business, your hologram may shatter completely or it will lose a limb or two. These ongoing losses need ongoing replacements. Your hologram is stuck in a lifelong tug of war between who it wants to be and what happens.

Just about everyone has a hologram they live by, but no two holograms are the same. Holograms are made of dynamic, innumerable identifications with things, people, ideas, events, memories, etc. By attaching to thoughts, you give birth to these identifications. These identifications are only as real as you make the thought passing through your mind to be. A thought passing through your mind is no different than a wave arising in the vast ocean. Waves can be fierce one day and at peace the next. However, waves do not affect or define the deeper water below.

Molding your hologram through identifying with thoughts is not your choosing. It happens to you the same way digestion happens. It is an automated process deeply embedded in the human psyche over thousands of years. Unlike digestion, this process can be interrupted and controlled. You must recognize the hologram to diminish the hologram. In your recognition, you are no longer attached to, but aware of your mind-made self.

Holograms are always up for grabs. Some may be harder to intimidate and manipulate while others may be easy. The existence of a personal hologram implies a fragility to what happens and futile search for enduring meaning and fulfillment against a backdrop of lack and fear. If a stranger walked up to you with a mean stare a few inches from your face and said, "You look like cooked bacon grease," what would you do? If said to me, my wife would probably agree and tell me to go shower. However, most people would instantly react in a holographic battle with actual consequences. Each time you resist and react, you grant the unconsciousness in others control over your vulnerable self. Perhaps you will remain calm on the outside, but offended on the inside. If so, curiously ask yourself why you feel offended? Who is it that feels taken away from? "Well, I do," says the ego, which really means the hologram does. Even if you accidentally sprayed hair gel on your face and look like cooked bacon grease, it still has nothing to do with who you are. Nothing said or done ever has anything to do with who you are. At best, concepts can point, but never truly define. Be wary not to neglect caring for things and people by saying, "This has nothing to do with me anyway." You must be carefully aware of the egoic voice muddling with your awakening and misusing pointers. You can learn from the situation and wash the grease, but when you make a situation into a personal problem, you are making life harder than it needs to be. Making life more difficult is not something you would do if you actually had the choice.

All insults are part of the collective human unconsciousness flowing through a person and into the world with great momentum. The ego is rarely completely gone due to our inheritance and reinforcement of intense human conditioning throughout the ages. When your hologram feels taken away from, there may be a leftover void that will cry for help. When part of your identity is shattered, your desire to be this or that will remain suspended over your hologram waiting for a passing thought from a passing event to reattach it. If no attachable thoughts come to fill your void, you will search to find or create a reason why you can once again be this or that. If this missing identity remains detached and suspended above your hologram for some time, this could lead to depression and desperation. "I need this identity and attachment to move on and be me," says the ego. Holographic lifestyles are the root cause of endless suffering.

For example, you take great pride in being a loving girlfriend. You've loved your boyfriend for many years and feel a great connection to him. All of a sudden, he tells you he doesn't see your relationship going much further and breaks up with you. Thus begins the egoic chase for completeness as you experience a holographic episode of emptiness. Emotions will likely rise and that is okay. Accept them as they pass through the body. You don't need to try and be an emotionless robot. There is no right or wrong way to be. This is not about becoming a different or perfect version of yourself. No one is perfect, but everyone is whole. Such perfection implies personal inflation. Wholeness implies universal intelligence. To inhabit your body at length, emotions need your attachment to a tempting storyline. Left alone, they are strong vibrations of energy that will pass quickly. If you cannot accept the story you impose on this neutral moment, then you have an opportunity to accept your feelings and emotions about it. You always have that second chance and third and fourth and so on. My good friend and performance coach Jay Abbasi called it, "The ever-present reset button." If no acceptance is possible, your hologram will likely mutilate itself and open an empty void. Once the void opens, you will have a suspended desire hovering over your hologram waiting for a passing thought from a passing event to cover the void. If the hologram gets its way, you will seek another partner to temporarily cover this void and seemingly make you happy and whole again. The ego is under constant threat because its very existence depends on fading forms. Deep down, the ego knows this very well and so the underlying state of fear persists beneath everything you do. This subtle fear can easily go unnoticed, but profoundly impacts your everyday life.

You are ultimately unidentifiable. There is never an actual identity to defend or love, just mental holograms to spend a lifetime chasing with an abiding sense of basic incompleteness. Your hologram lets in what adds to it and attempts to keep out what takes away from it in an endless dance with what happens. It's one thing to protect what you love and another to be at war over what you love due to a "loss of self." Your ego will try to protect its creation by saying, "I need to be me and don't want to give it up." This is especially true for parts of your hologram that comprise an identity you love, such as being a charitable human who is dedicated to helping others or a loving husband who cherishes his wife. This will appear as an identity you don't want to let go of. If so, that's great because you don't have to let go of such roles and functions! All you need to do is lose your sense of self you invested into them. The ego may be whispering, "Why in the world would I do that? Go jump off a cliff George!"

When you split yourself up and invest a piece of your identity in someone or something, who you are is at the unstable mercy of that someone or something. Similar to the stock market, your potential is limited and controlled according to what happens around your investments. You lose your ability to choose because choices are already made for you by different parts of you invested out there. Transcend this habit and you will see if you love to give, you will be able to give much more. If you love your wife, you will be able to love her even more. Loving without investing a sense of who you are into that love means you are free to love without relying on what you love to determine how and when you love. To invest yourself is to break yourself into pieces and choose where your identities will reside. Similar to invasive species, your identity now dwells in many places at inevitable odds with your surroundings. These places don't need your investment of self and you don't need to invest yourself. How to stop this habit? Realize the multiplicity of false identities you are not. Rest in what is left.

Falsely invested in who you are, you try to influence the turbulence of what happens to suit your holographic identity. For example, I used to invest who I am into my daughter which led me to overreact when she would do something "wrong." Deep down, I was afraid that if she didn't grow up to be the way I wanted her to be, then part of my hologram would shatter. I needed her to be the best she can be not just for herself, but also for me. From a place of hidden fear, I was on top of her for all the little things that weren't aligned with my vision and ineffectively pushed her to accomplish for her and me. I limited my daughter's psychological and emotional growth the moment I invested my identity in her. By doing this, I shrank my untold potential to a small world of protecting my self-image and prioritizing my expectations and desires over my daughter's well-being and growth.

It may be helpful to name your hologram so that every time you notice an automated desire to act on its behalf, you can say nice try to "Firestarter" or "Ghost." If you have someone close to you who often acts unconsciously, you can also name their hologram as "Con" or "Hoax." You can keep this to yourself or gently share this with those close to you and mutually agree on carefully helping each other this way. This helps not take life so seriously. Part of enlightenment is lightening up. Poke fun at the ego, but do not do it in a way that fuels the ego. The ego is not some giant monster; it is an inherited, little "me" that pretends to be you. As a reminder, when I use the term *act unconsciously*, I point to thoughts and actions that are imbued with an illusory sense of self. By giving a hologram a name, I don't mean to give it more meaning and reality than it already has. The purpose here is to notice, separate and watch a thought you have that is based on worry over misleading ideas of who you are. This helps prevent unnecessary defensiveness within yourself and further aggravation to situations. This way you can act with power and control without that unnecessary oomph that tends to make things worse. You can still be stern, of course, but you are no longer a problem-making machine. When someone calls you a name and you feel an arising defense, it may be helpful to take a second and internally say, "Nice try Ghost" or "Hello again Hoax." However, starting entire conversations with your hologram while someone is yelling at you likely won't help. If it helps, use playful names until you no longer need to.

Never forget that you are not the only one with a hologram. Virtually everyone carries their own hologram and holographic views of others. Holographic views are born of judgment and assumption, which happens instantaneously as a deep-rooted response. Internal or external conversations either partially or completely consist of holograms. If a hologram is who you take yourself to be, how often do you think you forget it? Not very much. This foundational knowledge influences and controls virtually every aspect of your life. Due to an inherent fragility, two holograms speaking to each other are always at the mercy of each other. This may not show on the outside, but it is there due to the subterranean fear that gives birth to the hologram. Living life as the egoic hologram, you forgo conscious choice-making as a norm and are barely even there. Do not judge or put down others when noticing their hologram. They are not wrong for having one and never had a choice in choosing one. Do not try to get rid of the mental representation of who you are. It is not a problem and has its temporary, necessary place. Instead, see clearly the distinction between your hologram and who you truly are. In doing so, its heaviness naturally and effortlessly fades on its own.

Chapter 4
Learn from Nature

George, the passionate environmentalist. This was one of my most cherished identities. I spent over two years building a non-profit educational website called *Everything Connects*. My intention was to inspire the notion that no one person is too small to make a difference, help people understand the importance of a healthy ecosystem and provide a platform for taking action. Hidden, however, was an enormous desire to build myself a bridge from emptiness to fullness. I remember the satisfaction rushing in the moment I finally clicked the "Publish" button and went live. To me, the button didn't say "Publish," it said "Who I Am." I celebrated in deep joy for figuring it out. I finally knew who I was because I had built myself an identity from scratch, or so I thought.

In the winter of 2014, under one of the missions of my website, my sister Ariana and I joined a volunteer-based organization, Project Amazonas, and together embarked on a journey to a secluded field station in the heart of the Peruvian Amazon rainforest. Upon our arrival, I was in complete awe at the symmetrical dance between danger and beauty. At night, the thunderous sounds of the wild created a remarkable chorus of life. It was a phenomenal experience until an all-too curious moth flew deep into my ear. I immediately tried to take it out with my finger, but accomplished the exact opposite as I pushed it further in. This moth remained alive in what felt like my brain, buzzing for two nights as a psychological nightmare. Somehow, as I wondered whether the moth was laying eggs, I managed to stay calm until we reached a doctor at the nearest city of Iquitos three days later. The lesson here? Don't illuminate your face with a flashlight in the middle of the night in the middle of a jungle! An emergency room doctor couldn't help me, but pointed us toward an ear specialist elsewhere in the city who finally removed it using a special tool.

Years later, after I recognized the voice in my head as the ego, I thought of the moth buzzing in my head. I remember smiling thinking, "Here we go again." This time, words were the pointing finger, life was the specialist and this moment was the special tool. The ego faced a similar fate as the moth because I focused on where the finger was pointing. Let this story serve as a reminder to go beyond what you read and not get caught on fancy wording. "Consciousness" and "Being" do nothing for you. They can be as much a barrier as a bridge. Use this book as a steppingstone, but do not start believing in it. Focus more on directly knowing and realizing what is being pointed to. You must see this book like the emergency room doctor in Iquitos who had the experience to point in a helpful direction, but could not do anything directly.

In nature there is only poetry, no chaos. Chaos exists only in our minds. The ego keeps our view narrow, blinding us from the whole. Where we see chaos, nature sees acceptance, interconnection and adaptation. Nature speaks in grand, yet subtle ways. Speaking nature's poetic, rhythmic language, there is much to learn:

As the seasons change, animals do not complain
For such actions would be in vain.
The squirrels dig holes, the birds set goals.
To resist change is to become estranged
From the present moment
That you should never make your opponent.

Watch a stream patiently
As it moves around the rocks graciously.
A stream does not shout at the rocks
For being in its way;
It remains aware of what is there
And gets on with its day.
Be like the stream,
At peace with reality,
Accepting all that happens
As your unshakeable mentality.

Nature achieves all feats without worry or hurry.
The past does not make the present moment blurry.
Nature's secret is perspective as one with the collective.
She whispers through wings, gills and paws:
"Resist nothing and evolve.
Accept everything and resolve."
Everything is respected because she is connected.
Everything is aligned because she is undefined.
Free of self-restraint, there is no room for complaint.
Free of delusion, there is no room for confusion.
Mentally confined, she would be like humankind –
Blind by her state of mind.

Watch the sky and realize what is true.
What is always there is the witnessing blue.
Clouds pass through but cannot define
That which has not been given a deadline.

Nature uses the least amount of energy
Quite cleverly to accomplish what is needed
And make sure all warnings have been heeded.
Those with impeccable energy efficiency
Have the least amount of deficiency.
Memory and anticipation help with longevity,
But she never forgets –
The here and now is her secret to serenity.

Animals lick their wounds
And get on with it without a fit.
They turn a bite into foresight.

Nature is completely aware of her surroundings,
Which leads to more intuitive findings.
Ears instantly move to the direction of sound.

Snouts instantly pick up the scent all around.
To be fully aware, she must be fully present
No matter how unpleasant.

Nature always says yes to the present moment,
Then decides how she will be in further enrollment.
The past fuels her instinct,
But to live there – she'll begin to go extinct.
The future fuels her devising,
But to live there – she risks a deadly uprising.
Misaligned with present-moment essence,
She would fall into obsolescence.
Rooted in Oneness,
She has infinite abundance.

When a lion attacks a porcupine,
It learns a lesson it won't resign.
It uses knowledge usefully
Rather than belittle itself fruitlessly.
The lion does not attach to memories,
It uses them as remedies.

In nature, everything that happens is a cup of wisdom.
She drinks each cup to master the system.

Chapter 5
Sitting for Nothing

"Me meditate? You must be kidding!" This was my usual response when asked if I wanted to meditate. I would sometimes try, but could barely last a few seconds. As soon as my eyes closed, all I would hear was, "You are wasting your time, here's a list of other things you could be doing instead." Without much hesitation, I gave into that voice time and time again. Meditation felt like a nice thing to do if I had nothing else to do and I always had something to do. "To meditate is to sit for nothing." This was my general attitude. Little did I realize from this "nothing" arises everything. Sitting for nothing, you bolster your foundation for everything. It allows you to pause doing and realize Being. Growing up, I only managed to meditate once at length. It was summer 2008 and I was in total party mode. I was vacationing with six other friends on the beautiful Mediterranean island of Cyprus. We spent our time there partying like it was the last day on Earth. In the middle of all the craziness that ensued, something happened that I wouldn't come to understand until almost a decade later.

During our trip, we visited Aphrodite's rock, which according to Greek mythology is where the Greek goddess Aphrodite was born. This rock was slightly offshore on a beautiful beach known as a sacred destination in Cyprus. After spending some time there, I decided to try and look cool to my friends by swimming a little further out beyond Aphrodite's rock to a tiny rock barely rising above the water. When I arrived, I climbed the rock and looked back at the shore with an excited smile. No one was paying any attention to me. As a result, I looked the other way toward the horizon and redirected my attention to peace and reflection. As I sat on the rock, my feet were dipped in the water as I stared out at the sea. Soon after, I spontaneously closed my eyes and began to meditate. During this fun-filled trip, the last thing on my mind was meditation. However, once I sat on that rock and noticed no one was paying attention, I heard through silence, "Good, go within." Sitting there with my eyes closed, hands locked and feet still dipped in the water, about an hour passed. Falling deeper into meditation, I was compelled to stand up. Without any urge to look back, I continued my meditation standing. I stood on that rock for over an hour slowly moving my arms and body in the direction of crashing waves and changing wind. It must have looked like a scene out of the movie Karate Kid, but instead with a hairy Greek guy in a speedo. I felt a strong inner stillness. I eventually opened my eyes, sat back down on the rock and looked out at the sea for a few minutes until I swam back to shore. That was my first glimpse of silence beyond the mind, but the endless torrent of compulsive thinking quickly reclaimed all my attention. As soon as I started swimming to shore, all I could think about was sharing the peaceful experience with my friends. Shortly after describing the experience, any desire to dwell on what happened disappeared into the next activity.

Looking back to that day, I realize I had absolutely no intention to spiritually awaken. I never cared for enlightenment nor did I think it even possible. I always thought it was reserved for spiritual masters and lifelong practitioners. I just thought, *Cool experience! Let me share this and get on with the day.* This mindset keeps the ego in control and prevents you from awakening. I was still and silent, yet unwilling to dwell in the stillness and silence. I was focused on doing, but dismissive of Being. I was not yet ready.

Meditation is the cornerstone for spiritual awakening, but it may not be the spark of it. Spiritual awakening can begin by reading and understanding, then deepen through meditation. Other possibilities are a spontaneous initiation or surrendering to intense suffering. No matter your pathless path, it can only happen now. You can read hundreds of books on spiritual enlightenment, but until you allow pure silence, stillness and spaciousness into your mind, knowledge can only get you so far. You cannot think your way to enlightenment. When you no longer exist as a mind-made entity within the confines of a mind-made reality, enlightenment remains with no one to claim it.

For me, it began with books and a willingness to understand. It hit me hard and made logical sense – to a point. Reality dawned on me when I sat to realize beyond the mind what I couldn't make sense of in the mind. You cannot understand through thinking what is beyond thinking. The mind tries to use time to understand the timeless. The mind tries to use form to understand the formless. When you think, you try to put things in order to make some sort of sense; but beyond the mind's grip, there is nothing to put in order and nothing to make sense of. The mind cannot understand who you are because there is nothing there to understand.

Meditation is not an escape from reality, but rather a retreat into it. It is not about having a particular kind of experience, but more so how you relate to all passing experience. It has no absolute rules to follow, just different methods to try. There is no right or wrong way with meditation, there is only what works for you. Ultimately, even meditation is not necessary to realize who you are. You can stand on your head or jump from a plane! I invite you now to find a comfortable and quiet location. If unable to find quietude, remain undisturbed by accepting all sounds. If you have access to music, you may play some light meditation music or nature sounds in the background if it helps you relax. Better yet, get out into nature. Remember, do what works best for you. You can do this intermittently as you read or after you read. Grab a meditation cushion or thin pillow, such as an accent pillow, to sit on. A chair works too, but I suggest keeping off the back of the chair to stay attentive. If you don't have any small pillows, use a pile of sheets. Get creative! After you sit, close your eyes, and feel the torrent of thinking that keeps you locked in time. This is the common trance behind all your suffering and demise of the planet. Acknowledge its existence and accept its presence. Thinking is not the enemy. It is our attachment to thoughts which shrinks our immeasurability and feeds the unrelenting torrent. Meditation doesn't mean sleepy time. Quite the contrary! You are most aware and focused while meditating, yet relaxed and at ease.

Continue putting attention on the thoughts you are having. They are there and they are not wrong. Do not expect them to go anywhere. As they come, become aware of expectations, not attached to them. Instead, watch them from afar. See them as bubbles floating at a distance in an empty plane of awareness. If it helps, create a visual to allow space between you and your thinking so that permanence doesn't attach to impermanence. When a spacious presence surrounds your thoughts, there are no attachments to limit your limitlessness. As they normally do, expectations and judgments will likely arise and that is okay. Without attachment, they cannot possess you. Be the watcher of what happens instead of attached to what happens.

After accepting that part of meditating is watching thoughts come and go, keep watching until you are at peace with watching. Allow everything to be without trying to be or do anything. If you become bored, then watch that thought too. Do not judge your mind for overthinking. That only adds more unnecessary thought. With complete neutrality, watch your thoughts until they disappear and clearly unveil in their absence an ever-watchful presence. The more aware you are watching thoughts from a distance, so to speak, without them touching who you are or your sense of absolute reality, the less compulsive your thinking becomes. Thoughts begin to lose their density and seductive, gravitational pull. Soon, there will be voids of no-thought. You are like a beaver building dams in a river. Each dam is a void where the torrent stops. When I use the word *void*, I point to your leftover essence in the absence of thought. Do not celebrate not thinking because that revives more thinking. As the awareness behind what happens, watch each thought arise and cease. Remember, don't expect, force or suppress anything. Simply allow what is to be. This includes all perceptions, thoughts, feelings and emotions. Don't try to stop your mind, just ease deeply into this moment. Sense your senses and the awareness that is aware of your senses. Rest in this awareness.

Once your thoughts begin to effortlessly slow to a halt, the void between thoughts increases in duration and frequency. Rather than think about this, just remain aware of the torrent subsiding. As your mind becomes still, your awareness reaches the leftover void when thinking subsides or, in other words, reaches Itself. You become aware of being aware. This is where you realize there is an undying reality beyond the thoughts that make up your dying reality. This is where you realize your Self. There is no form here; no time; no limitation; no separation; no definition. There is nothing perceivable or conceptual. There are no edges or boundaries. There is only a silent awareness. There is only a timeless stillness. This is your intrinsic nature, untouched by what happens, always the same and always here, now.

If you were just the thoughts you assumed yourself to be, then all you would know are thoughts. There would be no awareness of thought. When thinking ceases, there would be no leftover realization of the formless fabric of life. Thoughts are powerful tools, but cannot define who we are. Once you let them, you live at their unstable mercy. As spiritual teacher Michael A. Singer said, "The day you decide you are more interested in being aware of your thoughts than you are in the thoughts themselves – that is the day you will find your way out." Be wary of the ego whispering, "I am a human being. I am a father. I am a 30-year-old woman. I am a primate part of the evolutionary process. I am this. I am that." All you can ever truly say is "I am" in this moment. The sense "I am" is already whole, undefined and open to the infinite possibilities. Thoughts can only define form, but transience cannot define non-transience. By realizing thoughts cannot objectify the non-objective field in which they appear and from which they are seen, you draw a line between using thoughts and allowing them to define your undefinable nature.

When you let time go, reality remains. You remain. Every human being who identifies as a thought-made entity still breathes when thinking is no longer present. Every definition you ever gave yourself is a mere, fleeting thought. If thoughts are all you know yourself to be, then who remains in their absence? Did your thought-made self die and resurrect itself when thinking started again? Was it ever real to begin with? Do thoughts only allow for intermittent existence? If so, what is left in the absence of thought? Who is left in the absence of thought? What is always here and now in the background allowing and watching the foreground? You are. Without empty space, there would be no room for existence. Without silence, there would be no possibility for sound. Without stillness, there would be no origin for motion. We pay attention to everything that is born of space, silence and stillness but rarely to the space, silence and stillness. When your mind is free of thinking, you realize you are the light which allows, watches and contains the content of the movie screen. In other words, you are That which allows, watches and contains what happens.

What is a human being but a mental label? What is a bird but a mental label? What is Earth but a mental label? Labels cannot truly uncover an inherent mystery, they can only cover it up. By identifying with thoughts, you attempt to uncover an inherent mystery. This leads to suffering, separation and illusion. Use labels as tools for practical purposes, but not as answers to who you are. Your sitting meditation may be coming to an end, but your intrinsic nature has no end. Meditation helps create gaps in the torrent of thinking that begins to lessen the quantity and heighten the quality of thought. Thinking becomes more of a powerful tool instead of an entire reality to identify with and remain trapped in. Realize, "I am still here even when the thoughts I take myself to be are not." This realization can create a powerful wave of awakening that persists beyond your meditation and grows the longer you ease into it. Dwell in this realization and do not let it slip into irrelevance the same way I did on that rock a decade ago. This wakeup call is the most important realization you can have. As you slowly open your eyes from meditation, eventually you won't need to close your eyes to be awake. The duration and frequency of your meditation is not as important as the quality. The secret to meditation is to sit for nothing. Do not sit for freedom. Do not sit with an expectation. Do not sit as a means to an end. The only effort you need is to throw away all your efforts. Sitting for nothing, the seed of awakening grows in silence until it blooms in eternity. What is eternity? The absence of time, not endless time. Sit with this moment until only the moment remains. This rediscovery of what you have always been can only happen now.

Chapter 6
Past, Present, Future

Next time you visit a theatre to watch a movie, I invite you to arrive before they turn on the projector. As you take a seat and gaze upon the large screen, what do you see? The screen lacks content, sound and motion. The screen is empty, silent and still. In a few minutes, all this will seem to change, but does it really? As the projector turns on, does the screen ever stop being empty, silent and still? Can you still notice the screen beyond the lights, camera and action? The screen is always there untouched by the passing content, sound and motion. The screen allows the space, silence and stillness for content, sound and motion, but who pays attention to the screen? Do you ever notice the light projecting onto the screen?

As the movie plays, pay attention to the screen it plays on. Be aware of the light that projects onto the screen. Is the screen or light ever affected by what happens in the movie? Try to watch the movie from the perspective of its own light. You will realize there is nothing to watch from, just everything to see. You will realize there is nothing you can attach to, only a movie to watch. You will realize there is nothing to add or take away from you, only a movie to watch. As light, you watch, allow and contain all that passes. No matter the explosions, laughs, deaths and dramas that pass in a movie, the screen remains untouched. No matter if a character loves, hates, lives or dies, the light remains untouched. Imagine for a moment that a character in the movie becomes self-aware as the watchful light which allows, contains and comprises everything in the movie. Imagine for a moment that a character in the movie realizes the screen in which everything exists. Spiritually awakened, this character will be free from suffering. How do you think this will transcend the movie plot?

As you continue watching the movie, realize everything takes place within the screen. The screen is the only reality for all that happens. The content of the movie is transient whereas the screen is still. There is no past or future to play the movie in. When you rewind a movie, there is still no past to play it in. You watch it now. When you fast forward a movie, there is still no future to play it in. You watch it now. Here and now, life happens. What happened in the screen happened in a different appearance of the present moment and is remembered in the present moment. What is expected to happen in the screen is expected in the present moment and can only happen in a different appearance of the present moment. All that is remembered is remembered now. All that is expected is expected now. All that happens – happens now. The entire movie unfolds in the present-moment screen as does your life.

You may be thinking, "Well, this moment will change and what I do in a year won't happen in this moment, but a different moment. Also, what happened to me a year ago is different than what is happening to me now. Life is a series of moments. Who I was is different than who I am today." That is correct to a point. There is a relative paradox here. All we have is now, yet now keeps changing. Although this moment changes appearance, nothing ever happens outside of this moment. What will happen in ten years will be a different appearance of this moment. What happened ten years ago was a different appearance of this moment. All you ever have is this moment. Life seems like a series of moments, but it is always this one, ever-changing moment. Memories create a sense of continuity, but what are memories other than thoughts you have in this moment of previous appearances of this moment? From birth to death, every experience happens in this moment as time continues to alter its appearance.

The past and future have no separate reality from being a thought in this moment. You cannot separate the past or future from this moment because they are always thought of now. You can know this by trying to step outside the present moment. You can know this by realizing behind all your doing and thinking, there is a timeless tranquility. Time gives this moment a passing appearance, but this moment never passes. The same way the screen is still while a movie happens, this present moment is still while life happens. All your memories are just thoughts you have now, are they not? All your expectations are just thoughts you have now, are they not? Would this not generate the same answer if you were asked at the age of five? Has this not been the same moment, influenced by time? You cannot escape this moment. Your whole life is this one, ever-changing moment.

Let's say the time is 3pm. You just planned to watch your favorite Game of Thrones episode at 4pm. It is safe to say your mind is thinking, "I will watch it in the future." So, now we have something that will apparently happen in the future. Once 4pm comes, you are able to watch the show, but you are faced with a baffling question: am I watching the show in the future as I felt I would an hour ago or am I watching the show now – in the present? It turns out you can't watch the show in the future, you can only watch the show now. At 3pm when you were anticipating watching the show in the future at 4pm, you had this anticipation in the present, did you not? When 4pm came, did it come as the future? Are you now watching Game of Thrones in the future? It is still the present moment, only its appearance is different. Now that it is 4pm, you have the memory of anticipating this moment at 3pm. This memory is just a thought you have now, is it not? This means the past is always just a thought you have in the present of a previous appearance of the present. It is important to realize the past and future have no existence of their own other than being thoughts you have in the present. This was no different ten years ago and will be no different in ten years. At no point in your life does this change. Your entire life, which seems like a long story, is really just whatever appearance this moment is taking. After all, whatever long story you have, you have now. Life is always now. Ultimately, you do not have a life because you are life. You cannot have what you are. The past and future have no separation from the present. Everything is always contained in this moment. You cannot experience time, you can only experience this moment. This realization grounds you in the present moment, which is always the only reality there is, and breaks your enslavement to what Eckhart calls "psychological time."

Whether or not you realize it, you still only have the present moment. However, when you don't realize this, you treat the past and future as places to live more so than tools to use. When you don't realize this, you grant the past power to define you and future power to enslave you. When you don't realize this, you don't see the present moment as the most important alliance you can have. This moment gets reduced to a mere steppingstone toward future salvation or past reclamation. You miss the only reality there ever is. In your mind, your life unfolds from past to future with little reality in between. This reduces the only present-moment reality you have as a means to an end. You can accomplish your goals more effectively by treating each action as an end in itself. Inwardly accept what happens and your alliance with the present moment will never break. Inwardly resist what happens and your alliance with the present moment will always break. This alliance is your link to being One with Life.

When you treat the present moment as an end in itself, this doesn't mean you don't keep a peripheral vision of your goals. For example, if your main goal is to impress an audience while singing, then you're not fully present singing which means you're likely not singing your best. Let your main goal be to sing and you will likely sing your best. Sing to sing. Impressing the audience, which is a goal in your periphery, will then happen more naturally and effectively. This isn't about being perfect. It's about realizing how we get in our own way of being most effective by having no anchor in the torrent of thinking. Usually this anchor is dropped when we fully immerse in doing something we are good at or enjoy. For example, while playing a sport, the more present and focused one is without a thick veil of compulsive thinking, the better one typically plays. Any type of mastery requires presence. What would happen if you expanded this presence to all that happens while still learning from the past and planning for the future? This cannot happen if you rely on what is happening to be present because not everything will spark your interest or be desirable. This can only happen when you remain rooted in the present moment no matter its appearance. Fully accept what happens, then consciously choose how to influence what happens. Let your feet dig deep into this moment so that your arms can carefully reach back and forth. To do this, you cannot rely on your mind. You must go beyond thinking and sense the bare nature of the present moment to fully use thinking.

Do not rely on the mind to see your whole life as this one, ever-changing moment. Memories tell you otherwise. Thinking tells you otherwise. When your mind is still, you realize an ever-present timelessness that gives birth to the time-bound universe. The same way a movie plays, the universe flows in time against the timeless screen of the present moment. We don't realize the stillness beneath time because we are consumed in identification as characters in the time-bound movie. If all you know is thinking, then thinking will tell you all you know. Do you believe in the possibility of knowledge in the absence of thought? I invite you to sit for nothing and see for yourself! Stripped of all thinking, what is left to know but the Knower?

Inner silence allows true intelligence to flow through you. This doesn't mean you'll be the smartest person in the room, conventionally speaking. This deep knowing is born of effortless realization of who you are beyond name and form. On the mental and physical level, we all have varying degrees of knowledge and skill. In thoughtless awareness, we all share an uncreated intelligence of oneness. This non-conceptual intelligence is readily accessible to you right here, right now. To access it, you must be like a ripe and receptive fruit ready to fall from the tree of thought. To be ripe is to have had enough suffering and illusion. To be receptive is to be open to pointers. You cannot force your ripeness or receptiveness through doing or thinking something. Rather, it's a non-doing; a gentle, ever-easing into this moment to its formless, thoughtless essence. This is the intelligence that frees you from time. Here, you consciously unite with Life.

Be wary not to get caught on the concepts of ripeness and receptiveness. There is no necessary checklist to go through in order to be more ripe or receptive. Simply, draw your attention ever-deeper into this moment until there is only a directionless field of attention. In other words, let your flashlight-like beam of attention, which is normally and usually on something, turn to its radiant, undirected source. You are home.

We can say there is an outer present moment and an inner present moment. The outer present moment is all passing experience. The inner present moment is an eternal presence in which all experience passes. The inner present moment is the movie screen and the outer present moment is what passes through. Aware of only the outer present moment, we are bound to remain lost in time. Lost in time, we largely drift in thought from past to future with no real focus on reality. This is akin to stepping into a hurricane and being carried uncontrollably. The strong winds blow with pulses of thought created by the ego, which has become the norm humanity has settled for. From birth to death, we remain stuck in the unchosen direction of the egoic wind whispering to us who we are and what to do. To connect with the reality and power of this inexhaustible moment, you must first disconnect from the ego. Both happen instantly and simultaneously. You do this by realizing you are undefinable. Only the ego attempts to define who you are. Be wary of the ego cloaking itself with good intentions. Whether good or bad, all definitions are still illusory. You cannot define what is beyond words. You cannot add or subtract from wholeness. Transmute inner definitions into outer descriptions and use them as tools or do not mind them as they come. What you allow to inflate your ego today may be the reason why it deflates tomorrow. Your boundlessness is again shrunk to the dualistic mercy of what happens. Remember never to judge yourself for letting this happen. This was passed down to you from thousands of years of human conditioning and has tremendous momentum. With that said, take responsibility for unwanted attachments to what you do and think. If you make a mistake and redirect full blame on this momentum, it is the ego in you taking advantage of what you are reading. Use your awareness of this momentum as compassion, not blame. This momentum can slow to a halt and reverse its direction inward through spiritual awakening.

Anytime you judge yourself, there is nothing really there to judge, only your mind-made hologram. Having a relationship with your false mind-made self is having a relationship with utter instability for such a creation is shaped by an untamed, inner narrator and judgmental, unpredictable world. Drop splitting yourself in two and having a relationship with yourself, even if it's a love relationship, and focus on your relationship with the present moment, which contains all relationships. Instead of solely asking what your relationship to a person is, ask more frequently what your relationship to this moment is. In doing so, you immediately grow in presence and pull away from the grapple of thinking to better use thinking. How are you relating to this precise moment with which there is no personal history? Let your relationship with this moment be of utmost importance that broadcasts overarching ripple effects into all subsequent relations. Nothing and no one is left out. Create a sacred alliance. Create an unwavering bond. When you relate to this moment, you aren't stuck completely in the moment as some isolated character in a mental fiction. This helps you be present as a field of possibility, unidentified through the past. This practice helps until there is no longer a distinction between "you" and the "present moment."

Rooting in presence doesn't mean you will never make mistakes or have rushes of unchosen emotion passing through you. Difference is they pass quickly through awareness and acceptance. Nor does it mean you have to like or enjoy whatever appears in this moment because you won't always, but you are grateful for the present moment itself, which means you are grateful for the One who appears as the many. Be relentlessly grateful for the canvas, no matter the painting. This is freedom.

Be at peace with the present moment through unshakable acceptance of what happens. See this moment as the culmination of everything that has ever happened. This way, no passing event can seemingly possess you and shatter your alliance with what is. You are always responsible for your state of consciousness. No matter what happens, no one makes you attach to passing thoughts. Whether unconsciously or consciously, it is still of your own knowing or not knowing. Yes, what happens sparks thoughts, but what happens never forces you to become attached to those thoughts. This is where you take non-judgmental responsibility for the lack of space around your thoughts. It's okay to label things as good or bad, but carefully use this knowledge and don't let it use you. Good and bad labels can quickly become a slippery slope of unconscious thinking and acting. The more presence oriented your attention becomes, the more you understand and utilize the good and bad labels you need to get by in the world, but without attachment. To be free from the bounds of attachment, you must uproot your attention from time, reroot your attention in the here and now and relate to time-bound events from this rootedness.

The past can be a beautiful memory or a dreadful shadow. The past can be a useful tool or a blurry lens. Question is, do you get to choose? Does the past automatically restrict your vision of the rawness and freshness of this moment? Does the unwanted past seem to haunt you uncontrollably? Do you carry around memories that limit and hurt you? Do you settle for this being a normal human experience or do you realize your potential to redefine the human experience? Would you ever choose to let memories drag you down or would you rather accept and learn from them? Does the past get in the way of your goals? When you look in the mirror, do you see possibility or memory? Does the past use you or do you use it? You must realize a common denominator of most human experience is a past that controls and limits us.

You always have two buckets beside you. One is full of memories and the other of empty space. Both are useful, but do you automatically and conditionally reach into the bucket of memories at the mercy of your ego oblivious to the bucket of possibility beside you? When you first realize the bucket of empty space, you realize there is nothing there to define or limit you. Born of nothing is possibility for anything. To view this moment without a thick lens of judgment, expectation and definition, you must learn to reach one hand in each bucket simultaneously. This way you can use memory while cultivating possibility. Memory is useful, but we tend to live more there than here. Every word that rolls off the tip of tongues instantly perishes into the past. Every thought that arises in the mind instantly perishes into the past. Let all words and thoughts instantly rest in peace or use them as needed. This is how you use both buckets at will. This is how you awaken from auto mode to the freedom, possibility and power of the present moment. Never underestimate the power of presence. It's the only true power since it's the only power that doesn't come and go. It is not bound by time. It is boundless. No one can take it from you. Thoughts can obscure it, but it is always available to you. Make yourself available to it. Ease deeply into this moment, put your personal history aside, let all expectations go and endlessly see what remains. Take shelter in this moment and "the future" will take care of itself.

Treating the present moment as fresh possibility doesn't mean you turn a blind eye to habitual patterns in others. You remain aware of what may happen, yet open to what hasn't happened. Keep a peripheral vision of patterns in behavior, but don't attach to or shrink the other into a defined expectation. You don't have to let memories of how many times something happened pile on top of the only time it is happening, which is now. This pile up is the cause of untold suffering. This is where you create a fine balance to give the gift of presence without falling victim to a judgment or expectation. For example, if your partner became upset the past ten years each time you spent beyond your budget, there is a good chance he'll be upset the next time you do it. However, do not approach him in defense mode with a strong expectation of this. Have the understanding, but approach him with presence. Stay present no matter how you expect him to react or how he actually reacts. Sometimes, when handling unconscious behavior, all you can do is listen, nod in humane silence, and perhaps speak a few words. Unreceptive to deeper insight, some people just want to be heard and have their stories acknowledged and that's okay. Whether visible or not, your presence is contagious. Through your awakening, you water the seeds of awakening in others. Expectations of habitual patterns are likely to rise. The trick is not to become attached to them. Use them carefully if need be or just be aware of them until they fade back into the passing energy field from which they arose – until they fade back into nothing.

Life has dwindled to an almost continuous state of waiting for the next moment. Thing is, this present moment is it. Everything you perceive and experience is within this moment. You don't have to look for it, it is always right here. Whether or not you realize it, this moment is all you had, have and ever will have. You believe the story of who you are is an accumulation of memories that paint a picture of your life, but where does all this happen?

When do you think of memories? This one, ever-changing moment contains all memories, projections, perception and experience. What life do you have outside of this moment? Anything you do or think of is always contained within this moment. This has not been any different since birth and won't be any different until death. Yes, memories did happen in a former appearance of this moment, but they are only fleeting thoughts you have now which cannot define you. Either memories unconsciously guide and use you, or you consciously use them for guidance. Strip the past of unwanted repetition by seeing it as a useful lesson rather than a false reality. You are pure possibility untouched by storytelling. Use memories as tools to smile or learn, but do not let them define your undefinable nature. Do not let thoughts breathe life into a separate past or future outside of this moment. There is nothing outside of this moment. Problems need time to exist. This moment is timeless. Time is only in the mind. Without thoughts of past or future, who are you? Consumed with time, we cannot realize the timeless truth of who we are. Albert Einstein put it well when he said, "Time does not exist – we invented it. Time is what the clock says. The distinction between the past, present and future is only a stubbornly persistent illusion."

To truly understand time, you must realize the bounds of its grip. Then you know there is nothing to understand. As Eckhart said, you see the circumstantial evidence of time, but never any direct evidence. The same way you cannot hold the past or future, you cannot hold time in your hand. What you can hold is this book right now. Words like "past" and "future" refer to time, but they are always thought of and used now. Although life happens now, the past and future draw most of your attention, which means you miss life. This stops the moment you realize there is only this one, ever-changing present moment. This stops the moment you are fully here to live now. The ego needs time to survive. When you are fully here and now, the ego retreats to a distant shore as a faint whisper waiting for time and unconsciousness to set it free.

Have you ever experienced the past? Have you ever experienced the future? Have you ever experienced a day, week or year? How about a minute or hour? You cannot experience what has no reality. You can only experience the present because the present is all you have. Although the appearance of this moment changes, this moment remains. When you have a memory, you have it now. When you have an expectation, you have it now. You cannot experience a memory or expectation anywhere else but now. The past and future are always contained in this moment as passing thoughts. When you set a goal for the future, when do you accomplish it? When you reflect on the past, when do you learn from it? When else but now? What else but now? The answer is always now. Time may need to alter the appearance of this moment before your goal or lesson manifests, but it can only happen now. The past and future is never more important than the present. The past and future belong to those who awaken to the present. The best way to prepare for the future is to first realize there is no such thing. The best way to learn from the past is to first realize it has no power over this moment. This way, "past" and "future" become hollow tools to use with ease and effectiveness. They no longer dominate your sense of reality or who you are. As you wake up to this moment, your personal history loses its grip on you. You will awaken to greater potential. You will awaken to reality. Do not see this moment through the past. Do not imagine the so-called future. Who are you now?

Chapter 7
Accepting What Happens

Life doesn't always happen the way you want it to, but it happens nevertheless. When my parents divorced many years ago, I resisted that reality with every cell in my body. I was depressed, confused and angry. On my way home from work, I would sometimes drive to a wooded area of a cliff overlooking New York City and scream in hopes of solace. It barely dented my anguish. People would watch in astonishment, but I didn't care. In the midst of it, I once yelled angrily at a stranger, "What are you looking at!" I kept asking myself, "Why? What now?" I would sit there miserable staring at the city lights. I wanted to be there for my family, but how could I? I took any potential I had and squashed it with a strong resistance to a fact of life. It was so easy to be upset. It felt like the most natural response. I felt I had every right to feel the way I did and kept excusing my angry responses as justified actions. I loved them so much, which is why it hurt so bad. In the heat of the moment, if someone were to tell me to accept what happened, my pride may have punched them in the face! In that state of mind, acceptance to me meant throwing in the towel and feeling completely defeated. All I knew was to accept what I wanted and resist what I didn't. I took a difficult situation and made it impossible. I didn't know that I could accept the situation and still do something about it. Acceptance to me meant giving up and moving on. We've all been through this in varying degree for different reasons. This is normal. With that said, it's time to go beyond the norm.

One plus one equals two, does it not? Would you ever resist this fact? Would you ever say, "One plus one should equal three?" This is a fact because it is proven correct. Everything that happens is no different than one plus one equals two, except it doesn't have to be proven correct to be a fact. What happens instantly becomes a fact of life because it already happened. This may seem like an invitation to robotic la-la land, but this simple understanding is your gateway to freedom. From a space of acceptance, you can choose when and how you want to be passionate, funny, outspoken, powerful, emotional, reflective, charismatic, stern, authoritative etc. Whatever you choose, remain unattached so that you may keep choosing. Accept what is as it is. Then, you may work toward how you think it should be or remain at peace with how it is. Do all this because it already is.

In undesirable situations, it seems easier to resist than to accept. It seems easier to give in to the whispers of the ego than to watch the whispers fade until possibility remains. Until you awaken to your intrinsic nature, it will take great effort to accept all that happens as it happens. Although it's possible, it's not practical. The most natural state of acceptance requires an awareness of your most natural state of Being. How to get there? No distance required. How to do this? No action required. How long to wait? No time required. Simply, be here now and stay here now. Where you start, you finish. Where you finish, you started. Realizing this awareness is unlike anything you have done because it is not something you do. You must realize the one who seeks awareness is the one who blocks awareness. In this realization, the awareness is unveiled. Seeking is born of lacking and only the mind-made self lacks – never You. So long as you are the mind-made self, you will always be seeking. The felt-reality of your psychological identity must vanish meaning you still use it when need be, but no longer mistake it for who you truly are. This doesn't mean your memories and sense of aliveness disappear with it. As a matter of fact, you will feel a heightened sense of aliveness and control over your memories. A conceptual identity is created by attaching to thoughts you and others have about who you are. Remember, thoughts and memories are passing tools. Use them as such by unveiling your roots beyond them.

When I sat on that cliff overlooking the city, I kept reliving the past and worrying about the future. I could not notice the beautiful plants around me. I could not notice the ladybug crawling on the dirt. I could not notice the beauty of the sunset. You may be thinking, "There is nothing wrong with emotions. They are normal and should be expected. It is unrealistic to say we can and should accept everything." If so, you are right – there is nothing wrong with emotions. I want to remind you that I point toward wholeness, not emotionlessness. Yes, emotions may rise and that is okay. However, they do not have to possess you. As an emotion comes forth into your experience, you have just a few seconds to turn your attention to it and choose what to do with it before the egoic grip takes full hold. To make such a choice, there must be space between you and the rising emotion. Otherwise, the storyline and emotion that follows engulfs you. If this is an emotion you enjoy, you can still enjoy it without attaching to it. As permanence, you cannot attach to impermanence. Only your ego can. Resistance to what happens precedes unwanted emotion. Human beings are emotional creatures and that is not a bad thing. It is our attachment to emotions that condemns us to suffering and illusion.

Whatever you can do attached, you can also do detached, but without fear, lack, limitation, illusion, suffering or worry. Remain obedient to accepting what happens for effortlessness and effectiveness to prevail. Trying to accept everything using sheer willpower is very difficult and largely ineffective. It is unrealistic to expect full acceptance while still identified with your thoughts. Once you awaken to your intrinsic nature, acceptance requires little to no effort. You naturally abide in a state of acceptance, but do not hold onto this expectation. You must abandon all expectations of what it means to spiritually awaken. To whom do expectations belong? Realize there is nobody there to have expectations to free yourself from bondage to them. The realization that there is nobody there to become enlightened is enlightenment. Remember, concepts can be as much a barrier as a bridge. Use them until you are able to go beyond them.

As a reminder, when I use the term what happens, I point to everything that transpires on the level of mind, body, and universe. What happens is all inclusive. Nothing is left out. I once gave a talk on mindset to my team at Tesla and asked the question, "What is the most unstable thing in the universe?" I had a few responses, including black holes, customers, supernovas, family members, etc. I responded, "Yes, these are quite unstable! However, there is one thing which includes all of these and beyond. That is what happens." It's a sort of trick question since what happens isn't a thing per se, but it includes all things. What happens includes all natural and manmade events. What happens includes all thoughts and emotions. I told them I could take the hammer on the table and break the window right next to me and they couldn't do anything to stop me. I had a few laughs and nodding heads. I proceeded to ask, "Why then do we invest our fulfillment in such instability? Why then do we rely on unreliability for our inner state?" There was a pause in the room.

This time, no one had an answer. As silence filled the room, I let the pause remain for a moment and answered, "This is not a choice we make. This is the norm we settle for. This is the only reality we know. We are at the mercy of what happens because we only know what happens. When we search for happiness, there is a voice within creating and confirming our unhappiness. We are too busy searching for fulfillment to realize our inherent source of fulfillment. Immediately following what happens, we have two choices: resist or accept. Resist and you see life the way you would rather it be while rejecting the way it already is. Accept and you see life for what it is while spaciously choosing how you may want it to become. Resistance limits your choices by pitting you against your inner voices. Acceptance opens up your choices by allowing a space of possibility to take action or remain at peace. This inner spaciousness helps unlock your greatest potential."

Every time your mind resists what is, you step into a boxing ring with reality. When you accept what is, complaining becomes an old habit. You cannot both accept what is and complain about why it is. Full acceptance frees you from the conditioning of the mind. An incredible amount of energy is spent on incessant thinking. You can achieve more with less expenditure of energy. The more you accept, the less energy you drain. The more you resist, the more energy you drain. Resisting what is drains you of vital life energy. You will realize a surge of energy as acceptance becomes your unwavering foundation for all that happens. Whether beautiful or horrible, no feeling is final. Accept all that comes and all will go. The best way to change something is to first accept it. The best way to be at peace with something is to first accept it. Nothing happens by chance because everything is backed by billions of years of leading up to it. Nothing lives in separation from everything. There isn't anything that already is which shouldn't be. Meet all that appears in this moment with no resistance. Remember, your sacred alliance with what happens is the most important bond of your life because it contains everything.

There is a distinct difference between the present moment and your perception of the present moment. To accept what is, you must see what is as it is, not solely as you imagine it to be. For true acceptance, you must not personalize this moment with storytelling. To do this, you must separate from the torrent of thinking that tries to personalize what you perceive. Do not let stories cover up the simplicity and neutrality of the present moment. Do not turn the present moment into a story of "me" or "mine." In storyland, acceptance will depend on the story. This one, ever-changing moment is simple. Only the mind complicates it. If I knew this while on the cliff in dismay, I would have felt the soft breeze, heard the sounds of the birds, seen the setting sun and touched the flowers beside me. Even when you are surrounded by chaos, you aren't. Only in the mind you are. Without imposing a heavy overlay of thought, this moment is as it is. As simple as this sounds, there is great power here, which is why spiritual teacher Jiddu Krishnamurti said, "The highest form of intelligence is the ability to observe without evaluating."

What happens instantly becomes the factual what happened. It is what already is. It is nonsensical, futile and damaging to resist what already is. When you resist what happens, you are no longer dealing with the present moment, you are dealing with a time-bound story you imposed onto the present moment; you are dealing with a story in your mind you have mistaken for reality. Accepting what happens means you say an inner yes, not necessarily an outer yes. Acceptance is always internal, but it does not have to be external. By having an inward yes, you get to decide your outward flow with equanimity and clarity. By having an inward yes, you are aligned with what happens and uncorrupted by the ego. By having an inward yes, you are a space of possibility, not predictability. You allow yourself true choice in how you want to be and what you want to do. This all begins with an inner yes to what happens. The 2008 movie *Yes Man*, starring Jim Carrey, depicts in the most humorous of ways the importance of having an inner yes, not necessarily an outer yes. In the movie, the main character Carl meets a man who tells him, "You say no to life and therefore you're not living." Carl then agrees to say "yes" to everything, but instead of an inner yes, he says an outer yes no matter what the situation. As you can imagine, he finds himself in some ridiculous and hilarious situations! Such covenants are not required, only an inner yes is required.

Attaching to how things should be over accepting how things are fuels your endless searching with endless problems. The more you realize your intrinsic wealth, the less you need to search. What at this moment is lacking? Who in this moment is lacking? Our desire for joy, love and peace is an attempt to reclaim our natural state. Thing is, we cannot reclaim what we have never truly lost. We can only unveil its primal presence within. We mistake joy, love and peace as something to attain elsewhere when in reality, these are leftover feelings of presence. For joy, love and peace, you need nothing. It is your natural background state when you are fully here and now. For anger, regret, anxiety, fear and so on, you need something. You need to see this moment through the past. You need to worry about the future. Joy, love and peace are an absence, not attainment. The moment you yearn for such feelings, you create and reaffirm the fact that you do not have them and seek fleeting scraps of them outside of yourself. These feelings are found beneath your search, from where all searches begin and end: here, now; the timeless space in which the present moment manifests.

Even your best friend or amazing lover is pure instability because they are a part of what happens. Love them, but do not rely on them to feel alive and whole. Anchored in wholeness, you are free to love without fear of what happens since your sense of self is not invested in what happens. You can focus more clearly on what is happening since you aren't needlessly daydreaming about what could or should be happening. This doesn't mean you stop caring about what happens, only that you are free to choose how to handle what happens without it controlling and limiting you. You don't need to invest your sense of self in those you love to protect and love them more. Uninvested, you are unlimited in your potential. Awakening to who you are is the most loving and powerful gift a human being can be. This is why renowned Zen Master Thich Nhat Hanh said, "When you love someone, the best thing you can offer is your presence. How can you love if you are not there?" Your mere presence helps water the seeds of awakening in others. Here, no searching is necessary. You are completely aware that you are eternally whole. Wholeness may seem like alienation. In reality, it is your deepest connection. With a sense of wholeness comes oneness. This doesn't mean you must become a robot named i-Enlightened! On the contrary, you're more connected, caring and attentive because you're fully present listening without a thick lens of judgment, attachment or expectation. Stay aligned with what happens, not separate, higher or lower from it. As you let go of your assumed nature, your leftover nature takes hold.

If someone says you are beautiful, acknowledge their opinion and do not mind it. If someone says you are hateful, acknowledge their opinion and do not mind it. When I say, "do not mind it," I mean do not let words or concepts add or take away from who you are. Who you are cannot be added to or taken away from. Only the hologram of who you take yourself to be can be toyed with by words, thoughts and events. For example, you may be waiting for your body to be a certain weight before you can be happy and at peace with it. You are searching for the "right" numbers on a scale to tell you, "Okay, now you can be happy – while it lasts." Do not allow your body image to dictate who you are. The harder you try to do this, the more difficult and superficial the results. Trying to convince yourself not to worry about numbers on a scale doesn't work very well. Freedom from the scale is effortless when you realize you are not the body and it does not define you. However, you can't just read these words and realize this. You must take an inward pilgrimage to where the words point. Attached to your body image, you breathe life into your hologram that you have a relationship with and take to be you. Unattached to your body image, you still take care of it, but do not obsess over it or seek yourself in it. Like all things, you understand your body exists at the mercy of nature so you do not seek lasting fulfillment in it. The same way you see the body, see the seer of that seeing. Pay attention to both. When you sense yourself getting caught up on comparing your body to a preferable image, remember to also pay attention to the observer of all that happening. Cut up your attention in half, so to speak, and keep part of your attention on the field in which these images arise and fall. Link into this field. Doing so will help loosen your attachment because that field is freedom itself and you can only be free now.

Accept everything. Resist nothing. These inseparable statements spell an end to suffering. To accept everything, you must resist nothing. To resist nothing, you must accept everything. Focus on one and you will have both. Accept your body the way it is because it already is and take care of it from there. Engaging in a relationship with yourself is engaging in a relationship with your false mind-made self. There is never a separate "self" to have a relationship with, just an egoic hologram that runs your life. The voice of this hologram is what whispers to you, "Look at the numbers on the scale, you should be ashamed," or, "Look at the numbers on the scale, you can now be happy." No matter its whispers, they are illusions because they are coming from an illusion. As you fully accept the impermanent body through realization of your permanent nature, this voice loses its grip over you.

The human mind is like a microcosm of the universe. There are an estimated 100 billion galaxies in the known universe, each with about 100 billion stars of their own. The human brain has roughly 100 billion neurons. Your entire body is made up of atoms. Less than one percent of these atoms comprise protons, neutrons and electrons, and the other 99.9999999% is empty space. The universe is mostly empty space. Everything in the universe is mostly empty space. Science explains that humans are made of stardust. Science explains that all life is interconnected. Each breath is taken from the infinitely connected expanse of the universe. What happens in the universe turns into knowledge. Knowledge is a tool to use, not a tool to use you. Imagine someone lends you a screwdriver that starts screwing with your life. This is what happens with knowledge. The mind takes everything that happens and turns it into a piece of knowledge. What happens with this knowledge next? That may or may not be your choice. It depends on whether you accept or resist what happens. What you can accomplish by resisting, you can also accomplish by first accepting. Behind what happens are the infinite events that led up to what happens. The entire universe has led up to the passing appearance of this moment. To be aligned with the universe, you must accept all that happens as the universe speaking. Then, you may dance with the universe.

Chapter 8
Freedom from Attachments

The earliest fossils of modern humans came from Africa and date back 200,000 years. At this point, there was no enlightenment because homo sapiens, like all animals, were already merged with the divine. Without extraordinary cognitive abilities, there is no way to mentally separate from divinity. As we evolved these cognitive abilities, our unconscious connection to who we are became a conscious disconnection. We became capable of realizing who we are and falling victim to who we are not. The central nervous system, which comprises the brain and spinal cord, is the primary reason we are able to become conscious of consciousness. Otherwise, the human body would not serve as a medium for spiritual realization. It is through and beyond the body and mind that we can realize our true nature. This capability doesn't make us any better than a tree, just unique in our ability for spiritual awakening. We evolved into a species that specializes in thinking and knowing. During this evolutionary process, at some point we started consciously thinking. Imagine ancient humans having thoughts for the first time that they can now be aware of. Imagine a voice in their head that they can now be aware of. What to do with this voice? What to do with thinking?

At first, it gave us an edge in the struggle for survival. We have climbed to the top of the food chain as the most powerful species on Earth. We have succeeded, from a biological perspective, in reproduction and survival. However, we continue to destroy each other and the natural systems that sustain us. At some point we transitioned from using thoughts to thoughts using us. The great tool that thinking is turned into a self-defining machine that gave birth to illusion, separation and suffering. Thinking turned into a self-defining machine through self-attachment to thoughts. This attachment gave birth to the ego, which continues to take grip of humans. This was the turning point for humanity. Perhaps this is why Stephen Hawking said, "The greatest enemy of knowledge is not ignorance; it is the illusion of knowledge." Now, we must go back to merging with the divine, but not in the same way our ancestors were hundreds of thousands of years ago. We can and must now realize our shared divinity. This realization will unite humankind and free us from bondage to madness. Even if we find another planet to escape to, we will carry the same ego that is destroying Earth's inhabitants, habitability and environment.

All suffering is the effect of an ego-driven mind. You can mitigate the effects, but the root cause will remain. Unless you pull the roots of suffering, the weeds will never stop spreading. We planted the roots of unconsciousness and only we can remove them. This is done through an enduring awareness of the roots, not force. You are not incapable of this. All movements throughout all of history started with a yes to possibility. To give into impossibility is to reduce your possibility.

What exactly does it mean to be attached? When I use the word *attach* or *attachment*, I point to the lack of space between a thought we have and who we are. To lack space around thoughts is to be identified with thoughts. Thoughts cannot define you. Nothing can.

Why is attaching to thoughts such a bad thing? It is neither bad nor good, just illusory and limiting. The moment you judge yourself for attaching to a thought, you split yourself into the judge and judged. You have a relationship with your mind-made self. Instead, accept what happens and learn from it. Learn what works and doesn't, but don't start a civil war within.

How about my attachments to those I love? You don't need to feel attached to those you love in order to love them. Unattached, you are free to love without bound, neediness or excessive control because who you are is not invested into your love. Once you invest yourself in those you love, they decide when and how you do or don't love them. Unattached, you always have the choice to remain loving.

How do you create space around your thoughts? You don't. Empty space already comprises virtually all of your body, mind and universe. You can't create more of it, there's already an infinite amount. You must realize the space that's left when your mind is absolutely still and free of thinking. In this realization, spaciousness fills your mind like the first rains after years of drought. In empty space, there is nothing to attach to and no one to be attached. There is only possibility.

What if you already consider your life a great success? Why should you care about attachments if you already have your dream career, plenty of money, a healthy family and a loving partner? Why should any of this even matter to you if you are already joyful and successful? Your whole reality, no matter how good the story is, has become a reflection of the original illusion that you are your mind and body. You may be thinking, "Okay George, even if that's true, what if I like this illusion and don't want to change it?" I agree, you won't want to change it and don't have to change anything. I'm not asking you to shave your head and live in a cave. I'm not asking you to quit your job and meditate all day. Be wary of the ego whispering, "Why unveil another dimension to life when you are happy with the life you know? Won't that threaten everything you worked so hard for?" This fear is where the ego builds one of its many strongholds. To realize your whole life is built on an illusion is a frightening, threatening and seemingly ridiculous notion. To prevent your realization of this, the ego will fight like its life depends on it because it does.

You can expand the mastery of the life you know to a mastery of life itself in which there is no master or life to be a master of. To realize you are not the mind frees you from the limitations of the mind. You don't have to change what you do, but how you do what you do is transcended to greater potential. You are no longer separated from, attached to or a victim of what happens. You don't have to give up your career, money, family, passions and possessions. Just disentangle your sense of self in them. By investing pieces of who you think you are into people or things, your inner state is dependent on people or things. You limit yourself by worrying about a loss of self. Spiritually awakened, you no longer seek bliss because you've realized the source of bliss within. This inner bliss is utterly free and incomparable to anything fleeting. Instead of being enslaved by the mind, you are free to use the mind. A major evolutionary leap for humanity must be to derive a sense of identity from beyond the mind. This subtle shift silently changes everything.

Success is not about becoming something in particular because that unstable image is conditioned, fleeting and contains within it the fear of loss. This doesn't mean you shouldn't strive for success in this way, but that your inner state and sense of self is no longer reliant on or entangled in such images. True success is being here and now as the space containing the appearance of this moment wherein you feel total contentment, peace, love and unity. That is success and you can only be successful now.

To derive your sense of identity from beyond the mind, you must realize you are the awareness behind what happens, not a small piece of what happens. In this realization, your highest purpose unfolds as your intrinsic nature unfolds. Do you agree there is an awareness that is aware of this moment? Can you sense this awareness or only what the awareness is aware of? The easily observable objects of awareness, such as thoughts, feelings and perceptions, come and go. The subtle awareness, however, neither comes nor goes. It remains in the presence and absence of objects to be aware of. This awareness was never born and will never die. It was here before your birth and at the time of your birth. It is here now. It will be here at the time of your death and after your death. How can something unaffected by time and form have a beginning or end? Has the awareness, by which you know these words, ever changed? Has it aged? Has it suffered? Has it moved? Does it have any boundaries? Can it be split in two? Is it a perception? Is it a feeling? Is it an emotion? Is it a thought? Or is it the timeless, boundless spaciousness in which everything comes and goes? Do not turn to the mind for understanding here. In the absence of thinking, this awareness is immediately unveiled effortlessly. As you deepen into it, you sense it also in the presence of thinking. As you mature into it, the veils of form no longer easily obscure its felt-omnipresence. In this space, there is nothing to attach to and no one to be attached. You must remain aware of this awareness to be free of attachment.

For detachment to blossom, you must carry an awareness of who you are. Without this awareness, you drift in time and become what happens through attachment, which means events have weight over who you are. When you become what happens, passing events control and limit you. Attachment is born of illusion that you are attachable to and leads to inevitable suffering time and time again. Only your hologram can conceptually attach and detach itself. While attached, you are at the mercy of the dualistic nature of what happens. What conditionally lifts you up today can unexpectedly drag you down tomorrow. The dream continues. No one needs your attachment, only your alert wholeness and immeasurable peace and potential that ensues which serves better than any fabrication of self ever will.

No one is ever responsible for your state of consciousness, only you are. Attachments to thoughts, feelings and emotions happen within you. No one goes in there and does it. Although events spark the rise of thoughts and resulting feelings and emotions, you cannot blame someone else for your own attachment to what arises and passes through you. Even then, how responsible are you if you never had a true choice to begin with? If you can't shake the attachment, learn what you can and remain aware of it until awareness of the attachment replaces the attachment. You are the awareness that is aware there is an attachment. Remember this and attachments will lose their grip over you.

Attachments exist because your Self-realization does not. You are attached to being attached. It is hard to notice because it is automated, subtle and everyone does it. Your interpretation of the experience becomes more important than the experience. Your thoughts about how the present moment should be become more important than how the present moment is. How you relate to what arises in this moment is normally determined by who you think you are, which is your foundation for all interpretation. The ideas you have of yourself serve as a filter through you which see. Question is: who are you? Is this a question you can easily answer? Is your answer a role or function you play, such as a mother or pharmacist? Are you quick to know this answer? If so, that is okay. You are one among billions that are! Are you too busy to investigate the "I" you refer to so frequently? Would you rather settle for assuming what that "I" means? A common misconception with enlightenment is you have to give up your worldly possessions, job, loved ones, etc. Perhaps this is a fear you have? Perhaps you are afraid of detachment? Detachment doesn't mean disregard. Detachment means choosing what to regard and disregard. Contrary to appearances, there is nothing passive about detachment. Detached, you have true choice, clarity, unity, equanimity and inner possibility. Attached, your inner possibility is limited by an inherent susceptibility to the instability of what happens.

Attachment is based on fear and incompleteness. The desire for attachment is really a desire for completeness. You are already complete, but your attachments to thoughts and things are inherently incomplete and shroud your essential completeness. For example, I am George. Okay, so who is George? Well, let's ask the uncontrollable voice in my head and the rest of the world to see what they think today! All self-definitions are born in the mind, try to survive the mind and eventually die with the mind. They are born of instability, live on instability and die of instability. Rather than turn to the world for who you are, turn to silence. Silence can teach you more in a moment than a lifetime of studies. This is why Albert Einstein said, "I think 99 times and find nothing. I stop thinking, swim in silence, and the truth comes to me." Do not underestimate the wisdom and power contained within your silent depths.

All madness of human existence is due to thinking your existence is only human. Yes, the human is there, but where are you? Are you in the body somewhere behind the eyes? Are you the body itself? Are you just a bundle of thoughts somewhere in the mind? These aren't questions many of us ponder because we've had the answers since childhood. Why bother thinking about a question when the assumed answer already lurks behind all you do and think? A question like this seems reserved for a weekend getaway around a campfire. Do not underestimate the importance of this question. Your answer to this question determines your reality and profoundly impacts every aspect of your life. Any answer to who you are is only an ephemeral thought. You can only answer what you are not, which helps point to what you are. My pointing isn't intended to make you better. There is no you to make better. If this book is in the Self-Help section, it really belongs in a No-Self-To-Help section. This is the greatest "help" possible. I point toward liberation from the limitations of attaching to the idea of a separate self. Liberated, you are authenticated. When you no longer feel separate from anything, you are everything. As nothing exclusive, you are all-inclusive. You are the seed that sprouts a tree. You are the wind that moves sails. You are the water that gives life. You are all life, yet no particular life. As the infinite expanse of consciousness, there is no-thing that can describe nothing. The human body serves as an opening in consciousness to realize consciousness. However, it is not the human that realizes consciousness. Consciousness realizes itself through human transparency, meaning the human is no longer here as a dense, psychological entity. Self-realized, you are the still eye of a hurricane allowing, watching and containing the winds of existence.

Self-realization transcends the core of problem-making, which is the ego. All illusion, suffering and loss of inner control begins with an attachment to a passing thought that influences your identity. This is not done by choice. It is done through condition of knowing who you are, which leads to worry about a loss of who you are. To be free of conditions, you must see the conditions. This seeing takes place outside the conditioning and frees you from conditioning. Stay the seer to grow ever freer.

Surely, no one wakes up saying, "I want to suffer today, limit my potential and make life more difficult!" Yet, this is what we do. You must replace your sense of incompleteness, which drives attachments, with a sense of completeness, which frees you from attachments. A sense of lack accompanies your knowing who you are. A defined you will always lack, no matter how you polish this image. You reaffirm this lack when you break your sacred bond of accepting what is by attaching to thoughts that resist what is. You can have an outer resistance, but you must start with an inner acceptance of what is because it already is. The moment you resist what happens, a gap of insufficiency and neediness opens up within you. This gap is accompanied with complaints and frustration. To fill this gap, you need to create or wait for the right circumstance to give birth to the right thought that can attach into the gap and make you feel better – until circumstances change again. It is an endless cycle of suffering.

A sense of boundless wholeness arises by letting go of who you think you are. You hold on to being someone to avoid facing a deep-rooted, ancient fear of being no one. When you let go, the world is no longer a scary place to live in. When you let go, a space opens up. Unlike other spaces, this space doesn't need filling because it opens from beyond the mind. This space is pure possibility that contains, allows and watches all manifestation. This is your unmanifested home. This is your undefinable nature. Out of this space arises natural love, joy, peace and unity. This is a natural emanation from what naturally remains when you are no longer the voice in your head. Inner mastery replaces inner slavery. Letting go of your current mental version happens on its own by realizing you are not who you think yourself to be. To unclutter the mind, allow silence to flood the mind and halt the torrent of thinking. Rest in what is left.

Chapter 9
True Love

When I see a snowflake, I see you.
When I feel a raindrop, I feel you.
When I hear the wind, I hear you.
When I touch the soil, I touch you.
When I taste food, I taste you.
When I smell flowers, I smell you.

When you're no longer in the world, the world is in you. This realization gives way to unconditional love. True love is not exclusive, it's all-inclusive. You no longer pick and choose what to love when you see yourself in all the choices.

I've been chasing love all my life. After my first kiss, I knew my two main goals in life. One was to actually learn how to kiss. The other was to fall in love. My wife would argue I'm still working on the first! I always thought love was something to "fall into." I always thought love was waiting for me in my other half somewhere out there. From one girlfriend to the next, I kept seeking love to complete me. Just when I thought I had it, poof! I lost it. Near miss perhaps? That's what I kept thinking. Shortly after I met Alexis, as our relationship deepened, our differences began to surface and the built-in friction of "relationships" ensnared us. Our love was frequently obscured by expectations that weren't being met. One moment we loved each other, the next we couldn't stand each other. This is normal, but does it have to be? Is it possible to transcend such rollercoaster love?

Without a deeper sense of oneness, love becomes a mental image you create, need and chase. This image is destined to shatter because your expectations cannot always be met. Expectations are not wrong. It is when you express how someone should be before accepting how they are that expectations become a problem. Or, when you express how a situation should be before accepting how it is that expectations become a problem. When you accept before you express, peace never leaves you. True love isn't about wanting and needing; expecting and fearing; giving and taking. When we search for love, we are searching for an inclusive experience with another human being. We seek to include the other as part of who we are. Instead, we unconsciously invest half of who we are into our partners. When entering a romantic relationship, half of your idea of "me" is dependent on the other person. There are so many problems in relationships because we enter them half complete and expect completion.

The best way to be in a relationship is not to be in one. When you are fully present as the awareness behind what happens, there are no relationships containing separate, thought-made entities. There is only this moment and how you relate to its passing appearance. If you're in a relationship, then who's aware of the relationship? The moment you think you're in a relationship, you invite all the limitations and conditions of a relationship. While in a relationship, there's little difference between loving, wanting and needing. You want your love to be a certain way and need it to feel a certain way. If this doesn't happen, you fall out of love briefly or permanently with that person. This conditional love depends exclusively on the instability of what happens. Love blossoms when the stars of what happens align and withers when your expectations are not met. This is completely normal and has been this way for thousands of years. As long as your love is invested in what happens, it will remain conditional. To love someone unconditionally, you must not turn to them for love. They will fail you because no one can perfectly meet your expectations. Until you realize the causeless source of love, your love will always depend on conditions. This love is not dependent and cannot be corrupted. We settle for conventional love only in the absence of experiencing the purest love. This doesn't mean you must break all relationships. Instead, transcend them.

You never actually find love in something or someone. Feelings of love always rise within. It is always within you waiting to surface. Given the choice, would you ever conceal such a beautiful feeling? There is no choice because you aren't the one who chooses. The places you invest your love choose for you. If you invest your love in money, you're able to love as long as your pockets are full. If you invest your love in job performance, you're able to love as long as you do well. If you invest your love in marriage, you're able to love as long as your desires are met. If your investments aren't giving a favorable return, you'll enter a state of depression, anger, desperation, etc. Love only surfaces when life happens the way you want it to. How often does that happen? Stop relying on the world to show you love. Stop relying on people to bring you love. Stop relying on circumstances to allow your love. You must realize the source of love and remain there. The discriminatory mind is controlled by what happens and dictates your life based on what happens. This prevents you from living with freedom, power and bliss. To rewire your unchosen conditioning, you must realize the unconditioned space in which the conditioning plays itself out and ever-ease into it. The rewiring then happens effortlessly.

Pay close attention and you'll realize there's an undercurrent of fear, lack and unease that fuels your search for love. When you finally find love, this undercurrent seems to disappear – for some time. The person, object or event temporarily covers up the dissatisfaction. For this reason, you label the person, object or event as special and become attached to your special someone or something. You try to influence the volatility of what happens to keep your needs and wants satisfied. Inevitably, this cover-up reveals itself as inadequate. As long as you're identified with form, nothing can stop you from suffering. The ego will likely pin your suffering on your special someone or something when they have very little to do with it. They are but sparks for what is already there; a mere reflection of the undercurrent of dissatisfaction that's been unveiled when your cover-up fades away. To transcend the restlessness of the mind, you must experience everything as yourself. This is raw love. Do not use willpower for this. The mind cannot help you here. This all-encompassing love naturally exudes when you let go of being this or that. Free from illusion, a great weight is lifted. Spaciousness quickly floods your body and mind. From this space emanates an inconceivable love that I can barely put to words. This love cannot be sought after and found. There's nowhere to go and nothing to do. True love is your leftover quality in the absence of inequality.

This doesn't mean a glimpse of true love isn't possible in a mind-dominated reality, but it's usually short-lived and uncommon. True love is free from conditions because it arises from beyond the conditioned mind. Under the egoic spell, two of the closest ways to experience unconditional love is through a baby or pet. Among other reasons, this is easy because babies and pets can't talk back! An exception here would be my mother's dog who pees inside the house out of spite when she doesn't get what she wants. There are certain types of love, such as family love, that are virtually indestructible no matter your state of consciousness. However, even this type of love is built on the condition of kinship. If your sibling was born into the family next door, would you still love him or her the same? If you were born into the family next door, would your parents still love you the same? Can unconditional love evolve from an underlying condition? What is normally called "unconditional" love only appears that way because its conditions are forgotten or ignored as you bathe in deep love. The source of love within is frequently trapped or fades as it makes its way through the habitual mind. As long as who and how you are is dependent on external factors, your deep-rooted love loses its eternal shine. The most profound love is born of oneness and shines no matter what.

This doesn't mean your love is fake or you don't truly love your family. Be wary of the ego rising to defense. The purpose here is to completely free your outflow of love. To free your love from limitations and conditions, you must first realize you have them. Love is not about someone else; it is the ineffable fabric of who you are. Realize this by realizing what is left when you realize all you are not. This is why it's called Self-realization. It could just as easily be called Love-realization. You cannot know these things because the mind cannot tell you them. If you turn to the mind, you may hear things like, "I love my child unconditionally. How dare you tell me I don't! I love my partner with all my heart. Who are you to tell me otherwise! I would die for my brother. How's that not unconditional!" The ego rises to defense because it feels its loving image is being threatened. Rather than listen to that voice, go beyond these pointers to evolve your love to an unshakeable state.

The "completion" love you seek only exists because you don't realize the love that you are. This doesn't mean you shouldn't seek to share your love intimately. The question is: what type of love do you seek? Do you seek a love that will complete you? Rather than seek *for* completion, seek *from* completion. This shift of "for" to "from" changes everything. So much of what humans do is based on a sense of lack. This sense is an illusion created and perpetuated by the egoic mind. This raises another question: if you realize the complete you is boundless love, would you still seek another to share an intimate love?

Universal love has nothing to do with personality or physique. This transcendent love has no borders or conditions. When you can sense your timelessness, you can sense it everywhere within everyone. You must first realize it within yourself. Universal love isn't possible until you realize we're all manifestations of the same consciousness. Through manifestations, you love the consciousness that allows all manifestation. There is no discrimination here. Beyond the form you perceive, you love the formless you can't perceive, which contains all form. The consciousness that we are is where the sense of oneness is born. Call it Consciousness. Call it Being. Call it God. It doesn't matter what you call it. What matters is you look beyond these pointing words. As Eckhart said, "True love is the recognition of another in yourself."

True love doesn't discriminate or leave you, but the intensity at which it is felt can vary. You may feel love at a higher intensity depending on how love is reflected back at you. On the level of form, there can be a pull of attraction with another form based on physical appearance, personality or both. This attraction is perfectly compatible with spiritual awakening. Two human beings may complement each other, but not complete each other. You may feel a pull to another human being because something in their form resonates with something in your form. Although all form is of the same intrinsic nature, each form has its own extrinsic nature which is made of pure energy. As energies attract, this is where a higher intensity of love blossoms on the level of form. To strike a balance between universal love and form love is to relate to the other on the level of form, whether it's mental, physical or emotional, and the level of universality. This mix dissipates the deep-seated problems of relationships and transcends life as you know it.

If you're only relating on the level of form, you and your partner are bound to suffer. The more you decorate your relationships, the more power they have to control and hurt you. Without the deeper dimension of oneness, all relationships are destined to beg for mercy as they lay naked and afraid amidst the uncontrollable elements of what happens. Relationships teeter in the dualism of love and hate; happiness and sadness; compatibility and non-compatibility. So long as your love rises from the mind, it will always contain the seed of opposites. Everything that rises from the mind contains this seed. What makes you happy one day can make you sad the next and vice versa. Love can quickly turn to hate. There is a dimension beyond opposites that contains opposites. You cannot get to this dimension. You are this dimension. This dimension is all that's left when you let go of all you know and think you are. This leftover essence is the source of unconditional love. When you are fully aware of this dimension, the emergent love meets no opposition and has no sensitivity to the mind. It is utterly free as all distinctions lose their grip over you. Those you love no longer dictate when you show them love. Those you didn't love no longer dictate your lack of love. From the source of love through your physical form, love flows freely into the world.

This doesn't mean you must walk around telling everyone you love them. This doesn't mean if someone acts unconsciously toward you that you must go along because you love them. This doesn't mean if you see someone being abused, you stand idle because you're drenched in love. This doesn't mean you can't defend yourself from attack. The source of love is also the source of possibility. Rooted in possibility and love, you get to choose how and when you want to act. You're no longer a limited, predictable human being controlled by the forces around you. The ego may try to warn you that everlasting love is weakness and will hold you back from being successful in life. "The strong step on the weak," whispers the ego. Own a business? You don't have to stop being stern. Compete at work or for hobby? You don't have to stop being competitive. Love to hunt? You don't have to stop being a hunter. There's nothing limiting about realizing love as the essence of who you are.

The moment you resist what happens, love becomes obscured. To liberate relationships, there must be space between the seer and what is seen; the lover and what is loved. This means to allow space between who you are and what happens. This space allows you to watch without attachment, love without limitation and be without definition. You cannot look to another for space. You can only allow space within by realizing the space that you are. Sit for nothing until you realize a primordial spaciousness with no beginning or end. Be aware of this leftover space and ease into it without thinking about it. Let it fill you with possibility and free you from slavery. When you're in a romantic relationship, you enroll your partner with the absurd task of completing and fulfilling you. A great importance is placed on what he or she does or doesn't do which determines what you can or can't do. There's no space in relationships because who you are is so invested into them. The mind fools you into thinking you need love, are in love or can lose love. You cannot rely on the mind for love. Otherwise, you'll chase it, think you found it and try not to lose it. True love cannot be found in people, thoughts or things, doesn't contradict itself and cannot be lost. It touches everything.

Be wary not to create an image of what true love should look like and start to chase it. We tend to fall in love with images and fantasies more than the human being. Over time, especially when living with someone, these ideas will start crumbling as we realize no one can live up to our ever-lasting fantasies. This is also what can draw us out of relationships as we fantasize what life would be like with another human being. Fantasies replace human beings as tools to cover up our suffering. To love a fantasy of expectations being met is to smell the incense stick of a firecracker. This is the ticket you buy every time you attach to expectations. There is far more to your partner than a unique personality you have all figured out. There is far more to you than your habits and memories. It is an illusion to think all you know, see and expect is all there was, is and will be. Relating only on the level of form is why relationships contain two limited personalities at the mercy of each other. To transcend your love, you must realize your depths beyond what you think and feel. This realization carries a timeless sense of wholeness. Otherwise, you may have fleeting moments of true love when you are completely present to feel something very beautiful within and see it in your partner as well. When you no longer carry the tendency to define yourself, you can look at others without defining them. This loving gaze arises from beyond the mind and thus, does not rise and fall with what happens. When both lover and beloved disappear, true love remains.

Since time immemorial, love has been a result of what happens. Conditional love stems far beyond your partner and relationships. It comes along the package of being identified with your body and mind. In this state, no matter how many times the words "I love you" are said, when a few expectations or requirements aren't met, it can all fall apart. Was it ever real to begin with or just great memories of passing intimacy? Can true love really fade with the winds of circumstances? Conventional love has become more of a transaction between the needs of two individuals. Romantic relationships carry a silent expectation of experiential completion. It is very convenient to have someone else make you feel whole. This takes introspection off your list of things to do. In reality, romantic love is quite inconvenient because no one can truly complete you. You cannot rely on an ego that is always hungry for elusive salvation. Beneath the ego, you are already complete. Before you can open your eyes and truly love, you must first close them. Stop looking out there and start looking within. When the thick filter of time through which you look disappears, you will know it as love appears everywhere in everything. Who you are beyond who you think you are never leaves you, which means love never leaves you. You can only cover it up, but it is always here and now behind all you do and think. Spiritual teacher Rupert Spira said it best: "In ignorance, I am something; in understanding, I am nothing; in love, I am everything."

Unconditional love gets obscured in time beneath your attachments to judgments and expectations. When you are fully present, a space opens up wherein the detachment happens naturally. Presence is essential for enduring love. To love without limitation, you must first realize the unlimited. To love without condition, you must first realize the unconditioned. To love eternally, you must first realize eternity. True love doesn't come from what you do, it flows into what you do when you realize you're the source.

Endlessly searching for people, things or events to fill the "gaps" in your life only reaffirms the gaps, temporarily covers them up and prolongs the inevitable suffering they create. For example, you try your hardest to keep moving from one relationship to another. It may be that you fear being alone. It may be that you need a partner and not only want a partner. Deep down, you may feel a sense of emptiness without a partner to find yourself through. It is your very search for meaning through your relationships that brings you misery. Every time you search for fulfillment, you create and reaffirm your lack of it. There is a silent agreement here where deep down you are saying, "I need to find love to feel complete because I lack love and am incomplete." This statement is responsible for your feelings of incompleteness. It seems like circumstances are responsible, but really it is your inner whispers that are. The mind whispers, "Find yourself in me. Look for happiness, peace and love in me." Don't be fooled by these whispers. Instead, see where these whispers come and go. Even if you get what you want, it is fleeting and only dims your sense of neediness that persists beneath what you are grasping onto. You split yourself into multiple pieces and invest your identity in crumbling places destined to fail you.

Even when you find the fulfillment you're searching for, within that victory is the search to keep the victory. You are endlessly searching. When one search ends, another begins. Perhaps when you find your happiness, it may not be what you expected and so you start a new search to find something better. If you aren't searching to keep what you have, you are searching for more than you have. It is one thing to search for water and food and another for meaning and fulfillment. You aren't wrong for searching without for what you have within, only misinformed by the ego. The moment you begin searching for stable fulfillment, you strengthen a sense of lack as your base and condemn yourself to immediate failure and inevitable suffering. This doesn't mean you shouldn't be driven to accomplish goals. When you don't rely on what happens for fulfillment, you are free to fearlessly act from a space of completeness and possibility. There is great power here for you are not at the mercy of what happens nor are you reliant on anything for you do not lack anything. You are peacefully unleashed to your full potential. By remaining grounded in this moment, you can effectively choose how to handle what happens without possession by what happens.

When you bathe in the realization of how you are still here when thoughts you take yourself to be are not, you will no longer need to live off highs and lows to feel good. You will go from seeker to finder; from poverty to abundance. In this state, nothing is needed to feel what you naturally cultivate from an incomparable sense of timeless completion. This evolutionary leap surpasses the roller coaster ride of endless searching to endless finding. Everlasting fulfillment emanates from who you are. You cannot have love, but you can exude love. You cannot find enduring joy out there or hold it in your palm. Do not search elsewhere for what is already here. The wealth you seek is sitting right under your fears and delusions. Uncover it and let it draw breath. Instead of a moth chasing light, realize you are a firefly emanating light. Self-realized, you illuminate the dark obscurity you once took for reality and awaken to the treasure trove within.

Seeking blocks finding, but the desire to seek the truth of who you are can serve as a useful, disposable tool that drives your spiritual awakening. To go from seeker to finder, you must not seek the dimensionless truth of who you are in space or time. The moment you seek something somewhere, you immediately miss your essence, reaffirm your lack and agree to shortage. To find what you seek, the seeker must vanish. The lacking seeker is the reason you are seeking. Only the ego seeks because only the ego lacks. When the seeker disappears, your intrinsic nature is revealed. This unveiling is enlightenment. It is not something you become; it is a realization of what you already are.

Chapter 10
Investing Who You Are

As a child, one of my favorite toys was the genie from the movie Aladdin. I played with all sorts of toys, but I always had a special liking for the big blue genie. Perhaps it's because everyone told me I looked like Aladdin and the most fascinating part about the movie was the mystical genie. This toy was bigger than most toys and was easy to take apart. I would pretend to make wishes come true and cast all sorts of weird spells on other toys. My favorite part about the genie was taking him apart. I could easily remove his arms, hands, legs, feet, head, belt and even hair. I would throw these parts around the room and use different parts to play with other toys. I would disassemble the genie and reassemble him after making a wish that he would be whole again. Little did I know this play was analogous to what we do with who we are.

The moment I begin writing about who you are, I fail and call it pointing. The moment I begin writing about who you are not, I point and call it failing. This book is a dance between failing and pointing. Ultimately, no word can describe you, no sound can explain you, no thought can define you. Silence is the best medium for communicating who you are, but who has the ears to listen? In fact, we all do and this book points to using your profound listening skills. There is a deeply embedded primal confusion about the fundamental nature of reality: humans think they are like the genie. A highly automated and barely detectable human condition is investing pieces of who we think we are into places we hope fits and stays fitting. We expect our unwholesome investments to bring about wholesome results. We usually have no idea when, how, where or why this happens. We certainly don't decide to split ourselves into multiple pieces of seeming existence and ship our identity parts to other people, places or things and say, "Here I am, please fulfill me," with fingers crossed. It just happens. Does this mean you aren't responsible for your investments of self? Yes and no. No, because you have no idea you are doing it. Yes, because you never investigated who you are to the degree of detecting this.

Just because who you are cannot be known doesn't mean you should start telling people, "I am not Mike, I just am." This doesn't mean you should stop using words like I, me, mine and myself. There is nothing wrong with these words. Imagine trying to get by in life without using these words! Your boss would say, "Mike, please get me the income statement." Your response may be, "Well, who exactly is receiving the income statement?" Your boss says, "Huh? Me! Who else?" Your response may be, "Outside of this moment, there is nothing else. Also, who's Mike? There's no Mike here! Only possibility." Words like I, me, mine and myself are communication tools to get by in the world without letting them touch who you are. These words must be like footsteps along a sandy shoreline that disappear quickly with no trace. When you hollow out these words and start using them, suffering ends and greater possibilities begin.

When you invest who you are, you are really investing thoughts of who you want to be into expectations of who you can or should be. Investments of self are really an exchange of thoughts. The definition of who you are occurs in your mind. The splitting of who you are occurs in your mind. The investment of one of your pieces occurs in your mind. Whether or not the investment is deemed a success or failure occurs in your mind. Although self-investments happen entirely in your mind, they are externally dependent which means the instability of what happens decides the fate of your investments. This is why we suffer. Who you think you are is merely a bunch of scattered thoughts in your mind imbued with a sense of "me" and dependent on external conditions that you barely have any control over. Similar to the genie, you split yourself into many pieces and leave your identity to a child prone to toss you around the room and then hope the child puts you back together. The child, in this case, is the instability of what happens.

All this is within your perception. If the body and mind is perceived, then who is perceiving? The fact that you can perceive your body and mind shows you are not your body and mind. The very act of perceiving shows you are not the perception. All that is perceived is passing. You must realize the perceiver who doesn't pass and watches all that is passing. Is it possible to have perception without a perceiver? Can the perceiver be what is perceived? No.

You cannot perceive the perceiver for there is nothing there to perceive. You can only realize the perceiver through Self-realization. Although it's a good choice, even the word "realize" or "realization" cannot properly convey the unveiling of who you are. No word can. What is perceived comes and goes. The perceiving consciousness never came, never changes and never goes. All that is within your perception is not you. You are the unmanifested space from which all perception happens, but not the manifestation perceived. Not realizing this is the primal confusion that befalls humanity.

Keep in mind, the truth of who you are has nothing to do with words in a book and the thoughts they produce. You must claim the answer through direct realization. Be still and realize the subtle awareness that is left in the absence of all thinking. As complicated as all this seems, it is really very simple. As a matter of fact, its pure simplicity is why we completely miss it. The complication proliferates because you are trying to use your mind to understand what is beyond the mind. The answer contains the mind and is not a result of the mind. You cannot explore the perceiver the same way you explore a mathematical equation. Most humans are barely oriented towards such simplicity, yet we are all capable. We are so used to relying on time, effort and practices, which have their place and purpose, but when you realize the truth of who you are, you realize it was not because of time, effort or practice, but the absence of them. Those are meant to be disposable tools, like a raft that carries us across the river of thought to the silent shore of eternity in which no raft, time, effort or practice can reach; in which everything is let go.

In addition to thoughts, who you think you are is based on the limits to which bodily sensations occur. What you feel is who you are. What you think is who you are. This is all you've ever known about who you are. Stuck in the mental-emotional stream, you completely miss what contains, watches and allows all thoughts and feelings because all your focus is on what you think and feel. How much of what the mind thinks can you really control? How much of what the body feels can you really control? Who you are is invested in what you think and feel, which is determined by what happens. Like white puffs of a dandelion, who you are is carried with the winds of change. This is the underlying condition passed down to you. It is easy to mistaken your thoughts and feelings for who you are because they are most easily detectable and all you've known since childhood. This well-oiled machine runs itself and spews out a changing identity.

You can feel your breath. You can feel your heartbeat. You can feel sensations to the elements. You can feel emotions. You can feel pain. You are so convinced you are the body and mind because you feel everything about it. The human serves as a rare opening through which consciousness can become conscious of itself. The illusion is thinking you are this opening just because you can feel everything through it. Find the "I" that thoughts belong to. Find the "me" that feelings belong to. Where exactly is the owner? With a finger pointing inward, the ego says, "Well, I'm the owner because I have my personal feelings, thoughts and emotions. No one else can know them except me." This is no more than a strong scent you follow without question. All form rises from the same formless fabric of life – consciousness. Does this fabric change from human to human? If two people dropped their thoughts, would the leftover emptiness differ from one to another? There is nothing left to differ. There are differences only on the level of form, not formless. Do not take my word for it. You can realize this right now. With nothing left, there is no one to invest. If all your investments of self can disappear just like that, how real is your selfhood to begin with?

You must realize the answer to life's biggest question – Who am I? – doesn't come from the mind. Everything in the mind can quickly poof or change. This is not a place to resolve such questions. The resolving only occurs here because this domain is all you've known. Where else to go? Even if you travel the world in search of answers, it will ultimately be just another fleeting thought. You cannot find who you are anywhere in the universe, through the words of another or with anything passing. To invest who you are, you must first know who you are. How can you invest something you know nothing about? Yes, you can know your family and name. Yes, you can know your limitations and conditioning. Yes, you can know your memories and expectations. However, what does any of this have to do with who you are? This is where the illusion perpetuates. Outside of memories, who are you? Outside of expectations, who are you? You take yourself to be defined. You take yourself to be changing. You take yourself to be temporary. You do this because you haven't realized the undefined which allows the defined; the unchanging which contains the changing; the permanency which watches the temporary. Unrealized, you remain trapped within the surface level of reality. In such a reality, who you are is completely subject to the merciless laws of nature and judgment. Indeed, this is a scary world to live in.

For the ego, a truly scary concept is the word "nothing." When I say, "There is nothing left to differ," the ego may become deeply afraid at the idea of being nothing. Why? This spells certain doom for who you think you are. Stories of working hard for nothing come to mind. Stories of spending a lifetime in illusion come to mind. Stories of confusion, boredom and passivity come to mind. The mind creates many concepts about nothing when in reality, there is nothing to conceptualize about. This is a conditioning of the mind to try and explain something of nothing. Especially with the unexplainable, the mind is always trying to explain everything, or even nothing, in a nice, neat package for sharing and understanding. This is part of why there are thousands of gods created throughout the ages. An age-old conversation may have gone, "What are those green lights in the sky? Hmm, that must be the gods!" It is difficult for humans to say, "I don't know." The unexplainable begs for explanation because all we know is knowing and we want to know everything, or at least pretend to. This brings us a sense of comfort and security. Ultimately, even calling a tree a tree is false. It is convenient and useful for communication and practical purposes, but don't mistake four letters and vocal sounds for truth. Just because you call something a name doesn't mean it is ultimately that.

To understand self-investments isn't enough. You must recognize how they feel so you can detect when it's about to happen or is happening. Your mind can trick you, but your body never does. Your feelings and sensations never lie. If a loved one harshly criticizes you and you try to maintain a posture to appear spiritual or enlightened, but feel a deep frustration building up, that is how you truly feel and that is okay. Again, do not split yourself further by criticizing yourself on top of the criticisms you're already receiving. Don't get stuck on having to appear a certain way. Don't get stuck on perfection. Don't get stuck on concepts like enlightenment or spiritual. Don't allow a vision of how this moment should be overshadow how this moment is. Unlike pain, suffering is always self-created by self-investments. Only the creator of suffering can end it. This is why the Buddha said, "Pain is inevitable, but suffering is optional." If it's possible to create your suffering, then it's possible to end it. Do not export this ending to some future event after you've gained x, y and z. Only here and now can you end suffering.

The mind will tell you that you need to wait for enlightenment. It will tell you that you need more knowledge. Perhaps you will be ready after the next book? Perhaps you need to wait for some spiritual experience? Perhaps it will convince you that your ego is still too strong? Perhaps you need to wait for a quiet enough mind? Perhaps you need to wait for retirement so there is enough time for this? These whispers are normal and at the same time, completely false. These whispers prevent you from realizing who you are. No understanding is necessary. You don't need anything more. There is nothing you need to change. There is nothing you need to add or take away. You don't need to wait. Time will not help you. Time is all that holds you back. This realization is timeless. It is now. As your sense of self exits the mind stream, all it takes is one of these thoughts to drag you right back in. As who you are begins to escape the story of your life, all it takes is one of these thoughts to drag you right back in. Who you are requires no understanding just as breathing requires no understanding. In the absence of effort and time, you realize the truth of who you are. This is not something you do. It is an effortless and immediate way of seeing, not a doing. Just be here now. How much effort does it take to be here now? How much time does it take to be here now? Feel the witnessing presence of this moment. Be the empty spaciousness of this moment. Ease into the silent awareness of this moment. Do not look for it. Instead, look at the looker. Feel the space from which all looking happens.

Remind yourself as often as possible, "I am here now." Before you open a car door, pause and declare, "I am here now." As you lay in bed to fall asleep, pause and declare, "I am here now." As your phone rings, before you pick up, pause and declare, "I am here now." Before engaging in a conversation, pause and declare, "I am here now." As you sit to eat a meal, pause and declare, "I am here now." No matter what appearance this moment takes, this unstoppable declaration is always readily available and carries with it an immediate healing and freeing presence.

Investments of self don't always lead to immediate suffering. They can lead to happiness before the inevitable suffering. For example, you are at a casino gambling and take out more money from the ATM than planned. You know this is irresponsible, but you are on a high streak and feeling lucky. Before you gamble, you make a silent investment of self into the money and what happens with it. The money now has the power to determine who and how you are. What happens to the money also happens to "you" because a piece of you is in there. Investing pieces of yourself isn't something you pause and close your eyes to do. This happens automatically with great subtlety.

After playing a bit of money, you continue your winning streak and jump up and down in celebration. You can recognize the self-investment because you are fearful and timid before happiness floods your body and mind. You anticipate what's to come with a total reliance on what does come for your state of mind. If you win, you are ecstatic. If you lose, you are regretful and angry. Who you are depends on what happens with the money because "you" and "money" have conceptually merged.

You may have short-term self-investments, such as the previous example, or long-term self-investments, such as marriage, family and career. Who you are is all over the place! Even if you get what you invest your fulfillment in, how long will it take for the dual seed that sprouts that happiness to sprout its opposite? Who you are is broken up into fragmented pieces and scattered out there as various investments prone to the elements of judgment. Your self-investments exist in the duality of the world and negate the reality of your wholeness. When I use the word *duality*, I point to the seed of opposites and division of life. "Seed of opposites" means what makes you happy today can quickly make you sad tomorrow. "Division of life" means me and you; this and that, with no sense of deeper unity. With self-investments, what goes up must come down because it cannot be held onto forever. True happiness is more of a deep, uncaused, unsupported joy. It is an enduring reality when you touch its true source beyond what happens and maintain this connection. It is not something to hope comes out of the instability of self-investments.

Allow your mind to slow down, quiet and still. Pay attention to your senses and the awareness that is aware of your senses. What do you see right now? What can you hear? Who is aware of what you see and hear? Who knows your current experience? If the ego says, "I do," then who knows the thought, "I do?" Go from mind to body and from body to awareness. This takes no effort, time or distance. Don't see this moment through the past and inquire, "Who am I now?" The only thing that can feel like an isolated fragment in the world is a thought because only thoughts seem to have their own reality outside of this moment, but there is nothing outside of this moment and you are not a thought. You are the One who is aware of all passing thoughts and phenomenon.

There are small and large self-investments. The large ones are more easily noticeable. They may include your family, career, relationships, passions, pride, regrets, accomplishments, etc. The smaller ones are not so easy to recollect and notice because they happen almost continuously. From being cut off in traffic to receiving a compliment to making a mistake, all self-investments mean the forces around you determine who and how you are. It is one thing to act upon what happens and another to let it touch who you are and then act upon it. Nothing and no one can add or take away from who you are. Uninvested into what happens, you are limitless in choosing how to handle what happens. You act from a place of wholeness, not fragmentation.

This doesn't mean you shouldn't act or feel based on what happens. This doesn't mean you can't laugh and smile with what happens. You can act, feel, smile and laugh, yet not be bound by any of it. Be wary not to become uncaring to what happens in order to avoid self-investments. There is a big difference between not caring and caring without investing who you are into your caring. This is a fine line to walk and the more you ease into your awakening, the better you learn to walk this line. Free of self-investments, the ego of others may label you as insensitive because it doesn't recognize the deep love and peace within you. Instead, it may expect you to behave in a particular way that it considers caring and then attacks you for not doing so. For example, your pet dog breaks a leg and your friend is crying compassionately for the dog. If you are standing there in full acceptance of what happened calling someone for help, your friend may consider you cold-hearted due to your lack of tears or emotion that is expected in times like this. You must remember not to judge yourself if tears do roll down your face and emotions engulf you! Tears and emotions are not wrong. Accept what is happening always. Do not suppress your thoughts and emotions. Stay aligned with what happens within and without. Everything I point to is a natural emergence once you realize all you are not and rest in what is left. To realize all you are not is to realize no word can describe you, no sound can explain you and no thought can define you. The same way a feather glides with the wind, you will rise in conscious awareness. The same way you cannot find the voice in a speaker, you cannot find the being in a human. Where are you? Remove the parts of a speaker and what is left? Empty space. Remove the parts of a human and what is left? Empty space. Don't remove the parts and the same empty space remains. However, you need the parts to realize this undying emptiness and fullness. You need the human to realize your true Being.

When you make an investment into the stock market, everything is quite clear. You are the investor. Your money is the investment. The stock is where your investment goes. What happens to this investment depends on a multitude of factors. On the contrary, investing who you are begs a bewildering question: who is the investor and what is the investment? To invest yourself means you are both investor and investment. Is this really possible? The genie had seven pieces of himself tossed all over the place. How many pieces of you are there? Hundreds? Thousands? From wholeness to homeless you go. Human beings can just as well be called scattered beings. Unaware that you are already whole, you enroll the world with the absurd task of completing and fulfilling you. As it happens, become aware of the self-investment process. Remain rooted in this awareness to uproot this condition. You may be thinking, "Easier said than done!" You are right – if you rely on willpower to do the uprooting. Willpower can only get you so far with this. Awareness is effortless. You must go beyond will and realize a leftover sense of wholeness when thoughts subside. This sense may be obscured by the mind, but wholeness never leaves you. Just because a cloud blocks the sun doesn't mean the sun stops shining. Sit for nothing and everything I point to will manifest from your realization of the unmanifest. Here, even if you live on the streets, you are never homeless.

Chapter 11
Illuminating the Mundane

"Same shit, different day." This is a common term in New York City, especially within a familiar work setting that requires long hours doing repetitive work. For over a decade, I worked with my father managing restaurants and gift shops that were the bread and butter of our family income. They were located within various hospitals in New York City. In addition to administrative work, I mostly worked the take-away counter serving hundreds of customers a day. I got to know many of the doctors, nurses, employees and much of the local community. I also got to know terms like, "Same shit, different day," and "Another day, another dollar," which were the usual answers when asked, "How are you?" Not everyone expressed this view, but it was very prevalent and apparent. Through exposure and not knowing better, I picked up this mindset and although I never verbalized it, I felt it every day. I joined the crowd and stared at the clock waiting for my time to be up. Every weekday became a steppingstone toward the weekend, which was universally accepted as temporary salvation from an otherwise mundane existence. I was always thankful and knew how fortunate I was to have a steady income and security, yet I was miserable from the moment I woke up.

My father worked hard for decades to support the family and pass me the reigns of the businesses. From a young age, he would always say to me, "This is your future," with a conviction I never doubted. I completed a bachelor's and master's degree just to show the hospital administrators I'm educated and capable. I hated my area of study and blamed my father and situation for the eight years I spent in college pursuing what felt like his aspirations and not my own. Of course, this wasn't his fault. I just went along with what he thought was best for me. By the time I discovered the direction of my desired career path, which was to help people and protect nature, I felt it was too late. I was deeply invested in the businesses and already chose my education. After years of feeling trapped, depressed and desperate, I decided to take action. Since I didn't want to go to school again, I taught myself how to build websites and built www.everythingconnects.org to pursue my passions and use as a bridge to a new life. This worked and landed me in multiple documentaries and a job as a solar consultant with Tesla. As I published the website, I also met Alexis. I found my partner and built my escape route simultaneously. Prior to doing so, I was ready to commit suicide. I couldn't endure the sense of emptiness and lack of purpose anymore. My plan was this: I wanted to buy a one-way ticket to Africa with nowhere to go, no one to know and nothing to do. I told myself, "If this website doesn't work, that is what I'll do." *At least if I die, I'll die with the lions and be of some use to their hunger,* I thought. I always had a strong love and reverence for lions. I complained to my entire family, except my father because I didn't want him to feel bad. His intentions were always pure. Everything I did and didn't do was my own doing and deep down, I knew that. That knowing destroyed my confidence in life and almost led me to ending my life.

My endless thoughts about how things should or could be reduced the great exuberance and aliveness of the present moment to rubble. This reduction process was a slow grind that resulted in a numbing of almost all joy and peace. Except for the mere hope of a new life in some distant future, everything looked dead to me. I could barely see the majesty, wonder and beauty of life. Instead of accepting life, I played the "what if" and "how come" game. I asked myself over and over, "What if I get stuck here the rest of my life? How come I went along so easily for all those years? What if I went to school for something else?" This game is futile, endless and only feeds a hungry ego. I was completely possessed by past grief with little faith in any future relief. Of course, I didn't know I was possessed because all I knew was the possession. I thought, *This is it! This is the life I have and who I am. I am pathetic and don't know how to create a fulfilling life for myself. I am stuck and don't know a way out.* I couldn't realize this was only a revolving story that distorted reality and created intense suffering. I played the victim of circumstances and poor decision-making. This victim identity was no more than a story – a parasite – I carried with me for many years that ate me up inside. These were my ego's greatest days. My ego had the full run of the house and enjoyed a host who lived almost exclusively in resistance and illusion.

This is not my story. I have no story. These memories are a passing speck in the endless realm of what happens. There is only this moment and the memories I may recollect in this moment. Who I am watches the recollection of these memories, but is not touched by it. These memories have nothing to do with who I am or why I am. Without attachment to memories, what power do they have over you? They are just passing thoughts to use or let pass. Am I a mystic? No. Am I enlightened? No. No word or concept has anything to do with who I am. I simply am before "I am" is born into anything. You too can be free of "your story" right here, right now. Attaching a story to who you are only limits the boundlessness of who you are. Even if you enjoy the fleeting attachment, it is still illusory and contains within it the dual seed of inevitable suffering.

The world, too, is only a speck. The world appears momentarily as the perceptual and conceptual face of now. Memories, which create a sense of continuity, make you think the world continues; however, the world is a mere moment; the thin, outer layer of the eternal. The world is like a grain of sand on a cosmic beach. Do not live by memory alone. Live now. Let this moment be ever-renewed as fresh aliveness. Do not obscure this moment with the contamination of another moment to get to. You never get anywhere. Everything passes through here and now. Be still and watch all that passes. You will live naturally, effortlessly and with boundless love. You will have choice, power and freedom. Flow with life now, not against it in your mind.

To illuminate the seemingly mundane, you must not rely on what surrounds you to be exciting, beautiful or interesting. Rather than rely on what happens for fulfillment, you must consecrate the space which contains what happens. Nothing can be made divine for everything is already a manifestation of the divine. Knowing this beyond thought is effortless consecration. No matter what you do or where you are, there is always the same space within and around you. What is contained in space changes and passes, but space itself never changes or passes. It is not a manifestation of consciousness subject to time, but rather consciousness itself, which contains time. The consecration of space triggers an evolutionary leap that defies the Darwinian scale. From a charged space, you hasten your evolution by shedding your mind-made self and revealing your intrinsic nature. To consecrate space, you must first sense and realize its eternal nature. Life will retain its vibrancy, peace and aliveness no matter its changing appearance.

If you were asked to describe your life right now, you may say, "Well, I'm reading a book, see lights, feel the chair I'm sitting on, hear the neighbors and am surrounded by walls in a brightly lit room with plenty of furniture." There's nothing wrong with this description. As a matter of fact, the moment you make this description, you are present and not carried away by the torrent of thinking. With that said, there is more to your life than just this. You think the essence of your life is the thoughts you have and surroundings you perceive. Yes, you have your thoughts. Yes, you have your emotions. Yes, you have your perceptions. Is that all? Is that all there is to life? Behind all your thoughts, emotions and perceptions, there is an awareness that is aware of all your thoughts, emotions and perceptions. Otherwise, you would never know you are having them. You would just be as you are without awareness that you are. Question is: are you aware of this awareness?

In truth, you don't have a life, you are life and all manifestation of it. You cannot have what you are. Any talk of "my life" is always illusory and should be used strictly as a communication tool. Growing up, I got made fun of a lot. Many people would say to me, "Get a life!" This is a common saying in America. I believed them. I would make new friends and start new hobbies just so I felt I had a real life and not some miserable existence. If only I knew that life is not something you can have. It is not claimable or personal. "My life" really means my graveyard of memories. This is not life. This is your prison cell and it is time to break free.

Can you sense the awareness behind what is happening? Or, put another way, can you sense the awareness by which and in which you know your current experience? If not, try closing your eyes. It is here and now behind the noisy filter of thought. This is the missing realization for humanity. Although this awareness is always here and now, we are rarely aware of it, hence the madness of everyday life. This awareness is infinite, timeless, empty space. We pay attention to sounds, but rarely to the silence. We pay attention to motion, but rarely to the stillness. We pay attention to objects, but rarely to the space. You can only be aware of space, not as an object, but as awareness itself. Otherwise, you'll be like a bird trying to find the sky or a fish trying to find the water. It is everywhere, yet you can never really point it out.

Let's take a look at the different times there are. There was now. There is now. There will be now. There is no other time but now. How can you know this for sure? Try searching for something outside of this moment that you find outside of this moment. You will find this search quite difficult. Everything is searched for now. Everything is thought of now. Everything is discovered now. Yes, you had your breakfast yesterday morning, but yesterday morning is just a thought you have now that points to a former appearance of now. Yes, time may have begun billions of years ago, but "billions of years ago" is just a thought you have now that points to a former appearance of now. Yes, things have happened and will happen, but all happens now. The beginning of time, assuming there was a beginning, is also a part of what happens and thus happened simultaneously with the first appearance of this moment. In other words, it happened now, except "now" looked different as it always does. The beginning of time would be the first face of now. The paradoxical nature of time is difficult to fathom because the universe seems to unfold in a series of moments when all we ever have is this one, ever-changing moment.

The human mind has been conditioned over many millennia to believe the past and future have a reality of their own. When the clock ticks, it ticks now. Memories of former clicks are remembered now. Expectations of future clicks are expected now and can only happen now. It is an illusion to think there is a moment outside of now. Still, most humans live largely from past to future with little reality in between. All we have is now, yet we constantly project away from now. If you can't escape the present moment now, you couldn't when you were 5 years old and won't when you are 95 years old. If you can never escape the present moment, what else is there except different faces of the present moment? Even the story of "different faces" is just a thought you have now in the only face there is now. Although time alters the appearance of this moment, everything begins and ends in this moment. To be more precise, everything changes in this moment since form never really begins or ends, it just continues to change on a micro and macro level. Your body is just an accumulation of food and water and will eventually become the ground you stand on. It was never really born and never really dies. This is why scientists concluded that energy can be neither created nor destroyed. It just changes form in the cycle of life. All form is really a vibration of energy. You are so much vaster than that. You watch this cycle. You allow this cycle. You contain this cycle. However, you are not a small piece of this cycle. Your are its permitting light.

While working at the restaurants, every day felt more or less the same. Whispers in my head would go like this: "Here's the same window with the same view. Here are the same people with their same stories. My employees are complaining about their pay again. How many times are customers going to try and get a free meal by claiming our hair is in their soup?" And so on. My work wasn't the issue. My chronic, negative thinking was. My false sense of incompletion was. My reliance on what happens to feel fulfilled was. I worked from a place of deep lack. My workplace couldn't fill my lack and I didn't know where else to turn. I sought a girlfriend, but for six years or so, I was single. I turned to the online game *World of Warcraft*, but that only deepened my suffering. I turned to pets which made me happy for some time, but of course, it wasn't enough. Until you spiritually awaken, nothing ever is. I was stuck working somewhere with gaping holes in who I thought I was. I invested myself everywhere to fill these holes, but received very little in return. I pushed myself to the brink. Of course, this "brink" was only as real as I imagined it to be. Many of us wait countless years for the career of our dreams and treat other jobs as mere stepping stones to get there. Instead of getting somewhere, the "somewhere" appears to you in this moment. There is nothing outside of the appearance of this moment. You can think of an event you expect to happen soon, but that is just a thought you have in this moment which may soon become an appearance of this moment. Everything is contained in this moment. Instead of waiting to feel it later, feel the aliveness of life now. There is no later. Never was, never is and never will be. Have you ever experienced later? All you have is your experience now.

The appearance of this moment will never repeat itself. It is a one-time phenomenon that can never be experienced in the same exact way again. As the appearance of this moment changes, it is forever gone. This moment has offered the passing of measureless, fresh, ever-renewed, irreplaceable appearances. Whether enjoyable or not, each appearance is a one-time product of the cosmos with infinite details. You are never in the same place twice, looking at the same sight twice, talking to the same person twice, smelling the same scent twice, touching the same material twice, etc. This moment is always alive in a way it never was before. Without a deadening filter of the past, your sense of aliveness corresponds to this reality.

There are three words that would have transformed my workplace experience. These words are simple, but carry profound power: *work to work.* Don't work to earn money. Don't work to go home. Don't work to feel fulfilled. Have a peripheral vision of what you are working toward, but stay focused on what you are doing. Everything has become a means to an end. Let what you do be an end in itself. We step on this moment to get to "another moment" and call it working. All the while, we never actually leave this moment. This is why we miss life and limit our potential. Let why you do what you do fuel you, but remain focused on what you do. When you work to work, you are present and not carried away by the torrent of thinking. Otherwise, the actions you take are incomplete without their results. Let each action be complete in itself without needing a result for its completion. This way, you don't live half-complete, half-fulfilled, half-here, half-now.

If you are washing dishes, then stay focused on washing the dishes. Pay attention to all the intricate details, such as the formation of bubbles, and know that each dish is the entirety of life in that passing appearance. If you work as a taxi driver, realize each passenger interaction is all that's going on in your life. If you fly a plane, I don't think I need to tell you to pay attention there! If you work to work, you are fully focused in the moment doing what you are doing as your goals manifest more naturally and effectively. If you need to get home quickly, stay focused on working to work. This will help you work better with less stress while getting you home faster. If you have your boss hovering over your shoulder, stay focused on working to work rather than worrying about what he or she is thinking. If you have a deadline to meet, work to work rather than work to meet the deadline. This way, you are more focused on your work and don't create unnecessary limitations and suffering in the process with stress about the deadline. The mind piles thoughts on top of each other to create stress and maintain importance. It strategically whispers, "I am doing a million things right now! There is too much going on!" Reality says otherwise. Reality says, "You can only have one thought at a time. You can only take one breath at a time. There is only ever one step at a time." Rather than working for yourself or others, work for the work. Again, do not make your work, or anything, a means to an end. Let each action be an end in itself. There is never a future moment more important than this moment because "the future" always appears as this moment. Past and future are inseparable from now. This is why your relationship with this moment is of utmost importance. It's all you ever have so you might as well make friends with it. What may happen can only happen now. Working to work intensifies your presence, improves your performance and limits your suffering. This applies to anything you do wherever you are with whomever you're with.

If you enjoy your job and remain present while performing your duties, that is great, but what happens when you go home? Are you going back to the prison of a time-bound existence? Or are you going home in the same presence you carried throughout the day? Presence isn't a day job, it's the only reality you have. If you don't like your job, then you have a workday of spiritual practice. If you do like your job, you still have a workday of spiritual practice. Everything that happens is a spiritual practice because everything happens from spirit. Let all that happens open a doorway to where it is happening from, which is spirit. You must keep this door open to stay grounded in who you are.

While rooted in this moment, you are naturally more focused in life because you are aware of what life is, which is all that appears in this moment. You must realize that whatever appears in this moment is your entire life. There is nothing else happening in your life. This realization keeps you grounded in the present moment and fully alive to where you are, what you are doing and who you are with. Again, this doesn't mean you stop planning or suppress memories. The purpose is to anchor in reality to use thoughts effectively and end your thought-made suffering. Suffering requires you to lose grounding in this moment. Past and future cause suffering. Both need you to live elsewhere but here. There is only one place other than here: illusion. Life is always here and now.

Keep in mind, it's likely you won't stay fully attentive to life, which is to say fully attentive to the present moment, all the time. Sometimes I daze off thinking about all sorts of random things, such as the time I got slimed on the American television show *Double Dare* or when I peed my pants during class in the fifth grade next to a girl I liked. Do not think there is anything wrong with dazing off. When this happens and you become aware of this happening, gently return your attention back to the here and now. Don't make it into a judgment against yourself. Don't expect or strive for perfect presence.

How do you become alive to this moment? By realizing the aliveness of this moment. As you read this, become aware of your breathing. Your breath is a great pathway home when thoughts carry you astray. As vital as breathing is, it is also very subtle and seemingly mundane, which is why many of us pay little attention to it. We pay attention to everything apparent, but rarely the subtleties. When you inhale, there is no limit to where that breath comes from. When you exhale, there is no limit to where that breath goes. Is there a definitive line to draw between local air and cosmic infinitude? No, because they are inextricably connected. Nothing has its own existence. All definitive divisions are on the map or in your imagination, but not in reality. Conscious of your breath, you are in tune with the universe. Start with your breath and expand your attention to the entire appearance of this moment. Do not start labeling everything. Labels have their place and purpose, but they have become all we know and do. Like machines, we automatically turn all perception and experience into pieces of knowledge. We make final conclusions about everything and everyone when in reality, we only cover up mysteries with words, thoughts and sounds. This cover-up obscures the wonder and beauty of life. The ego silently yells, "Know, know, know! Do, do, do!" If life is only what we know and do, then we suffer at the mercy of what we know and do.

As you expand your attention to everything in this moment, what do you see? Notice the colors of the wallpaper or sky. Notice the floor, ceiling and everything in between. If you are in the same place you usually are, then notice something different about your surroundings. There are infinite details. Focus on one object after another. Try looking at an object without calling it this or that. Without a name, what is it? A mystery. With a name, what is it? A thought, which is also a mystery. You ignore reality when you all you do is conceptualize it. Stay focused on the appearance of this moment and not just the thoughts you superimpose on the appearance of this moment. There is this moment, which is as it is, and there is your layer of thinking which endlessly defines, labels and judges this moment. You must see the world without a heavy overlay of preconceptions and labels hanging over everything. Thinking is not bad; however, it's analogous to the overconsumption of sugar. The body needs sugar, but when you have too much of it, you tend to have a problem. As you focus on your visual perception, realize it is very limited. Everything is in constant motion, yet much of what we see seems solid. "Solid objects" are mostly empty space with constant motion on the molecular level. Pay attention to the colors around you. If you are near a tree or plant, see the symmetrical designs on each leaf or focus on the irregular shapes of bark. The light waves from objects are reflected through space into your retina and processed in your brain. In other words, everything you see, you see in your mind. Nothing is seen out there. Everything is seen within.

As you expand your attention to everything in this moment, what do you hear? Pay close attention to all the sounds. Close your eyes and focus just on your hearing. You can easily hear the loud sounds, but try to hear the quiet sounds. Listen to a noise that was previously obscured by thinking. All surrounding sound waves travel into your ear canal, hit your eardrum, which vibrates with sound, and causes tiny hair cells to send electrical signals to the brain. When you can hear the faintest sounds, you are present and not overthinking. Everything you hear, you hear within.

As you expand your attention to everything in this moment, what do you smell? Close your eyes and focus on your sense of smell. Some animals rely almost entirely on their keen smell for survival. To smell something, there must be molecules emitted into the air from a nearby object that travels into your nose. If there is a nearby flower, walk to it and soak in its fragrance. Focus entirely on this fragrance. Molecules from the flower travel into your nose and stimulate neurons that pass electrical signals to the brain. Everything you smell, you smell within.

As you expand your attention to everything in this moment, what are you touching? Pay close attention to the sensations created by your sense of touch. Focus on the sensation created by sitting. If you are standing, direct your attention to the bottom of your feet. What do they feel like? If you are carrying something, such as this book, what does it feel like at the tip of your fingers? Run your hands across a nearby object and feel the irregularities or smoothness of the surface. Let your whole life be your sense of touch. Just feel what it feels to feel. Close your eyes and feel the sunshine or raindrops hitting your body. Feel the movement of wind. Become fully alive to the elements. Smile at them. Your skin, which is the largest organ of the body, contains nerve endings and touch receptors that send electrical messages to the brain. Everything you touch, you touch within.

As you expand your attention to everything in this moment, what are you tasting? You may not be eating, but you can still taste the saliva in your mouth. It may not taste like much, but you can use this sensation as a focal point in the midst of unwanted thinking. When you feel trapped in the torrent of thinking, use your breath or one of your senses as a focal point to refocus your attention from unnecessary thoughts to this moment. If you are eating, turn it into a practice of presence. Focus fully on how the food tastes. How hot is it? How cold is it? What is the texture? Let your eating or drinking bring you directly into this moment as a conscious participant of life. When you eat or drink, little bumps on your tongue called taste buds, which have very sensitive, microscopic hairs, send electrical messages to your brain encoding the taste. Everything you taste, you taste within.

If you see, hear, smell, touch and taste within, where is your experience of life? Within. Where do thoughts come and go? Within. When does all of this happen? Now. Realize the source of this dance. Touch the base of this play. Sense the inner spaciousness in which life happens. We think life happens out there as something to keep up with. Although all of life happens within, most humans are largely focused on the outward flow. There must be a balance here, which Eckhart calls the balance of doing and Being. This balance is coming to fruition as millions of humans are realizing the futility of an exclusively outward-bound life. Life is an inclusive experience. You must realize the source of this inclusiveness. Everything, including stars and cars, is because you are. Everything "out there" is really in here. This moment is contained within you. As timeless spaciousness, you allow the manifestation of this moment and watch time change this moment. Only through thinking does it seem you are located behind the eyes as a separate body in the world. As Rupert Spira often emphasizes, all we ever experience is the knowing of something. If pain arises, we know the pain. If pleasure arises, we know the pleasure. Whatever perception arises, we know the perception. Whatever thought arises, we know the thought. There is no experience outside of knowing an experience. There is only ever-present, unchanging Knowing in which a changing experience is known. Experiences come and go. Knowing remains. Be the Knowing of what is known.

Reality is made up of something and nothing, form and formlessness. Everything you perceive and experience is only the tip of reality. You must remain grounded in the tip of this dying reality to access the undying reality. The tip, of course, is, has been and always will be the appearance of this present moment. You remain grounded in reality when you accept what happens because it already happened. You lose grounding in reality when you resist what happens because it is not what you wanted to happen. All of your thinking happens now, but is never about now. All thoughts carry you back and forth from past to future with brief intervals. When needed, memories and expectations serve as great tools for the present moment; however, they have become a false reality in defiance of the present moment. The torrent of thinking has become the only reality humans know. This torrent ignores the tip of this dying reality, which is the appearance of this moment, and therefore denies humans access to the undying reality, which is Life itself. Although the torrent of thinking also happens as part of this moment, it uniquely generates a false reality that seems to exist outside of this moment. This is where humans fall victim to illusion. The appearance of the present moment always is as it is. You can either align yourself with reality or suffer in your imagined reality. When the torrent of thinking is all you know and root in, it seems to have everything to do with reality and who you are. No one consciously chooses to suffer. It's a deeply conditioned response triggered by a resistance to what is and built on the assumption that we are our perceptions, thoughts, feelings and emotions. You must realize deeply that thoughts are just passing tools, not actual self-definitions or reality in themselves.

In the midst of unwanted thinking, how do you slow or stop it? Find an anchor in this moment that can help you ease back into this moment. First, accept the content and presence of your overthinking. Do not make thoughts into the enemy. Do not try to stop thinking. That is just more unnecessary thought and does not help. Then, use one of your senses to ground your attention here and now. Listen, look, touch, taste or smell your way home. Use whichever sense you feel most connected to. You can also carry around a small object that you can look at or feel to help your attention retreat to reality. If you have a tattoo somewhere easily visible, perhaps look at it and use your sense of sight to retreat to reality. Your breath, too, is an excellent anchor. The more you focus on your breath, the slower your breathing and thinking become. You reorient to now. The power and direction of your focus determines your reality. You feed what you focus on. If you are focusing on unwanted thoughts about the past or future, this is not done by choice. This is an unconscious conditioning of the mind. You must peacefully shift your focus from thinking to your immediate surroundings. When you do this, try not to label your surroundings or carry a sense of desperation. Start by easing into your breathing. Feel the energy field of your body. Become fully alive through one of your senses to the physical world. Choose any sense. You may alternate from one to the other. If you are listening to someone, try not to listen solely through the filter of thinking, but also through a sense of aliveness, which allows space between thoughts and who you are. When you are fully present, you are grounded in aliveness, not reactiveness. This is more important than spending the entire time you are listening trying to think of what to say back. From a space of presence, listen with the intent to understand and feel rather than just to reply. This helps prevent a superficial reply. Let there be space between what is said and your response.

Everything appears in your mind. Your mind appears in consciousness. Do you take yourself to be an image in consciousness or consciousness itself? I can easily keep writing, "You are consciousness," but the next time a difficult situation comes along, you will forget who you are. This is why you must realize this answer beyond the words you read and knowledge you know. You are consciousness beyond the concept of consciousness. Forget me, forget this book and look within. Let go of imagining yourself and realize what is left. Do not carry expectations of what will happen because nothing will happen, yet everything will change. This will be your last change. After this change, you are the Watcher of change.

Chapter 12
More Time, More Suffering

You may burn my body.
You may curse my mind.
You, however, can never touch who I am;
Only who you think I am.
Who I am watches the burning.
Who I am watches the cursing.
Who I am remains the untouched space
After the mind is cursed and body is burned.
The pain will pass.
The suffering is optional.

Suffering is neither foe nor friend. What is it then? The greatest motivation for awakening. If Gautama Siddhartha never escaped his palace and experienced suffering, would he have become the Buddha? Like everything that happens, suffering has its necessary place in the evolution of human consciousness. You have let suffering serve its purpose. Now, it is time to let it go. There is no need to continue serving an illusion that torments and controls you. Have you had enough? Would you like to continue? Self-affliction has become so normal that we rarely question it. It is hard to see the madness because it seems someone or something else is responsible, which blinds us from realizing we are responsible. In reality, we cause our own suffering. If we can cause it, we can end it. Don't fall into the trap of thinking you need more time to suffer before you can end it. More time creates more suffering. It is your natural state to be free of suffering and you can only be in your natural state now.

Do not mistake the end of suffering for the end of ego. Don't ever take for granted that your ego is completely dissolved. Just when you think the ego is gone, you may be in for a rude awakening. It may be gone for days, weeks, months, years or decades, but until your heart stops beating, it is always hiding somewhere. In small, dark corners of your mind, the ego waits patiently to use a person or event to pull you into unconsciousness. You know what that pull feels like. We all do. It's mesmerizing, powerful and happens very fast. Depending on how deeply rooted you are in the truth of who you are, you may or may not feel this again. Whatever the case, do not claim your ego dead. If you do, you may be surprised to see its resurrection as the walking dead or vengeful living. This element of surprise will add more power to the ego's return because it will cleverly whisper to you, "I thought I was enlightened. I can't believe I did that! I thought my ego was gone!" This self-judgment breathes more life into the ego and strengthens its return. You may even blame its return on the person or event that seemingly drew the ego out of hiding. Perhaps the return will be a subtle feeling, strong possession or it will never return. The best way to part ways with the ego is to consider it retreated to a distant shore as a faint whisper. Enlightened to the truth of who you are, you may still hear this whisper from time to time, but it has little to no weight on you. If it does have weight, that is okay. If it comes quite often, that is okay too. Everything that happens is meant to happen because it took a cosmic chain of causation for it to happen. Again, this doesn't mean you have to go along with all that happens. Maintain an inner alignment with what is, then choose your outward flow.

The ego plays an integral part in your awakening. Learn from the ego its mechanics. Let it teach you what triggers it and what is of absolute importance to it. Remember these lessons and fortify your presence when you sense these triggers appearing. The ego will show you all of its attachments. Study it so that you can use its teachings to go beyond it. This doesn't mean to disregard its attachments or what your ego considers important. Everything that happens should be regarded and accepted, but not everything needs to be entertained. Try making a list of the top five most common triggers of your ego. The next time you feel one of these triggers about to happen, do the exact opposite of your normal, conditioned response. Do nothing or respond in alignment with what already is. See what happens. You will notice a feeling of powerful lightness and sense of inner freedom and control. To the ego, it's death. In reality, you are much more alive and capable. It may not initially change anything on the outside, but how you experience life changes significantly which transforms life as you know it. When I speak of triggering the ego, I point to a heightened experience of the ego. Do not think the ego is gone and then something triggers it back into power. For most of us, it is the basis of all thinking and doing. The ego is who you are, or at least who you think you are, and establishes itself as your foundation for living. So long as you live from past to future, it's embedded in virtually all you do and think. It's the lack that drives all your seeking for fulfillment and meaning. It's your sense of separation that judges what happens. It's your attachment to what happens. It's the dense torrent of thinking that obscures reality. It's your lack of choice. It's your automated conditioning and reactive nature. It's a chronic illusion that has befallen humanity and if left unchecked, may eventually destroy humanity and most life on Earth.

It is easier to get rid of the ego than to solve all the problems it creates! Of course, making the ego into a problem won't help you to solve it because the act of problem-making is the ego. Instead of making the ego into a problem, learn to differentiate between your ego and who you are. This lack of distinction is the origin of all your problems. You create the ego, then suffer from your own projections. You are like a forgetful spider stuck on the very webs you create. Remember who you are and you will remember how to walk across the webbing. So long as you try using your mind to be free of the ego, you will find it very difficult because it is your mind. The ego will contaminate all attempts in the most clever and sneaky ways possible. Put your sword and shield down. Let your willpower go. This is unlike anything you've done because it's not something you do. When you let go of doing and thinking, the ego retreats on its own as you realize who you are in the absence of who you think you are. This process is effortless. This doesn't mean you should never do or think anything. On the contrary, your thoughts and actions are now aligned with reality, powered by unity and manifest from possibility. This realization will eventually replace the ego as pure potentiality. You will be home free. In truth, you already are free! You have only borrowed from your memories the idea that you are not and fooled yourself into believing it. This idea crashes here and now. If you believe you are not enlightened, from where does this idea arise? The past. Now, draw your attention into this moment. Allow your memories to subside and tell me, who is left to be enlightened or not enlightened? Both are ideas. You are neither. When there is no one left to chase enlightenment, enlightenment is left with no one to claim it. This is why spiritual teacher Michael A. Rodriguez said, "Awakening heals you of the belief that you need to be healed."

This doesn't mean you'll never make mistakes. This doesn't mean you no longer have to do the laundry, clean the house or take the garbage out. This doesn't mean you are now perfect. Let go of any fancy expectations you have of what it means to spiritually awaken. Expectations are no more than projections into a future that doesn't exist. They are useful for practical reasons, but not fancy ones. The more you decorate your expectations of enlightenment, the less enlightened you'll be. This book is a disposable tool and steppingstone. It speaks to and through the false in you while whispering, "Step on me. Do not start believing in me. Go beyond me." Feel free to place this book on the floor by your bed and step on it every morning as a reminder not to turn it into a belief! Remember and use the insights you read, but do not let them use you. If you don't live up to your own expectations, accept what happens and learn what you can, but do not judge yourself. That is just more ego. You must enter a state of inner alignment with what is. Let this book point your way home, but do not carry it above your head like a judge ready to slam the gavel. Everything I write about will begin manifesting quite naturally and effortlessly upon your first glimpse of who you are beyond name and form. If it doesn't, accept that it hasn't and keep quiet. A silent glimpse is all it takes to unveil the seed of enlightenment. The more you ease into this realization, the more water and sunshine you allow the seed. This seed is contained within all human beings and requires no expectations. When you let go of all your expectations, striving and thinking, the seed is there. You are there.

Despite the effortlessness of enlightenment, it may take great effort to become effortless. This is a reality many of us experience. Once you set out on a grand mission to become enlightened, you make it into a journey, which needs time. Time is the greatest deterrent of enlightenment. Once you make it into a journey, you breathe reality into a future that doesn't exist. The paradox is enlightenment takes time, but it can only happen now. Since birth, it takes time; however, believing you need more time is exactly what prevents your awakening. The ego makes you believe you need more time to prevent you from realizing your timeless nature. When will you be ready? Now. Why does it seem like you need time? Because everything else does. Many seekers spend their entire lives waiting to accumulate more knowledge and experience before they feel ready or even worthy to be enlightened. Enlightenment is not something you need to prepare for or earn rights to. It is a realization of what you already are. It is your belief that you must prepare or wait for enlightenment that prevents it. Trying to get enlightened keeps you from being enlightened. The word enlightenment is a trap. Use it, but don't try to become it. This is not about becoming something in particular, but rather unbecoming, meaning unassigning our sense of self from thoughts, feelings and emotions. Do you really need more time to sit and allow your thoughts to subside for at least a few seconds? Think of all the hard work you've done throughout your life. Think of all the sweat, blood and tears you've shed. Is any of this necessary with enlightenment? No. The only thing you need to "do" is sit for nothing. Even this is not ultimately necessary. You can stand on your head or jump from a plane and realize who you are. All it takes is a moment of consciousness turning its gaze upon itself. This is not done in the mind, but through a silent mind. If time is what you want, then time is what you'll get. But remember this: time is never what sets you free – this moment does.

I've never been a seeker of enlightenment. I grew up Greek Orthodox, but deep down, I always settled for, "I don't know and it's okay." That is as far as it got for me. Ultimately, that still stands. What I do know is what I'm not. What I can't know is who I am. My wife once told me, "You don't have a spiritual bone in your body." She was right. I would always lean heavily toward logic and science. I had no idea the three can co-exist. After randomly stumbling upon and finishing Eckhart Tolle's audiobook, *The Power of Now*, I felt an immense shift in me, but I still couldn't grasp what was happening. I tried so hard to understand it. I finished the audiobook while driving home from work and kept thinking, "Okay, I understand the logic, but I still don't understand who I am." I kept trying to figure out who I was. Thing is, you can't figure out who you are because there are no puzzle pieces floating around to put together. There is no real definition. Any definition you come up with is just a thought, which cannot define you. If you don't remember it's just another passing thought, then the thought becomes your reality.

The first time I listened to the audiobook version of this book, I was intrigued, but almost fell asleep. By some act of grace, I thought, *Let me listen to this again.* The second time, my mind completely stilled in which there was no mind since mind and time are synonymous. I never had the intention to spiritually awaken. I barely cared for spiritual truths, let alone enlightenment. I was looking for a self-help book to improve my psychological sense of self. Instead, the structure that held up my psychological sense of self collapsed revealing a timeless, leftover essence. It was a spontaneous, immense inner shift from slavery to freedom. Prior to that shift, I was a complete victim to people and circumstances. I lived entirely from past to future with no reality in between. I was deeply depressed, fearful and anxious, almost continuously. There was no effort, expectation or journey. I was like a bundle of kindling, prepared by suffering, waiting for a spark of truth to light my storehouse of illusion, attachment and fear on fire. That spark of truth was *The Power of Now.*

A half hour after finishing the audiobook, I arrived home and felt compelled to sit and meditate. Mind you, I've never been a meditator. I liked the idea of it, but rarely did it and when I did, I usually thought about what else I could be doing. I was home alone and had the day to myself. I walked straight to my basement and sat on the floor. I closed my eyes without expecting anything. I didn't close my eyes with a question to answer or problem to solve. The same busy mind I've always known all of a sudden didn't exist. I became still and silent; totally empty. Suspended in total stillness, I could have sat there for days, weeks, months or years.

That is all there was to it. It is really not a big thing. It is so simple, subtle and immediate. Its sheer simplicity, subtlety and immediacy, however, is why most of us completely overlook it. I didn't have to travel to the mountains of Tibet, meditate in a cave, shave my head, read more books, gain more experience, feel more qualified or wait more time. There is nothing wrong with doing these things, but you must realize there are no requirements other than using the human body as a vehicle for awakening. Human beings are the only known vehicle for consciousness to become conscious of itself. I am not special. In this sense, we all are. Go to your basement or wherever works best for you and sit for nothing. Do not expect anything. Just sit with a disposable intention to let your mind slow to a halt and realize what is left. Rest in that realization without thinking, "I did it! I stopped thinking!" Ultimately, no practice or method can take you there because you already are there; you already are That. Practices and methods are all within the realm of doing. The mind, of course, doesn't want to hear this. It needs something to hold onto and carry forth as a practice toward a goal. The mind tries to use an object of consciousness, such as a thought, practice or method, and carry it into a future that doesn't exist to realize consciousness. This habit is futile. To be, there is nothing you need to do. Just stay silent. The George I always took myself to be died in the basement that day. This is the most important thing that can happen for you. You must die to who you think you are before this rare gift of a human body no longer allows you to do so. As in nature, death sparks birth as you fully come alive, One with Life.

Eckhart Tolle, who I later found out is the world's most popular spiritual teacher, was only the beginning for me. One book pointing my way home was all it took, but only because I was ripe to go home. I was fed up of suffering and ready to let go. Are you fed up? Are you ready to let go, then let go of the concept of letting go? Lao Tzu, author of Tao Te Ching, wrote this difficult to grasp, yet powerful pointer: "By letting it go it all gets done." Deep down, I already knew that I was ultimately responsible for my inner state. I knew I was doing it to myself. I just didn't know how to stop it. I knew nothing of the present moment. I knew nothing beyond thinking. After the basement experience, I began reading and listening to many spiritual teachers, including Sadhguru, Mooji, Ram Das, Nisargadatta Maharaj, Ramana Maharshi, Papaji, Rupert Spira and others. I began writing down my thoughts and experiences as notes to organize what was happening. Years later, I had thousands of notes. I organized these notes into topics. Topics became chapters. Chapters became this book. Writing down my thoughts and eventually this book helped deepen the initial realization. In truth, I am not even writing. I watch the writing happen. Through this body and mind, the book wants to be born, so to speak. I feel no desire to write, yet the writing happens. The writing is not happening so that it can get published, it is happening for itself effortlessly, naturally and spontaneously. I have surrendered to the unnamable Author who writes, thinks, acts and speaks through this body and mind. If I could, I would remove "George Tsiattalos" as the author of this book and leave a blank space. Ultimately, there is no author and no reader. Writing happens. Reading happens. We are the awareness that is aware of all this happening. This nectar of truth must permeate through every cell in your body and not get lodged in your mind. This is freedom.

When I first sat in my basement, I knew I could have sat there indefinitely. It felt like the last thing I needed to do. While deeply rooted in Being, your body enters a sleep-like state becoming very still. Eventually, I was compelled to get up the same way I was compelled to sit down. This is where I realized it was not yet time for me to tip the balance of doing and Being. There was a pure outflow of love and peace ingrained with an intention to flow into the world. This is all I felt. It was pure love looking to express itself. I felt light as a feather, yet heavy with possibility and ready to flow with the winds of change. My work here wasn't done. I worked full time to support a family of four. I didn't have much time to write, so I made time. I woke up every morning between 4 and 5 to write this book. Perhaps this is why I'm so short, I never get any sleep! Despite my waking up early, I had more energy because I didn't expend it throughout the day on incessant thinking or unconscious behavior. I still washed the dishes, cleaned the cat litter and picked up my daughter from school. I showed up for work the next day, helped prepare dinner that same night and upheld all my responsibilities. Very little changed in what I did, but it no longer felt like "me" doing anything. I realized nothing actually happens to me, only within me. I disentangled myself from what happens by rooting in the awareness behind it.

This story is rather simple, is it not? I arrived home, went to my basement with a mind ready to empty, sat for nothing and realized who I was. There is nothing magical or supernatural about it. You won't hear about it in the news or see any fireworks in the sky. Do not try to sit without expectations or thoughts. It only becomes difficult when you try to stop your thoughts or expect them to go away. There is no need for this. You can't think your thoughts away! That is just more thought. Sitting for nothing means sitting without effort to start or stop anything. Just sit and watch all that arises until watchfulness replaces thoughtfulness. Carry a light intention for this, but not a heavy desire. When you rest in full watchfulness, the only thing left to watch is the Watcher. You are home.

What if instead of sitting, I gave into thoughts of not being worthy? What if I thought I needed to read more books or wait more time? These thoughts never arose because I never had the goal of enlightenment. Having such a goal, you may convince yourself you need a lifetime – or many lifetimes – of patience, practice, experience and study before awakening. Who I was all my life just disappeared. I knew rethinking myself back together would be just another image that would also, eventually, disappear. The egoic structure that held up my self-image was gone. Everything I thought I knew about life was now in question. All I had was a light intention to realize who I was. When I first sat, my mind was busy. I didn't make the chatter into an enemy or let it control or touch who I was anymore. I didn't resist or entertain it. I was simply aware of the chatter until it faded away. Do not wait for your thoughts to fade. Waiting is expecting. Instead, become deeply present and it will happen naturally. You don't need to wait to realize what is left when your inner chatter fades away. Find out right now. This is the only time you can.

The only time it takes to get a glimpse of who you are is the time spent fully immersed in who you are not. This time is necessary and unavoidable. Once you feel an intention for enlightenment, you no longer need time – you need presence. The common trap, however, is consciously allowing more time to pass before believing you are ready for enlightenment. Most who identify as a seeker have fallen into this trap. The ego plants this trap by whispering, "This is how you operate with everything else, why should enlightenment be any different? Very few people are enlightened, what makes you think you can be one of them? You need more of x, y and z before you can be enlightened." Acknowledge, but ignore these whispers! The ego wants you to suffer. It uses time to make you. It uses resistance to break you. This is how it survives and thrives. Waiting for the future to free you from the past only delays your freedom here and now. Psychological time has its place, but it is a disposable illusion created by memory and transcended by presence. As spiritual teacher Papaji put it in his satsangs, "This instant of time is beyond the concept of time."

There are distinct differences between pain and suffering. Physical pain isn't enjoyable, but it serves its purpose as a survival mechanism. It signals the brain that the body is in danger and requires attention. On the other hand, suffering occurs entirely in the mind as resistance toward what happens. When we are unwilling to accept what happens, we suffer. When we cannot flow with life, we suffer. When we cling to unwanted memories, unmet expectations or fearful thoughts, we suffer. When we avert or attach to what happens, we suffer. As Socrates put it, "If you don't get what you want, you suffer; if you get what you don't want, you suffer; even when you get exactly what you want, you still suffer because you can't hold on to it forever." Suffering may seem like an unavoidable reality, but it is really the denial of reality. Suffering is a result of not accepting this moment as it is before wishing it any different. As a reminder, you don't need to resist something to do something. To remain aligned with reality, you must accept what happens because it already happened, then choose how to proceed without letting people or situations choose for you. This choice in how to proceed after something happens is only available when you remain aligned with what happens. Using willpower here can only get you so far. Through enlightenment, accepting what happens becomes quite effortless. Once you truly accept the inherent volatility, unmistakability and ephemerality of what happens, you begin to let go of how things should be and first align with how things are. You don't need to wait or train for this. It is your natural background state beyond the fear and lack which haunt humanity. I use the word "haunt" because the dominant background state of humanity, which is fear and lack, is 100% imaginary. To be fearful is to create "ghosts of loss" from an imagined future to haunt you as thoughts now. To quote Will Smith from the movie *After Earth*, "The only place that fear can exist is in our thoughts of the future. It is a product of our imagination, causing us to fear things that do not at present and may not ever exist. That is near insanity Kitai. Do not misunderstand me, danger is very real, but fear is a choice. We are all telling ourselves a story and that day mine changed."

Fear is always about what will happen, not what is happening, which means it is always about that which doesn't exist. In other words, fear exists in time, not at present. It is pure imagination. If you think you need fear, this is just another fear of being fearless. Fear is not a product of reality. It is an unwanted prediction of what may happen. Fearless, you can still predict what may happen and act upon it, but you won't become a slave to the prediction. Instead, you are the master and your thoughts are the slave. To become an enduring master, you must be rooted in reality, not in your mind. The master knows there are no accidents and internally yields to the flow of life to remain One with Life. Fear is always coming for who you think you are, but can never touch who you really are. Fear arises from your sense of personhood. All fear is really the fear of death, whether it be psychological or physical death. When the image of who you are is threatened, you become afraid of losing your preferred sense of self. When your body becomes threatened, you become afraid of what may happen to it. Anything you can do afraid, you can do unafraid, but without suffering.

Despite the potential usefulness of fear, fearlessness epitomizes usefulness. Anything you can do fearfully, you can do fearlessly. Do not underestimate the potential of a clear mind that uses knowledge. Rooted in the truth of who you are, you are limitless in your potential. Instincts and adrenaline still kick in, but they are surrounded by spacious awareness. Fearlessness born of the present contains within it the seed of possibility and awareness whereas fearfulness born of the future contains within it the seed of illusion and limitation. We only settle for fear and praise it as necessary because we barely know another way. I invite you now to discover another way by discovering who you are. Fearful, you believe something, which has never truly been gained, will be lost. How can you lose what you have never gained? Is anything ultimately yours? Is anyone ultimately yours? Are you ultimately your body and mind? Fear exists in time, not in reality. You don't need it. Fearlessly redefine what it means to be human by unveiling your roots beyond the human. Fear and lack are co-creators for all unconscious behavior. They mold virtually all thoughts and actions in the subtlest ways. We only praise fear because we barely realize its impact on almost all we do and think. We are fooled into thinking it's necessary since everyone is unconsciously clinging to it. Illusions are never necessary. For raw freedom, only the truth of who you are is.

When fear does arise, it appears both physically and mentally. To overcome fear, you must first locate the physical sensation of it. Is it a tightness of the chest? Is it a constriction of your gut? Is it a pounding of your head? Close your eyes and find it. Become fully aware of this feeling. Go into it instead of away from it. Accept what you feel. Use your focus of the physical sensation to stay grounded in the present moment. Once you lose your grounding in reality, you must find an anchor back to it. Use the most dominant force of the moment to anchor in the moment. When you are afraid, the most powerful appearance of the moment is your physical reaction to fear. Use this to your advantage. You must uproot from fearful thoughts and reroot in fearful sensations. Shift your focus from thinking to feeling. Fear seems to exist where nothing can exist: the future. Your fearful thoughts have no grounding in the present moment; however, the physical component of fear does. Shift your attention from mind to body and let what is real, which is what you feel, ground you here and now. Step out of your mind and into your body and allow your body to free you from your mind. Full awareness of the physical effects of fear can free you from slavery to its mental causes. Focus on what it feels like rather than why it is there. This will divert attention from feeding your fear to accepting and overcoming it.

My car was recently totaled in a car accident. While driving to work, I got hit at 45 mph on the passenger side of my car. I never saw the car coming and had no time to react. I only knew about the car when the front of it slammed through my passenger door. My car ended up on the sidewalk with all the airbags out. My arms and legs were burnt, bruised and bleeding, but thanks to the airbags and seatbelt, I had no major damage. It caught me totally off guard. I've been in a major car accident before, but this time was completely different. I wasn't afraid. I remember looking down at my arms and seeing blood, but I didn't worry or stall. It certainly hurt, but there was no suffering at the mercy of fearful thoughts over a future that didn't exist. I didn't try to accept what happened. I just did. It was effortless. This allowed me to think clearly and take immediate action. I searched for my phone, stepped out and immediately dialed 911 while walking to the other car to offer help. There were seven people in the car, but miraculously, none of them were seriously hurt. What is the moral of this story? You don't need fear to take effective action. Sure, it can help, but is never absolutely necessary. If you don't want to let it go, then don't. If it has you convinced you need it, then keep it. More than anything, it exists as a subtle undercurrent that dictates who and how you are. When you are ready, which you can only be ready now, the power of fearless presence awaits you. Fear cannot prevail in your presence, only your absence of presence.

Despite my previous story, I am not incapable of fear. A few days after my son Leonidas was born, my wife and I were driving home from the hospital to begin my one-month paternity leave. From decorating his room to purchasing enough supplies for a year, we were well prepared for his arrival. The doctors and nurses told us Leo was perfectly healthy. As soon as we got home, we went upstairs to our bedroom to change Leo's diaper. I enjoy pretending I'm busy when it comes time to change his poop diaper so that Alexis can do it. As soon as I smell the poop, I hand the baby to her and say, "Be right back!" I then disappear as she realizes he has a poop diaper and is forced to change it! This makes us laugh! Well, mostly me at least. Although it's impossible to prepare for everything, we certainly tried our best. What we didn't prepare for was our two cats, Polly and Molly. For the record, I wanted to name them Zen and Master, but Alexis disagreed! Nevertheless, as soon as Alexis began changing his diaper, Molly jumped on the bed, hissed and attacked the baby's face. She got one good swipe. I immediately grabbed the cat and tossed her out of the room. I remember as soon as I closed the door, I paused before turning around to see the damage done. In that moment, I was afraid. I was certainly worried over what happened to Leo. I turned around and saw three scratch marks with blood. One was on his forehead, the other on his eyebrow and the third on his eyelid. Molly barely missed Leo's eyeball. We got lucky and learned our lesson. Here I am writing about fearlessness and there I was afraid. Now, what is the moral of this story? Shit happens, including ego attacks. The trick to shit happening is not to consider it shit. Have a peripheral vision of good and bad, but don't let a mental label paint your entire world. As I said, you may never experience the ego again, but it's rarely completely gone. It's always on standby waiting for you to believe in a past or future that doesn't exist. I resisted Molly's actions and was afraid of Leo living with one eye or contracting cat scratch disease. I fully accepted my fear the moment I felt it and spent no time judging myself for being afraid. I didn't split myself into the judge and judged. I focused on the sensation of fear and not its fictional causes, which allowed me to return to the present moment. This is why my ego attack was short-lived. Remain aligned with your misalignment. Don't hold yourself accountable to expectations of what it means to be enlightened. There is no separate "you" to hold accountable. There is only this moment and how you relate to its passing appearance.

The entire fabrication of reality begins the moment you say "I" and take "I" to be you. This sparks all your suffering, illusion, attachment and limitation. When suffering arises, it strengthens through the illusion of "my" suffering. When you claim ownership to suffering, you exacerbate and prolong it. In suffering, you ask many questions except the most important: who is it that suffers? Try to find the sufferer. Point out who is suffering. No matter how many fingers you point inward or times you say, "Obviously, I am," you can never truly pinpoint the sufferer. Every attempt to own your suffering is just another passing thought to disown reality. There is no owner of suffering, there is just suffering. You watch it, but you are not it. You feel it, but it is not yours. Anything you can perceive is never you. How could it be? If you take yourself to be that which is perceived, then who is the perceiver? We are so fixated on what we perceive that we miss the perceiver who is prior to all perception. Once you realize no suffering is your suffering, you are riper to end suffering. To end all suffering, you must end all illusion. End the illusion of time. End the illusion of personal. End the illusion of separateness. End the illusion of birth and death. There are so many illusions, but it only takes one realization to end them all. This realization is Self-realization. Let go of all you think you are and the illusions will disappear the same way they appeared – automatically. Waking up is like falling asleep. In the last moment, right before you fall asleep, you simply let go. You let go of all your identifications, attachments, memories and expectations. You let everything go. It is effortless. You rest in deep peace and rejuvenate. You can't think your way to sleep just as you can't think your way to waking up. As you let go, there is an opening. This opening is enlightenment.

Pain and suffering are not punishments. They are signals. Pain signals to the body the same message that suffering signals to the mind: something is wrong and needs attending to. Pain says, "This is where something is wrong. Attend to me." Suffering, which has more of a hidden message, says, "You have mistaken who you are for a bunch of thoughts and feelings." Both are useful signals meant to make us aware of what is happening, not hinder us. We all get the memo with pain, but not so much with suffering. It's clear that pain isn't enjoyable, but without it, it would be difficult to take care of a body you are out of touch with. It's also clear that suffering isn't enjoyable, but without it, it would be impossible to spiritually awaken. You cannot awaken by bliss alone. Suffering has its necessary place, but there comes a time that you must see it for what it truly is: a signal to wake up from the illusion of a separate self. This signal has within it the seed of motivation for enlightenment. The silent destiny of this signal is its transmutation into an intention for enlightenment. This is why you suffer. As Eckhart said, "Suffering is necessary until you realize it is unnecessary." The fact that you have read this far shows that you have likely transmuted this signal and fulfilled its destiny, but perhaps your ego is convincing you that you need more time. Perhaps you need to read another book or meditate a few more years? Perhaps you need a guru? These events can certainly help and there is nothing wrong with them, but only this precise moment can open the doorway to liberation. So long as your mind is run by the ego, you cannot be too quick to trust its whispers. It will fool you to control and limit you for its own survival. You must trust, but not in your egoic mind. Trust, at its deepest level, is the absence of fear. Instead, trust Life, your Self, the universe or however you want to word it. Inherently trustworthy, you know no matter what happens, you remain the untouched Watcher of it all. With more time, you can receive more pointers, but all signposts will always point back to this moment. All pointers are the same. All answers are the same. They come from different angles, but all say, "Be here now." Wait if you wish, but know it is your waiting that allows more suffering and prevents your awakening.

Chapter 13
Nothing to Forgive, No One to Defend

Since time immemorial, the Earth has been a battleground of illusions. Humans have been in the grip of the ego for thousands of years. The difference today is we have armed the ego with weapons of mass destruction. Never in human history has it been more important to realize who we are. From dysfunctional relationships to global warfare to ecological destruction, the veil of illusion has torn humanity into insanity. This veil obscures the presence of everything we are searching for – completeness, joy, peace, love – and tricks us into search and destroy mode. As Eckhart puts it, "There is only one perpetrator of evil on the planet: human unconsciousness. That realization is true forgiveness." This, too, is why Jesus said, "Father, forgive them; for they do not know what they are doing." Only the light of consciousness can dispel unconsciousness. How to shine this light? Forgive all unconscious behavior by realizing nothing anyone says or does reflects who they truly are. Unconditional forgiveness is a very powerful tool. The ego labels it as weakness because the ego shrinks when you do it. Do not rely on what happens to determine your forgiveness. Such discrimination spits in the face of reality, which is always what already is. You can better influence the next appearance of reality by first accepting all former appearances. Acceptance is forgiveness. This doesn't mean if someone has a gun to your head, you yield because you forgave the man pointing it at you. You can still kick him between the legs and escape! Difference is you don't carry any suffering in your heart. Let all unconscious behavior meet your unwavering forgiveness. Then choose how to proceed.

It may sound unrealistic to be forgiving all the time, but what is truly unrealistic is the illusion you are defending when you are unforgiving. To refuse forgiving what happens is to hold onto what didn't happen, which doesn't exist. It is always an illusion because it only exists as a preferred scenario that doesn't exist. When someone curses or judges you, they are cursing and judging only the idea they have of you. It is an exchange of thoughts in their own head and has nothing to do with this moment or who you are. Unless you consider yourself just a bundle of thoughts at the mercy of other thoughts, then no concept can touch who you are. Most people obsess over their opinions, which consequently become who they are and have incredible force behind them. The third patriarch of Zen accurately said, "To know the truth, only cease to cherish opinions." This doesn't mean not to have or disregard opinions. Rather, don't attach to or give them absolute importance. An opinion is just another passing thought; a tiny perspective and angle that can never, in and of itself, express the whole truth. Nothing said or done can. To help extract the power opinions can have over who you are, take the advice of author Byron Katie and always question: "Is it true? Can you absolutely know that it's true? How do you react, what happens, when you believe that thought? Who would you be without that thought?" These are powerful questions meant to extricate you from your opinions and allow a freedom no longer imprisoned by your opinions. Anytime someone tries to tell you who you are, see it as just another passing concept that has nothing to do with who you are. No thought can touch you unless you touch it. Inquire right now, without the lens of the past, what anything or anyone has to do with who you are? If four questions are too much, then always ask this one: "Who?" Who is vulnerable to opinions? Who starts at birth and ends at death? Who feels taken away from? Who feels added to? And so on.

The parable, *The Tao of Forgiveness*, by Taoist master Derek Lin, tells a powerful story of potatoes and forgiveness: One day, the sage gave the disciple an empty sack and a basket of potatoes. "Think of all the people who have done or said something against you in the recent past, especially those you cannot forgive. For each of them, inscribe the name on a potato and put it in the sack." The disciple came up with quite a few names and soon his sack was heavy with potatoes. "Carry the sack with you wherever you go for a week," said the sage. "We'll talk after that."

At first, the disciple thought nothing of it. Carrying the sack was not particularly difficult. But after a while, it became more of a burden. It sometimes got in the way and seemed to require more effort to carry as time went on, even though its weight remained the same. After a few days, the sack began to smell. The carved potatoes gave off a ripe odor. Not only were they increasingly inconvenient to carry around, they were also becoming rather unpleasant. Finally, the week was over.

The sage summoned the disciple. "Any thoughts about all this?"

"Yes, Master," the disciple replied.

"When we are unable to forgive others, we carry negative feelings with us everywhere, much like these potatoes. That negativity becomes a burden to us and, after a while, it festers."

"Yes, that is exactly what happens when one holds a grudge. So, how can we lighten the load?"

"We must strive to forgive."

"Forgiving someone is the equivalent of removing the corresponding potato from the sack. How many of your transgressors are you able to forgive?"

"I've thought about it quite a bit, Master," the disciple said. "It required much effort, but I have decided to forgive all of them."

"Very well, we can remove all the potatoes. Were there any more people who transgressed against you this last week?" The disciple thought for a while and admitted there were. Then he felt panic when he realized his empty sack was about to get filled up again.

"Master," he asked, "If we continue like this, wouldn't there always be potatoes in the sack week after week?"

"Yes, as long as people speak or act against you in some way, you will always have potatoes."

"But Master, we can never control what others do. So what good is the Tao in this case?"

"We're not at the realm of the Tao yet. Everything we have talked about so far is the conventional approach to forgiveness. It is the same thing that many philosophies and most religions preach – we must constantly strive to forgive, for it is an important virtue. This is not the Tao because there is no striving in the Tao."

"Then what is the Tao, Master?"

"You can figure it out. If the potatoes are negative feelings, then what is the sack?"

"The sack is… that which allows me to hold on to the negativity. It is something within us that makes us dwell on feeling offended. Ah, it is my inflated sense of self-importance."

"And what will happen if you let go of it?"

"Then, the things that people do or say against me no longer seem like such a major issue."

"In that case, you won't have any names to inscribe on the potatoes. That means no more weight to carry around and no more bad smells. The Tao of forgiveness is the conscious decision to not just remove some potatoes, but to relinquish the entire sack."

What exactly is the entire sack? Your ego. Emptying the sack is great, but relinquishing it is enlightenment. When you accept what happens, there is nothing to forgive. When you realize who you are, there is no one to defend. As explained in the parable, striving to forgive is an endless dance with what happens. You cannot rely on such dance partners. Everlasting forgiveness is not something you strive for; it is effortless love and wisdom shining onto every passing appearance of this unified moment. To shine such a beautiful, unconditional light, it must originate from who you are and meet no resistance in the mind. To originate from who you are, you must realize who you are. As you ease into this realization, your clear mind allows the light of Being to shine through your doing. Otherwise, the light of forgiveness originates from the mind. Such a light is destined to dim and brighten until it disappears.

When you are rooted in this moment, forgiveness blossoms because there are no problems in this moment. Problems need time to seemingly gain reality; otherwise, they do not exist. Worries and regret are never about what is happening; they are about what happened or may happen, which means they are about that which doesn't exist. You cannot overcome what doesn't exist because there is nothing there to overcome. You can only see it as non-existent. In this seeing, you are free from the ghosts of your imagination and ready to use your imagination. Memories and expectations can serve as useful tools to learn or prepare or they can enslave you as a servant to feed your ego. Everything that happens is a cup of wisdom urging your quenchless thirst. You experience problems for the transcendence of problems.

Ease completely into this moment and you will realize there are no problems. Problems are born of attaching to how things should be over accepting how they are. To exist, problems need a past and future storyline that at present doesn't exist. When I say, "There are no problems," be wary of a reactive ego, which relies on mental friction for its identity and survival. Something that already is isn't a problem but rather a fact of life. Accept it and see what, if anything, you can do about it. You can better handle a challenge without making it into a problem. If a lion suddenly barges through your front door, that is a challenge demanding your immediate attention. The mind doesn't have time to make it into a problem. With acceptance, you invite unrestrained unity, clarity, possibility and equanimity to a situation by not getting in your own way. Once you turn something into a problem, you make the situation more difficult than it has to be.

Problems are born of inner resistance, which creates fragmentation and suffering. They cannot exist in your acceptance of what is. Problems exist only in the mind. The mind exists only in time. In the reality of this moment, there are no problems. With acceptance, challenges still arise, but without casting a hypnotic spell on you that decides how you handle them. First, see things as they are rather than how you think they should be. Do not try to rid your life of problems. Use logic, but you must go beyond it. Sheer willpower will not free you from the problem-making machinery of the human mind. You cannot tear away your attachment to thoughts, but you can allow space to surround your thoughts wherein the detachment happens naturally. Realize your leftover essence in the absence of thought. This spacious awareness fills you as you realize it is You. Here, life is very simple and you are most powerful. Before we take on the complexity of the human mind, we should first take on the simplicity of the present moment.

Problems are the spark of our endless search for fulfillment and meaning. They initiate our search out there to fill the lack we create right here. We can only search for what we do not have. Perhaps you do have what you are searching for, but it is not enough. When will it ever be enough? When will your searching end? Does it ever truly end or momentarily rest when you get what you want? Do you initiate a new search to keep what you found in your previous search? Are you always searching? To search for what we think we need to finally feel complete, we must create the problem of shortage to begin with. To search for peace, we must create the problem of not having enough peace. It is our very search for peace that is responsible for our lack of peace. Peace is always available to you. Question is: are you available to it? Or are you waiting for it after x, y and z happens? It seems so real that we do not have enough peace and so we look to change our situation out here so we can be more peaceful in here. This also applies to love, happiness, security, etc. This is normal and doesn't warrant any type of self-judgment! It is your very search for fulfillment that creates and reaffirms your lack of fulfillment. Remember, what happens out here is pure instability. Do not rely on outer instability for inner anything. On one level, it certainly helps to change your outer situation to benefit your inner situation. However, once you realize your eternal abundance, both inner and outer merge into a sacred alliance of unwavering alignment.

Only your ego chooses slavery over freedom. Until you forgive someone, they are in charge of your happiness. Author and journalist Lance Morrow put it well when he said, "Not to forgive is to be imprisoned by the past, by old grievances that do not permit life to proceed with new business. Not to forgive is to yield oneself to another's control, to be locked into a sequence of act and response, of outrage and revenge, tit for tat, escalating always. The present is endlessly overwhelmed and devoured by the past. Forgiveness frees the forgiver. It extracts the forgiver from someone else's nightmare." Challenging people force you to go deeper because if your attention remains solely on the surface with them, you will suffer. No matter how dreadful they appear, maintain a deeper gratitude for their reminding you not to rely on the instability of what happens. This hidden reminder would be wise to remember. When encountering unconscious behavior, let your presence immediately deepen as you fortify your attention on this moment and the awareness that is aware of this moment. Practice this immediate deepening every chance you get and let it replace the compulsive strategy to resist and react. If you had not suffered and were never challenged, you would lack conscious depth. Everything has its place. Ultimately, there are no mistakes.

Take a look around you. Feel the tension of any grudge you are holding onto and realize what is actually happening around you. Does the appearance of this precise moment have anything to do with your grudge? Rather than carry unnecessary resentment, open your ears and heart to reality whispering, "Come to me, you are free here." In other words, ground yourself in this moment without letting memories cast a dark shadow over it. As Eckhart said, "Nothing ever happened in the past that can prevent you from being present now." This moment does not condemn itself as good or bad, only your thinking does. It is okay to use such labels, but are you really using them or are they using you? Are the labels you impose on the appearance of this moment causing you to act or feel in ways you would never choose? This question helps you notice your unconscious behavior and thinking. The act of noticing unconsciousness frees you from it. As you notice, a space opens up between you and the unconsciousness passing through. How long this space remains open depends on how deeply rooted you are in the truth of who you are. Once you notice an illusion as illusion, you are no longer identified as an illusion. The moment you know it is an illusion, you step outside the illusion. This simple sidestep is your eternal vantage point.

When someone commits a crime against you, what part of consciousness gets hurt? If it's a physical attack, the body is damaged. If it's a mental attack, the ego is damaged. Are you either or? No. Does this mean you shouldn't care about any form of attack? No. If someone attacks a loved one, should you disregard it because you know they can't be hurt? No. Do not mistake detachment for disregard. When who you are is detached from your body, do you believe it is still possible to protect and cherish your body? When who you are is detached from your mind, do you believe it is still possible to use and train your mind? In the absence of illusion awaits endless possibility. In the presence of illusion arises limited possibility. You don't need to believe you are the body to protect the body. You don't need to believe you are the mind to use the mind. Illusions are the root cause of all unconscious behavior. So long as you think you are the body and mind, your underlying state of consciousness is unconsciousness.

Our tendency to focus largely on the gross aspects of life prevents us from noticing the subtle aspects. When you start paying close attention to how deeply ingrained your selfhood is in all you do and think, you will understand the importance of realizing who you are. Your idea of who you are completely molds your reality, yet we are rarely taught to question who we are. We are rarely pushed to investigate who we are. If we are taught to question and investigate, it is usually on the level of thinking, which keeps the wheels of illusion spinning. Since childhood, our parents and society tell us who we are over and over again. Slowly, these definitions mold into an automated assumption infused with a personal reality within a fragmented world. Like playdough in the hands of a child, the molding of who you are changes over a lifetime according to what happens. If we could time-lapse the ideas we have of ourselves from childhood into adulthood or even throughout a single day or week, this would be very evident. Were any of these ideas ever real? Who knows these ideas? Who's always known these ideas? In what do these ideas rise and fall? If you had a list of all the ideas you've had of yourself, would you pluck one or two as your final answer? Do you consider yourself a fleeting, changing idea or the immovable, unchanging consciousness in which ideas appear and disappear? Where are you?

In defenselessness, you are safe. In forgiveness, you are sane. As stated in the book *A Course in Miracles*, "A defense which cannot attack is the best defense." You may be thinking, "How so?" Nothing ever happens to you, only within you. Capture this insight and you have captured the essence of spirituality. This doesn't mean you can't build a defense in court. This doesn't mean you have to stand idle while being physically attacked. I keep repeating what pointers don't mean because it is very easy for the ego to manipulate you into feeling weak-minded or stepped on by others. This is where the ego tries to build one of its many strongholds. I intend to catch your ego in its tracks as you read this book, but I cannot pinpoint all of your egoic reactions. Be wary of your reactions and where they come from. Pay close attention to who feels stepped on. Pay close attention to who feels weak-minded. Find this "you" that needs defending. Realize the illusion you are holding onto when you are unforgiving. No matter the insights you read, it is up to you to notice the basis of your habitual thinking. Is it a little, separate "me" prone to the elements of what happens? Ask yourself often, "Who is this thought in service of? On whose behalf is this thought? Is it on behalf of my ego or does it stem from presence?" The moment you pose these questions, you create space for, as Buddhists say, right action to occur. The ego is like a seemingly insurmountable mental fortress that disappears as you shine your light of attention onto it. The closer you pay attention to your mind, the more you see the ego for what it is: a mental phantom that has you convinced you are its image and consequently gained control of your thoughts and actions. In seeing the ego for what it is, you banish it. This seeing is where you must reside. To remain the seer, you must unveil a deep, timeless stillness from which you have a clear view of your diminishing conditioning. You can access this vantage point through a silent mind, then use the mind while resting in eternity.

This parable, whose author is unknown, is about elephants and ropes. A man walking by passed some elephants and became confused by the fact that these huge creatures were being held by only a small rope tied to their front leg. No chains, no cages. It was obvious that the elephants could, at any time, break away from their bonds, but for some reason, they did not. He saw a trainer nearby and asked why these animals just stood there and made no attempt to get away. "Well," the trainer said, "When they are very young and much smaller, we use the same size rope to tie them and, at that age, it's enough to hold them. As they grow up, they're conditioned to believe they cannot break away. They believe the rope can still hold them, so they never try to break free." The man was amazed. These animals could at any time break free from their bonds, but because they believed they couldn't, they were stuck right where they were.

What rope-beliefs bind you? Look down at your feet and see if you can envision your rope and storyline. The elephants had an actual rope keeping them together, but it was their stubborn belief system that empowered the rope. For humans, our ropes are invisible, but profoundly impact our potential and experience of life. As children or young adults, most of us have a particular experience that drastically shapes who we think we are. More times than not, we unconsciously carry this identity into adulthood and allow our own thinking to shrink our untold potential. No matter what story you have, it's only that – a story. What does a story have to do with who you are? If your story is, "I was abused as a child and keep my distance from people," then you must first identify this as a memory that has held you captive for years. The master in this scenario is the memory of what happened. Your victimhood mentality has turned you into its slave. Memories don't ask to become your master. You create their altitude with your attitude. This is an automated conditioning of the egoic state. I don't think you paused and said, "This experience was horrible, but you know what? That's not enough. I'm going to make it last forever by dragging it with me everywhere." This is not what happens. You can't fight this memory or try your hardest to get rid of it. You must surrender to it, which means to fully accept that it happened, and realize it has nothing to do with reality, which is the appearance of this neutral moment, or who you are. Let memories teach you, not own and deceive you. There is great power in surrender. No one can take this power from you. No one can take this peace from you. You've stripped people and circumstances from having that right by staying aligned with reality.

Due to their youthful experience of being unable to break free of a rope, the elephants were conditioned to mentally shackle themselves for decades. To unravel your conditioning, you must realize the unconditioned within you. Just as light resolves darkness, the unconditioned resolves all conditioning. What is the unconditioned? Your intrinsic nature. Realize who you are and the mind-made ropes clear because your mind clears. Stay with this clear mind by staying with the realization of who you are.

Former American President Bill Clinton once shared what he learned from former South African President Nelson Mandela on forgiveness. In one meeting of the two men, Clinton asked, "I wonder what you must have felt toward your jailers when you were walking out of that prison after those 27 years. Weren't you angry at them?"

"Yes, I was angry. And I was a little afraid," answered Mandela. "After all, I've not been free in so long. But," he added, "When I felt that anger welling up inside me, I realized that if I continue to hate them after I got outside that gate, then they would still have me." With a smile, Mandela concluded, "I wanted to be free, so I let it go."

When anger arises, yes, it is there, but where are you? If you are the anger, then who is aware of it? We endlessly question the storylines that spark feelings, but rarely do we question to whom the feelings belong. Rarely do we question whether those feelings are truly who we are. If you really are your anger, or any psychological makeup of your conditioned mind, then who is aware of it? Can you be both 'aware subject' and 'fleeting object'? If you are your anger, then there would be no witnessing awareness of the anger. All there would be is anger. The fact that you can observe your anger shows you are not your anger. The anger comes and goes, yet you remain. The anger arises and ceases, yet you remain. Who is it that remains? Not the anger. Anger is not a choice you make because no one would consciously choose to suffer. It's an unconscious automation of the conditioned mind that your sense of self is entangled in. That's all. This is normal, but there comes a time to rise beyond the norm. That time is now.

Become aware of the awareness that is aware there is anger. Become aware of the awareness that is aware of this word. Become aware of awareness. Turn your attention onto itself. Instead of continuously fixating your attention on something, fixate it on nothing. Become attentive to the field of attention in which everything passes. Anger cannot exist in the light of your awareness. For anger to exist, you must internally resist what happens, which means you have mistaken a story for the reality of this moment. All stories, meaning all thoughts, are based in time and have nothing to do with reality. They have their place and purpose, but we must cultivate the ability to differentiate between what is real and what is not real; what is ours and what is not ours. This wisdom will free humanity from their mind-made prisons so that we can truly use the mind as the wonderful tool it's meant to be. This wisdom, it seems, has now become essential for the continuity of the human race. It is no longer a luxury.

Forgiveness, acceptance and surrender are one and the same. Whichever word you prefer using, they all lead to the same outcome: peace. At peace, there is no threat; therefore, there is no defense. When you defend your mind-made self, you empower the apparent threat you are defending against by making it into a threat to begin with. The act of seeing a threat as a threat creates the threat. When you feel threatened, it is never real. You watch threats happen, but can never ultimately be threatened. Only your ego and body can. Again, this doesn't mean you shouldn't care about what happens. Useful instincts and adrenaline still kick in, of course, but deep down you know that "Nothing real can be threatened. Nothing unreal exists. Herein lies the peace of God," as stated in the *Course of Miracles*.

Imagine carrying around a ghost that you defend to the world. Look to your left or right and envision a phantom that follows and looks like you, but is not you. This image has become a central theme to your reality. If you watch someone verbally attack the sky, you may scratch your head, but you would find no reason to react. Similarly, who you are needs no defending because who you are is untouched by what happens. Why bother defending what can't be attacked? We think a lot about how to defend ourselves and why, but very little about who exactly we are defending. The more we delve into this question, the less we find. Eventually, there is no one to defend. See life as it is without personalizing how you think it to be. In the absence of realizing who you are beyond name and form, a personal "me" is created as an alternative identity to defend and enhance. This identity then becomes the root cause of all suffering and illusion. Eckhart explained this well when he wrote in his book *Stillness Speaks*, "All the misery on the planet arises due to a personalized sense of 'me' or 'us.' That covers up the essence of who you are. When you are unaware of that inner essence, in the end you always create misery. It's as simple as that. When you don't know who you are, you create a mind-made self as a substitute for your beautiful divine being and cling to that fearful and needy self. Protecting and enhancing that false sense of self then becomes your primary motivating force." All personal characteristics, that we tend to mistake for who we really are, are just an expression of the collective human conditioning. They are inherited and reinforced over a lifetime, but they are not you. In this moment, what personal characteristics do you have? Do not visit the past. Do not imagine the future. Now, tell me, who are you? You must take the form of sugar and plunge to the depths of the ocean. Who is left? What is left? The ocean itself.

This parable, whose author is unknown, is about learning from the dead. A novice once went to Abbot Macario to ask his advice on how best to please the Lord. "Go to the cemetery and insult the dead," said Macario. The brother did as he was told. The following day, he went back to Macario. "Did they respond?" asked the Abbot. "No," said the novice. "Then go and praise them instead." The novice obeyed. That same afternoon, he went back to the Abbot, who again asked if the dead had responded. "No, they didn't," said the novice. "In order to please the Lord, do exactly as they did," Macario told him. "Take no notice of men's scorn or of their praise; in that way, you will be able to build your own path." This parable points to inner completeness, which allows the flowering of true forgiveness. Accept and acknowledge what is said or done, but do not let it add or subtract from who you are.

When you encounter the unconscious momentum of the human mind, whether within or without, welcome it because it is already here and allow the challenge to deepen your presence. Everything that happens is an opportunity to realize where it is happening from: consciousness. When you defend one of your mental versions, you allow the past to disguise this flawless moment. Attached to such a defense, you are guided by unconscious automation, identified with a mental position for the sake of strengthening your ego. This is typically done through being right and making others wrong. Your pseudo-sense of self inflates when you are right and deflates when you are wrong. You become like a balloon in need of constant helium for your fulfillment and meaning. As Eckhart Tolle says, "There is nothing that strengthens the ego more than being right." Remember, there is a distinct difference between being right and being attached to being right, which reflects clearly in your communication of righteousness. When you listen to others defend or attack, listen from a clear space of pure alertness and non-reactiveness so you don't unconsciously participate in fantasy storytelling. Sometimes, bathing in deep peace invites others to join you in humane silence and be free of suffering. This is why the Dalai Lama said, "Silence is sometimes the best answer." Otherwise, the best you can do is let their unconsciousness play out with minimal involvement while maintaining present-moment grounding in who you are. If you get drawn into a story and begin defending yourself, you strengthen the unconsciousness in you by trying to fight it in another. You cannot fight unconsciousness with unconsciousness. Contrary to potential appearances, the ego always proliferates in this scenario. Even if you prove your point, you have contaminated your sense of satisfaction by reinforcing the momentum of your ego. If you don't attach to a mental position, you can't be destroyed. It is impossible to argue with peace. Even if you speak the truth, the truth never needs attaching to.

Do not mistake what someone says or does for who they really are. This is forgiveness in the deepest sense. See the ego in others and realize it spawns from an impersonal, collective unconsciousness and not specifically the other person, who is just a medium for human unconsciousness to pass through. Although it seems you are responding to the other person, you are really responding to your interpretation of the "other" person. One thought in your mind is responding to another thought in your mind. All of life is a subtle dance in your mind. Rather than focus solely on the dancers, which are thoughts, shift your attention to the dance floor, which is the present moment. Make the choice to live by choice, not compulsion. A simple, yet powerful action you can take is to pause after someone says something and choose your response instead of just react. This pause allows space to expand between who you are and what is happening. This spacious awareness prevents the vacuum of unconsciousness from pulling you in. You are free.

Rather than make explicit points, try asking questions that spark your point. Making statements through questions carries great potential. For example, instead of stating, "Take a good look at this moment, there are no problems right now," you can ask, "Take a good look at this moment, what problem do you have right now? Can you sense the awareness of your emotion or only the emotion?" There are many ways to ask questions that open up space in a conversation. Spacious awareness unbinds what happens from who you are. Simple, yet powerful questions can help, but do not attach to an outcome or judge yourself for what happens. Your questions will reveal themselves to have been hidden demands if you attach to an outcome you never receive. Have the intention, but not the attachment. Plant the seed, but do not judge its lack of growth. Be wary not to overdo it or be pushy. Be sure to first accept and acknowledge their concerns and emotions. Give up judgments. Give up mistaking words and actions for who someone truly is. When you judge others, you also strengthen your fear of being judged by reinforcing the reality of judgements. Through questions, you can help someone realize your insight without needing to tell them directly. This can strengthen the power of your message since the person you're speaking to finalizes the message. When someone speaks your insight by first discovering it on their own, they generally absorb it better.

When confronted with unconsciousness, the most important aspect of what is happening is your underlying state of consciousness, which determines whether you are ripe for possession by what is happening. As the Indian guru Nisargadatta Maharaj said, "In reality nothing is lacking and nothing is needed, all work is on the surface only. In the depths there is perfect peace. All your problems arise because you have defined and therefore limited yourself. When you do not think yourself to be this or that, all conflict ceases. Any attempt to do something about your problems is bound to fail, for what is caused by desire can be undone only in freedom from desire. You have enclosed yourself in time and space, squeezed yourself into the span of a lifetime and the volume of a body and thus created the innumerable conflicts of life and death, pleasure and pain, hope and fear. You cannot be rid of problems without abandoning illusions." All branch illusions spawn from the primal illusion of personhood. Once you abandon your idea of "me," all other illusions begin to disappear. Free of illusion, life goes on, but without your exchange of peace.

Chapter 14
Conscious Parenting

When I first met Alexis, we waited some time before I met her daughter Adriell, who was six years old at the time. I had very little experience with serious relationships, let alone ones that involved children. I didn't know the first thing about raising a child, yet I somehow trusted that everything would work out. When I first met Adriell, her biological father was still in her life, but not for long. His own troubles inevitably tore him apart from her. Being a stepfather just got a lot more complicated now that Adriell began blaming herself for her father's disappearance. Thrown into the lion's den of parenting, I began learning what works and doesn't. I'm still learning and always will be. At no point can you know all there is to know about anything. Fast forward five years and we have welcomed another child to love: Leonidas. There are countless books on parenting, but very few tell you that a child comes through you, but is not yours. This can be a difficult insight to grasp. Yes, you have their birth certificate with your name on it. Yes, sex led to conception. Yes, they came out of you and because of you. They are still not yours.

Consciousness doesn't give birth to the baby in your arms and says, "This is mine." It allows, watches and contains everything. Only the ego says, "This is mine," and means it absolutely. This is a reminder that the ego has many faces, which can appear as something wonderful such as "owning" a child. Through the human being, the totality of all that is presents itself as a passing appearance of the present moment. If you consider something that passes to be yours, then everything is yours. Either nothing is yours or everything is yours. Only the ego cherry picks because only the ego creates the duality of "mine" and "not mine." Treating children as property only limits your parenting through attachment under the pretense of ownership. Just because you are the official owner of a house does not mean it is really yours. On one level, it does belong to you. Ultimately, nothing is yours. As the sky, you don't own the birds. As the ocean, you don't own the fish. You contain, allow and watch them. It is important to strike a balance here so you take responsibility without attachment. This is the essence of what it means to be responsible. On one level, you uphold your duties. On a deeper level, you watch the upholding take place without letting it touch who you are or claiming true ownership. When you feel an absolute ownership over someone or something, you have split yourself into yet another piece to be invested in this apparent possession that now dictates who and how you are. Ultimately, your greatest responsibility is maintaining your roots in the present moment, alliance with what happens and realization of who you truly are. This is the hat trick to eternity.

My wife and I have a piece of paper proving that we own a house. Does that mean it is really ours? Yes and no, but mostly no. I am in my home right now typing this. I'm looking around at all the objects. In this precise moment, to whom do these objects belong? Without imposing a story onto an object, whose object is it? Without past and future, who is left to claim ownership? Without the lens of the past, in this present-moment reality, what do you really own? Take a look right now at something or someone nearby that you would normally feel an ownership over. Ease completely into this moment, let your mental identity go and allow the time-bound stream of thinking to subside; then ask, "What in this very moment is mine?"

When Leo was born, I felt an urge to run to the supply store *Staples* and stamp on his head, "Property of George Tsiattalos;" not literally, but in the sense of "mine." It felt natural, but I instantly knew it was the ego, which only obscures your divine nature. Attached to this urge was a sense of fear. "Mine" and "fear" go hand in hand for anything that is yours, you feel you can lose as a piece of who you are. I remember standing in the operating room holding my wife's hand while watching the cesarean delivery. As the doctors lifted Leo from the womb, they did a quick check up, then handed him to me as they stitched her up. When I sat with the baby in my arms, I thought, *Wow, you really did take after me, your shoulders are so hairy!* I later found out that's normal and has nothing to do with me. I was deeply at peace, filled with the freedom of detached love wherein fearlessness allows pristine blissfulness. As the Indian mystic Sadhguru says, "Your body is just a scoop of Earth." As a scoop of Earth, we belong to no one. Our physical roots endlessly trace back to the beginning of time, assuming there was a beginning. What we tend to do is look at the latest trace, which we claim to be the ultimate trace, and therein arises the delusion of "my" and "mine." Use possessive pronouns as tools to communicate, but once you give them absolute truth, they delude and use you as tools for the ego. This absolute ownership mentality is especially true with babies. If you are to choose an owner, then choose Earth. After all, our bodies are no more than a gathering of food, water and elements, which is orchestrated by the orchestra of life. What does Earth belong to? The Sun. What does the Sun belong to? The solar system. What does the solar system belong to? The Milky Way galaxy and so on. Which is the rightful owner?

You may be thinking, "Tell me again what is the purpose of this realization?" When you psychologically extend your identity to an apparent possession, this possession determines who and how you are in grand, yet subtle ways. You continue spreading the roots of egoic entanglement oblivious to who you are. You don't need to claim ownership over someone or something to wield love and care. You are more capable of loving and caring when you are free from illusion and attachment exposing you to the mercy of what happens. Children don't need your attachment; if anything, they need your enlightenment. You are bigger, smarter, older and stronger than your child. You can tell your child what to do, where to go, when to be home, how to act and who to spend time with. You can take their things away or reward them with things. Despite all of this power, there is no real elevation or distance between you. Striking a balance here, you are able to fulfill your child's needs on all levels. You are more capable of guiding your child next to them, not strictly above them with a gavel. This doesn't mean you can't be stern or authoritative. This doesn't mean you can't correct or teach them. This means you build a closer bond to correct and teach them from. There are no limits when a child lets you into their world. As a matter of fact, from the inside, you are able to better influence their world with them rather than trying to do it from the outside above them. Although they need your guidance and correction on the level of doing, all children have a deep yearning for equality and recognition on the level of Being. This is the most important longing of a child you can fulfill.

Jesus was right when he said, "Truly I tell you, unless you change and become like little children, you will never enter the kingdom of heaven." This means to learn from children how to be free again. When you look into the eyes of a toddler, you aren't worried about being judged. These are the eyes we must return to. These are the eyes that will free humanity from insanity. Children are freshly manifested from the divine, not yet directly subjected to our egos. Although they inherit a great deal of human unconsciousness, they don't have a fully developed ego, but do have a lot to teach us. To be an effective parent, you must be an effective listener. As much as you think you know, your child has many lessons to teach you. Their very first lesson is, "I am going to suffer and you can't do anything about it." This may seem obvious, but deeply rooted in this lesson is the acceptance of the necessity of suffering. Without suffering, there would be no cause for awakening. Let all suffering you have endured serve its purpose as fuel for enlightenment, which as the Buddha says, is the end of suffering.

One of the keys to helping children with their suffering, whether it's anger, complaining, sadness, worry, anxiety, jealousy and so on, is not to join them in that state. Whatever state of mind you are in transfers to your child and feeds their state of mind. No matter your words, if they are spoken with resistance to what happens, mixed in with your message is a promotion of self-enslavement to what happens. Children usually pick up on this as a long-term lesson more so than your likely soon to be forgotten message. As Eckhart says, your underlying state of consciousness, or "the how," is always most important because it determines "the what." In other words, the *how*, which is your inner state, determines the *what*, which arises from your inner state. And, as Buddhist Ajahn Sumedho says, "If it arises, then it belongs." Everything you do is a lesson to your child that whispers, "This is the way you should be too." Children remember "the how," which is like an energetic stream of conditioning, more than "the what," which is a lesson that may or may not stick amongst the endless realm of things said. This doesn't mean what you say isn't important! All you do and say matters, but your underlying state matters most because it determines all you do and say. Children pick up on how you do what you do with everyone and everything. How you relate to your partner is just as important as how you relate to your child. As the Chinese proverb says, "A child's life is like a piece of paper on which every person leaves a mark." Your presence flows into your child like oxygen flows into your body. You can't see it, but it makes all the difference. As you live it, you teach it.

Children can be notorious for a lack of listening and glut of attitude. These tendencies can easily trigger your ego as you resist what they do or don't do and reprimand them thereafter. No matter the outcome of your lesson, your negative energy will feed their buildup of unwanted emotion and cycle of suffering. Although suffering is initially unavoidable, this does not mean it should be exacerbated. Scolding your child reinforces the heart of their ego by silently teaching, "This is how you deal with things. When someone doesn't meet your expectations, you should resist and react." Learning this, children don't realize their potential to accept the seemingly unacceptable and choose how to proceed without suffering in the process or limiting their potential. If you demonstrate habitual resistance over and over for years, they grow up learning, "Since my parents resist what they don't like and accept what they do like, I will follow this pattern and rely on an unreliable world to dictate who and how I am." Children don't pause and make this declaration, it's a subtle strengthening of their inherited conditioning which spreads to other children and into the world. Despite their notoriety for a lack of listening, they are wonderfully sponge-like in the sense of absorbing with great intensity the information from the world around them. In truth, children do listen with an absorbent mind, they just don't always respond or acknowledge that they do, which makes it seem like they don't, and aren't always capable of upholding all your demands and expectations. After all, who is? We tend to view this "lack of listening" as personal and disrespectful, which of course, is always the ego. You can still teach respect without demanding respect or feeling disrespected. You, too, must return to a sponge-like existence and soak in the present moment without incessantly imposing time-bound thoughts onto the present moment.

The passions of a child evolve with the latest trends of their mind and society. One of the most powerful ways to connect with your child is to join them in their passionate world. Whether it's a toy, game, electronic, social media, fashion, music, sport, dance, outdoor activity or any pleasurable pastime, be sure to open your heart to their world. No matter how silly or mundane their passion may seem, it paints their entire world. No matter how often they seem to go on and on about the same thing, hear them each time like it is the only time because it always is. No matter your level of interest, be involved with total involvement. Although they would love it, children don't require you sit with them for hours on end playing. As little as 15 minutes at least once a day can mean the world to your child. Make time to hear them speak about their day, express their passion, play a game or read a short story. Listen to them with genuine ears and warm eyes. Ask curious questions. I never thought I'd learn so much about "slow-rising squishes," which Adriell used to adore. Children need more than an adult telling them what to do all day. They crave your recognition beyond the role of a parent. If you teach your child that, as Mark Twain said, "Life is just one damn thing after another," then you have uninvited space to be and invited a race to do. Yes, they need your guidance and correction, but they also need you to let go and just bask in the moment with them. This helps build a deeper connection, trust and love, which allows them to fearlessly turn to you for everything.

More times than not, children fear their parents because they lack a deeper connection and trust with them. What does this lead to? Lying, hiding and avoiding in order not to get in trouble. Once children truly experience your ego, it begins cementing their own. Trust, which is the absence of fear, can easily become an uphill battle and lifelong blur. To have your child want to cooperate, feel safe to tell you things and listen more effectively, you must stop looking to them and start looking within. Your inner state conditions their own. A child, like the universe, is a two-way mirror. All outbound frequencies determine, to an extent, the inbound frequencies. Keep in mind, no matter how enlightened you are, you cannot control your child who will not always cooperate, feel safe to tell you things or listen effectively. Do not let this spur self-judgment; rather, let it be a reminder that children are also a part of the instability of what happens that you mustn't rely on or invest yourself in. Moreover, remember there is never a separate "you" to judge. A good way to get your child used to cooperating with you is to ask them as often as possible to do things that are easy or they enjoy.

When children act up, they are learning to regulate and express their emotions in situations they wouldn't prefer. Punishing a child without effectively talking to them first does not teach them how to regulate their emotions and erodes their trust in you by instilling fear. Relying on fear may force artificial cooperation, but deep down, children are demotivated to naturally cooperate. In times of disobedience, punishing your child is easier than lovingly guiding them through their emotions because it is quick, simple and satisfactory to your ego. Children are a favorite target of the ego because you don't worry about appearances, your word is easily the final word and you can always be right. When you punish a child, they learn what not to do, but at what cost and how effective is it really? Does it help their emotional control? Does it help them trust you more? Through conventional punishment, children tend to build a resentment, plunge deeper into suffering and predominantly learn to hide things so they don't get in trouble. You can still teach right from wrong without becoming a slave to it and teaching your child to do the same. Through example, you inadvertently teach your child to be everything you ultimately want to be free of. Until you are free of suffering, limitation and illusion, you will advocate this way of life to your kin. Lovingly guiding your child through his or her emotions promotes problem-solving skills, inner discipline, unconditional love and a strong moral sense. The more love and trust your child feels, the better they will absorb your lessons and cooperate. This is what children need and it starts with you.

With that said, if your child is getting ready to go on a playdate and they all of a sudden hit or curse you, you don't have to say, "Okay son, I accept what you did, now go have fun!" This is borderline positive reinforcement for negative behavior. With children, there is no one size fits all in terms of what to do. However, what does "fit all" is how you do what you do. So long as you don't conditionally react, make your child feel horrible or criticize and condemn them to a bleak future, you can effectively withhold your child from doing something they enjoy to question their behavior, open up a conversation or go for a walk to help them cool off and open their little world to the world at large. You can also delay the playdate until after you talk. There is no right or wrong way, there is only what works, which depends on innumerable factors, especially the child's age, conditioning and your intuition. No matter a child's irrationality, accept their behavior first and foremost. Remain grounded in the moment without judgment. Do not let what happens become more important than your state of consciousness. Through acceptance and presence, you can effectively choose how to proceed by remaining unpossessed by thoughts of, "I can't believe he's doing this. This shouldn't be happening. She's disobeying again." This entire book can be considered a book on parenting.

For the most part, our belief that kids are misbehaving is really a cover-up for their behaving as kids do at their age. We think kids are constantly misbehaving, but mostly, they are behaving like kids. By nature, kids are abundant with playfulness and mischievousness. Although it may seem so, kids don't consciously set out on a grand mission to be bad and get punished. They have a great deal to learn about handling their emotions, focusing their attention and getting by in the world. Perhaps they are acting beyond what you consider "normal" because their emotional needs aren't being met? Perhaps they are overstimulated, not feeling well or experienced ridicule in school and don't know how to handle it, so they act up? There is so much going on in their little heads! If a child is upset and making demands, especially angry ones, try not to give in. This teaches the child in order to get what they want, they need to act up. If you consistently give in, this lesson will permeate into adulthood. Even if you want to grant them their wish, wait until they relax or the next day to do it. When children rebel, sometimes the best solution is to stay quiet or say as little as possible. If you say no, stick to it! Children frequently rebel just to get attention. Whether you scold or lovingly guide them, you are still reinforcing their belief that rebellious behavior earns attention. It is good to find a balance here and not always feel obligated to guide them every time they act up.

It also helps to remember that if you had their same exact energetic inheritance, upbringing and experiences, you'd also act in that same exact way. This applies to children and adults alike. If held onto, this understanding helps you remain nonreactive, compassionate and more effective in situations because you know if you had their "life package," you'd act that way too. This isn't meant to excuse or disregard their behavior, but rather to maintain an unconditional inner alignment with what happens as it happens.

An effective way to guide your child is by having them visualize a positive outcome. Rather than say, "Let's not be late for school," you can say, "Let's get to school on time." Another example is instead of saying, "Don't forget to make your lunch," you can say, "Please remember to make your lunch." This way, you are painting a positive picture of them achieving a task, which can help incrementally reduce their fear and build their confidence. Don't ask these questions with firm expectations that your child will better perform the task. With children, changes in their behavior takes consistent changes in your own. Depending on your child's age and level of conditioning, it could take days, weeks, months or years.

In his book *A New Earth: Awakening to Your Life's Purpose*, Eckhart Tolle has a simple, yet powerful series of questions you can ask a child after they act up and calm down, even if it's the next day. He suggests you don't tell the child what happened, but instead ask questions such as, "What was it that came over you yesterday when you wouldn't stop screaming? Do you remember? What did it feel like? Was it a good feeling? That thing that came over you, does it have a name? No? If it had a name, what would it be called? If you could see it, what would it look like? Can you paint a picture of what it would look like? What happened to it when it went away? Did it go to sleep? Do you think it may come back?" If your child names their ego, then use that name to refer to it going forward. Eckhart designed these questions for children to feel space between their ego and who they are. If the child names their ego, then you can name yours as well so they don't feel it's out of the ordinary to have one. If they ask why they don't see yours much, you can say, "It's still here, it just doesn't come out often." Based on your child's understanding and conversations you've had, you can elaborate.

Rather than strong-arm your child through fear, let love guide a path of redemption for your child that supports their own desire to listen, cooperate and fearlessly communicate. This prevents untold suffering by weakening their ego from a young age. An alternative to on-the-go punishment is planning together with your child a simple system of rules that take effect upon certain events and set the right expectations. The important part here is to plan it with your child so they feel they actually have a say in their life and take more responsibility if they break one of their own rules. Rules need not be solely for the child. Children love when you hold yourself accountable as well.

I suggest the first rule is limiting screen time with electronics. This way, children develop strong attention spans and become less dependent on continuous stimuli for their sense of aliveness. It seems most of humanity has become disconnected from the outdoors. Where has our attention gone? Into a screen. All screens, whether it's a television, phone or video game, offer a high level of mental stimulation because every few seconds, there's a new image. This weakens our ability to focus without feeling pulled towards a new fix every few seconds. The screen can easily pull a child, just like it has most adults, into an addicting, trance-like state of hypnosis. With most of society glued to their screens, it seems the zombie apocalypse has already arrived! You can make rules, such as after a child showers, finishes their homework and eats dinner, they can have an hour of electronics on Wednesdays. Better yet, you can give them a few hours a week that they can use however they choose. This way, children learn patience and planning skills. Weekends are usually a bit more flexible, but are also a great opportunity to get outdoors and do other things. It's important not to let your child lose touch with nature. Most children are too engrossed in their gadgets to experience nature, which is a great doorway to who they are. Perhaps you won't allow any screen time. Be careful not to plan every hour of their day for them. Leave room for children to decide on their own what to do, which encourages creativity and a sense of freedom. Children need to feel as though they are building their lives alongside you. Of course, if they want to eat candy for dinner every night, explain to them compassionately or humorously why they can't. Explain, "If you eat candy for dinner every night, then your teeth will look like this," as you smear almond butter on your teeth. Patiently helping a child understand why it's not a good idea to do something in a way that keeps them motivated in your absence is more effective than just blurting a few angry words and punishing them.

A second suggestion is the "Back to Now" or grounding rule. This rule teaches a child that when they feel something they don't like, such as sadness or jealousy, they can take three steps to let it go. First, let them talk to you about it and express what they feel without shame or guilt. Give your full, loving attention, which is vital for a child. Before addressing the lesson or course of action, try saying, "Let's first accept your feelings and what happened. Remember, we accept things because they already happened, not because they are good or bad. This means everything that happens should first be accepted before you take any action." This can take many years for a child to grasp, but it helps to start planting seeds. Secondly, to generate presence, have your child describe what they hear, smell, taste, touch and see right now. Adriell once humorously responded, "I smell your fart!" Finally, talk about the lesson or course of action to take. This three-step process addresses a child's underlying state before the issue at hand. This doesn't need to take long and can be done on the go. Keeping this simple and doing it whenever possible will slowly begin undoing your child's egoic conditioning. At first, this may seem pointless, but over time your child will learn the power of this rule and begin implementing it on their own. Keep in mind, if the child is uncooperative, do not force this. This typically works best for light ego-attacks, since children are still somewhat receptive, not heavy ones. Only you can know when is a good time to try. Sometimes, all you can do is patiently wait for their attachment to a story repeating in their heads to fade, which generally takes less time than it does for adults.

Furthermore, it is important to encourage children from a young age not to confuse mental labels with absolute knowledge, experience or reality. As Eckhart Tolle says, "When you teach them what something is, encourage them to touch it, to see it, to feel it, not just to say, 'this is called such-and-such.' Continue to look at it. Otherwise, you stop experiencing – and all you have is a mental label." Teach your child that just because we call a flower a flower doesn't mean we ultimately know what it is. Teach them we need names to communicate, but not to mistake those names with the complete truth of what something or someone is. Help them pay more attention to how something feels, smells, tastes, looks, sounds and not to get solely absorbed in the mental experience of it. This helps ripen your child's inner freedom and birthright potential for spiritual awakening. There is a beautiful and mysterious quality to life when nothing is defined absolutely. Allowing concepts to fully explain what things and people are diminishes that quality. It dulls the experience and reduces the aliveness and essence of an object or person to some fleeting thought. As innocent as this seems, it is the most tragic way to look at someone or something. Once you reduce the essence of a person or group of people to some abstract thought, the conditioned mind can easily take full control since it seemingly has full understanding and justify any judgment, attack, etc. When you look at someone, do you actually see them or do you only see the bookshelves of stories behind them? The trick is to balance both visions meaning to see them truly as they are in the moment and keep a peripheral understanding of the stories. If you only see the stories, then their immensity – and your own – has been reduced to a mere concept.

A third suggestion is if anyone yells aggressively, including the parent, then take a few minutes time-in. Try calling this time-in, not time-out, which is typically thought of as punishment. If it helps, you can sit with your child during time-in, but try to keep it a session of silence. In the heat of the moment, a child may be incapable of this. If so, then revert to the "Back to Now" or grounding rule or simply wait for them to calm down before talking about it. Paint this as a practice of presence, not punishment. As simple as possible, explain to your child why it is important for either of you to take a few minutes break and focus on being present. For example, you can say, "The reason you are upset is because you keep thinking about the past or future. In the present moment, there is nothing to be upset about. Go ahead and take a look around to see for yourself." Even if there is a nearby broken toy, it is their future thoughts about not being able to use it anymore that makes them upset. Although it can take many years for a child to grasp this, it helps to begin at an early age. Especially to a child, it is amusing to watch an adult sit because they yelled, but they highly admire you for it and are more receptive to doing it when their time comes. If you can't take the few minutes right away, then promise you will later and ensure they see you. Try not to talk during time-in or make them sit somewhere they absolutely hate. Be sure not to enforce this like a drill sergeant. You don't always have to ask them to go on time-in. One of the most essential gifts you can give a child is space to be. Also, you can use time-ins to positively reinforce good behavior! You can take a few minutes time-in to point out something admirable they did. They may have done something wonderful without even knowing it or thinking much of it, which is why it's good to draw attention to these behaviors.

Keep in mind, kids will be kids! Your words may go in one ear and out the other. It's difficult enough for adults to grasp all this, so don't hold any firm expectations over your children! This is meant to plant seeds only. The most effective lesson is leading by example day in and day out. Through consistent observation of you practicing what you preach, children will absorb your lessons far more efficiently. If you say one thing and consistently do another, it won't work very well. Especially if you decide to take something away or keep them from going somewhere, stay focused on how you are communicating more than anything. If your child refuses to follow a rule, try to let them calm their nerves before sitting to talk about it. Be there for them rather than against them. Try asking, "How could you have done this differently? Why do you think you act in ways you would never choose? What can we do that will help you follow this rule next time?" For example, if your child hits another child, you can ask, "Can you tell me the rule about not hitting other children? How could we have done this a different way?" Ask these questions with a sense of curiosity, not judgment. It can help to be stern, but not aggressive. This reinforces your bond allowing you more power and influence to guide and teach your child. One of the best ways to prepare a child for the world is to show them how not to be a slave to it. All this starts at home, with you.

Chapter 15
Between Nothing and Everything

I don't exist,
I allow existence.
I don't exist,
I watch existence.
I don't exist,
I contain existence.
I don't exist,
I am existence.
I am existence-less.
Between nothing
And everything,
I am.

The title of this chapter was inspired by Nisargadatta Maharaj, who said, "Love says, 'I am everything.' Wisdom says, 'I am nothing.' Between the two my life flows." I was recently asked over the phone, "Where are you?" Of course, the person asking meant where am I in relation to arriving at their home. Before responding, "I'm 15 minutes away," I remembered what Nisargadatta said and thought, "Between nothing and everything. That's where I am." If I responded this way to my customer, he may have very well locked me out with a note taped to the door: "Weirdo!"

Throughout history and especially today, I am just one of many known and unknown mediums to communicate the insights of this book. When I say "many," I mean in relation to one. Relative to the human population, there aren't many, but more and more people are realizing the collective dysfunction and therefore rising in consciousness. Despite the endless means of communication, we all point to the same nothingness. Trying to use something to communicate nothing is a necessary, oxymoronic failure that serves its purpose as a disposable tool. This is why I equate this book to a pointing finger or steppingstone. To communicate nothing using nothing, you must embody a stainless window to Being. This means through your gaze, presence and energetic field, you help transport the conscious focal point of others to consciousness itself. Upon successful transmission, the focal point dissipates into nothing and everything. This is a silent communication that everyone can receive, but few can process. Soon, you, me and this book will wither away. Our purpose here is to unveil what doesn't wither and eternally remain as such.

While working for Tesla, I sat at a kitchen table with a family who invited me over to discuss the process and benefits of switching to solar energy power. To get to know me better, they asked, "So, who are you?" Intuitively, I wanted to respond with a smile, "The same one asking the question. The same one giving the answer. The same space from which both question and answer appear and disappear." This is a reminder that you don't have to "enlighten" everyone that crosses your path every opportunity you get! Only you will know what works best for the moment. You don't need to feel as though you must always respond with deep insight. If a stranger picks up your wallet you accidentally dropped and hands it to you saying, "This belongs to you," you don't have to say, "Thank you, but nothing belongs to me." A simple thank you should suffice. Especially toward someone living with you who is not interested in hearing about presence or who they are, it is usually best to find a balance and not be pushy. It is okay to give generic answers if you feel it fits the moment best. This is part of the balance of doing and Being. It is also okay to never give a generic answer and radiate these insights no matter the appearance of this moment. Point is, there's no right or wrong way to be. There's only what works and doesn't. Let there be intuitive, natural, spontaneous action arising from presence in alignment with all that is.

I am. If held onto with earnest inquiry, these words have profound potential as pointers to who you are. "I" is consciousness. "Am" is existence. "I" is nothing. "Am" is everything. Without "I," there would be no "am." Because you are, everything is. The sense "I am" doesn't identify with anything in particular. It doesn't say, "I am I," or "I am this or that." Simply, I am. I am leaves out all else you think you are and you can only know it by what you are not. I am is already whole, remains undefined and is open to the infinite possibilities. I am is the merging of nothing and everything wherein "your life flows," as Nisargadatta said. This doesn't mean you shouldn't say statements like, "I am tired. I am not happy. I am excited. I am Andy." These are tools to use while holding onto the deeper "I am." When you say with utter conviction, "I am this or that," you attempt to define the undefinable. This or that has nothing to do with who you are. The immensity of who you are shrinks to a fading title because you missed the two most important words that precede much of what you say: I am. Nisargadatta put it well when he said, "Before all beginnings, after all endings – I am." Can you truly say, "I was not before birth" and "I will be no more after death?" What you can most profoundly say is "I am" in this moment and add nothing to it. Stay with what remains.

Through the inner stillness of a human being, consciousness can become conscious of everything and nothing allowing your life to flow between the manifested and unmanifested. You are able to realize what has form and That which is formless. Thing is, most of us are too entangled in the level of form to realize the subtle, omnipresent level of formlessness. In other words, most of us are one-dimensional, trapped in the dimension of doing and thinking. To be conscious of everything is to be conscious of the material universe. To be conscious of nothing is to be conscious of consciousness itself. Of course, when I say, "itself," I don't literally mean an "it" or thing. No word can properly fit here, but we must work with the language we have. It seems dualistic to say, "Be conscious of consciousness." It seems there is a subject and object. This is not the case. When consciousness is aware of itself, there is an indescribable felt-realization, not a dualistic sense perception. All subjects and objects fade into oneness. Freely arising from this felt-realization is wholesome love, peace and joy, uncontaminated by the egoic mind. No words can properly describe what is happening because this inward gaze is beyond words. Yet, we only have words to work with here. Don't be fooled into thinking there is any separation for separation exists only in the mind, not in reality.

What the unobserved mind loves to do is toss your sense of self on an imaginary cutting board and cut you up into different pieces to be invested wherever possible. What the untamed mind loves to do is anything it can to prevent you from realizing who you are. Mooji expressed his "I am-ness" by saying, "I am the indescribable, untouchable, unknowable, beyond experiencing of the mind. Stripped of every definition, every title, every association, and all quality. Stripped of whatever is perceivable phenomenally, stripped of the five elements and their play. I am. Not 'I will be.' Because I cannot speak of myself as 'I was' or 'I shall be.' I am is the most truthful expression. It is the very vapor that arises out of this infinite beingness. Stay here. For those who have come here, whatever arises for you, the invitation is to touch base, dissolve, and be as base. Thereafter, do what you like."

You can use "I am" as a mantra meditation. As you meditate, begin by focusing on your breathing. Redirect attention from mind activity to your breath. Feel the in-breath and out-breath for some time. You will likely bounce back and forth from mind activity to focusing on your breathing and that is okay. Never make your mind activity into a problem! Instead, accept it and let it be. Like any organ serving its purpose, there is nothing wrong with thinking. With that said, your mind has a deeper, more hidden purpose: to serve as a silent doorway to who you are. If you turn both purposes against each other, you will empower your ego and create more unwanted thinking. Do not be in a rush to stop thinking. Accept all that happens and, in your acceptance, your mind will stay quieter and more at ease. You can't force peace of mind. In truth, there is no such thing as peace of mind, or even a silent mind, because the mind is not meant to be at peace. True peace is of no-mind.

When you sit, you've already done all that needs to be done. From there, let go of all striving and expecting. After focusing on your breathing for some time, you will know when to silently chant "I am." On the in-breath, chant "I." On the out-breath, chant "am." Let this be a slow chant, leaving space between breaths and words. At the ending of "I," when you fully breathe in, before beginning to breathe out, there is a moment of inner silence. Likewise, at the ending of "am," when you fully breathe out, before beginning to breathe in, there is a moment of inner silence. The "I" symbolizes this inner silence and the "am" symbolizes your chanting and breathing. In other words, "I" is consciousness and "am" is the form that arises in consciousness. When you say or think "I am" and add nothing to it, you will notice a pristine peace emerging. After chanting "I am" for some time, you will know when to let this disposable pointer go and rest in who you are.

The Heart Sutra, which is among the best-known Buddhist scriptures, states, "Form is emptiness. Emptiness is form." This can also be stated, "Everything is nothing. Nothing is everything." This means all is One. How did the Buddha come to this realization over 2,500 years ago? He realized who he was beyond the form he took. Who was the Buddha? He is who you are. What is the purpose of this scripture? To transcend from one-dimensional to two-dimensional through the conscious merging of nothing and everything. This is his essential teaching. How does one attain such insight? This wisdom is available through any human being that, through silence, has accessed a deeper, universal intelligence. Silence is your greatest teacher. Through silence awaits innumerable insights. Books, words, thoughts and sounds do very little justice in comparison. This, too, is why Jesus said, "Be still, and know that I am God." To "be still" is to silence your mind. To "know that I am God" is to rest in what remains through a silent mind. This indescribable, formless and timeless remainder is your true self. How can a silent mind be your greatest guru? It isn't. A silent mind doesn't teach you anything. It simply opens the doorway to a non-conceptual intelligence wherein silence whispers its teachings from beyond the mind to the mind. These teachings are doused with incredible sweetness and truth.

Again, do not get caught here by making all this into a conceptualized goal for the future. You can't conceptualize "nothing" because there is nothing to conceptualize. Remember, use everything as pointers to nothing. Through words, this may seem incredibly complicated. It really isn't. It seems so because you are using your mind, which is the wrong instrument, to understand nothing. The mind always needs something to make sense of. Otherwise, it will likely get frustrated, shrug this off as not important and create something of nothing to grasp onto. To access the inner realm of universal intelligence and knowing, you cannot use your mind. Rather, your mind must silently open to naturally allow the whispers of nothing to flow into everything. Once your mind receives these whispers, it lets go of all ideas of who you are and becomes empowered with the reality of who you are.

The ego says, "What is the purpose of realizing 'nothing?' Even if my life does 'flow between two dimensions,' how does this help me pay the bills and feed my family? I have more important things to attend to!" Reading this far, it is likely your ego's momentum has begun diminishing. Nevertheless, questions like this can still arise, which is why I'm reminding you the importance of these insights. As spiritual master Paramahansa Yogananda wrote in *Autobiography of a Yogi*, "The more he realizes his unity with Spirit, the less he can be dominated by matter." The ego will spark the rise of whatever thought it needs to stop you from realizing who you are and keep you trapped in past-to-future mental cycles or, as Eckhart says, "psychological time." The insights of this book point to your breaking free of the mind-made prison you've inherited and reinforced since childhood. This prison cloaks your essential completeness forcing you to endlessly chase completeness. Within your prison walls, your identity is shrunk to flesh, bone and thought. You make this identity the center of the universe and mistake it for who you really are. This misconception leads to a lifetime of suffering and illusion. Despite the conditional highs of life, you miss the eternal ecstasy of who you are, which has no comparison. You settle for a rollercoaster ride whose ticket you never chose and whose tracks span your mind, not reality. By dwindling from eternal to temporal, who you are is shaped with what happens by the merciless whispers of your inner voices. Free from inner slavery, do you believe it is still possible to pay the bills and feed your family? Possibility becomes your very nature!

I recently saw an intriguing documentary called *Everything and Nothing: The Amazing Science of Empty Space*. To unveil empty space, scientists have been trying to rid space of all content. In their attempts, it turns out empty space is rather stubborn! Something kept popping up from absolutely nothing. Just when they thought they finally had empty space, mysterious particles, known as quantum fluctuations, kept blinking in and out of existence. This is similar to never-ending attempts to locate and understand consciousness. Everything we experience is not a fundamental reality, it is a passing experience. The lasting awareness underlying all passing experience is the fundamental reality. From the lasting arises the passing. From nothing arises everything. When human beings are inwardly still, only through and beyond form can empty space be revealed, not as an observation, but as a subtle realization of who we are. The moment humans embark on a journey to find consciousness, or empty space, through instruments, thoughts or perceptions, the journey is tainted with immediate failure. You cannot find externally what dwells internally. You cannot use something to find nothing. From the point of searching, you already missed your target. The search begins where your answer awaits. Once you start searching without for what is within, you miss it immediately and continue searching from the very space that contains your solace. By becoming so engulfed in the experience, we miss the experiencer, who is prior to all experience, which without, there would be no experience. As the infinite space in which all events rise and fall, we cannot search for the substratum of form, which is a geologic term Eckhart likes to use, within the realm of form. The substratum of form, or empty space, contains form and can't be found by or in form, only through and beyond form in silence and stillness as formless essence. This is one of the most difficult things to communicate because it is not meant to be communicated nor is it even a thing. Yet here I am writing an entire book on nothing! I find myself amused, yet know this is necessary.

All we see are objects in space, but not space itself. All we hear are sounds in silence, but not silence itself. All we feel is motion in stillness, but not stillness itself. Realize you are the space, silence and stillness containing, allowing and watching everything. You may be wondering, "I'm still not sure what to do with empty space?" There is nothing to do with it, but rather an awareness to have of it. Allow space to surround your thoughts so that you do not automatically and conditionally attach to them. Allow silence to soften your mind so that you may quiet the torrent of thinking that masks who you are. Allow stillness to flood your body so that you may heal and be at peace. Be wary of the voice in your head shouting, "Madness!" This voice doesn't want you to go beyond the mind and experience what is being pointed to. This voice fears your knowing the truth of who you are. This voice needs you to ignore what you are reading in order to survive as a mind-made entity. Do not go to war with this voice. Accept that it is there and become aware of it as the ego. The moment you become aware of the ego, it dissolves allowing your awareness to immediately expose its directionless, shapeless source.

In the Chinese classic text *Tao Te Ching*, which is based on teachings by Laozi, "nothing" is referred to as the valley spirit. The text states, "The valley spirit never dies." Why is consciousness, or nothing, called the valley spirit? The word valley can be defined as a low area of land between hills or mountains, typically with a river or stream flowing through it. The valley spirit, or nothing, is who you are whereas the hills and mountains, or everything, is all you are not. This all-pervasive meeting point is where your life flows. "Everything" is the ultimate seduction of humankind, typically capturing all of our attention. "Nothing" is the hidden dimension within humankind, typically evading any of our attention. The hills and mountains are obvious, but the valley spirit is very subtle, yet always here and now beneath the hills and mountains. To glide effortlessly from the changing mountaintops down to the everlasting valley for eternal grounding and remembrance, you must simply let go. Let go of knowing who you are. Let go of all attachments and expectations. Let go of endlessly trying to understand That which cannot be understood. Let go of your entire conceptualized reality and instantly glide inward to the deathless valley spirit of who you are. Do not fear letting go. You must also let go of the concept of letting go. As Nisargadatta said, "You are afraid of what you are. Your destination is the whole. But you are afraid that you will lose your identity. This is childishness, clinging to the toys, to your desires and fears, opinions, and ideas. Give it all up and be ready for the real to assert itself. This self-assertion is best expressed in words: 'I am.'" Once you unveil and realize the valley spirit, you may begin using concepts more effectively without the madness of an entirely conceptualized reality. Beneath the changing is eternal changelessness. This is the valley spirit and It awaits your realization now.

Keep in mind, when I use the word, "nothing," don't be fooled into fear, lack, boredom, disconnect or pointlessness. As Mooji says, "Take nothing to be yourself, and yourself will remain. It is so, whether you realize it or not. Realize it and live in the fullness of emptiness." He continues, "Get used to yourself as emptiness – empty beyond the concept of empty." Don't look for emptiness. If you are looking for emptiness, then you must be somewhere outside of it. Don't let the word emptiness become a useless thought in the mind. You've spent your entire life realizing something. It is time to realize nothing. Don't judge realizing nothing as nothing useful. From this nothingness unconditionally arises all the joy, peace, love and completeness you've been chasing since childhood. From this nothingness arises spacious choice-making, freedom from suffering and present-moment grounding. Who you are cannot arise from something you will have to let go someday. Only from nothing arises the realization of who you are. With this realization, your feet disappear into nothing while your arms reach back and forth on the level of everything. With this realization, your life consciously flows between nothing and everything. You are home, now and forever.

Chapter 16
Peace with the Unknown

What is God? This age-old, unanswerable question has many answers. If you search, "What is God" on Wikipedia, you will get this answer: "In theism, God is the creator and sustainer of the universe, while in deism, God is the creator, but not the sustainer, of the universe. In pantheism, God is the universe itself. In atheism, God is not believed to exist, while God is deemed unknown or unknowable within the context of agnosticism." With all of these "isms" to choose from, we have many options to separate ourselves with. What do all of these definitions have in common? The fact that they are definitions. Rather than experience the reality of God now, we get caught on the idea of God and wait to experience God in the future, even exported to death. Of course, at that point, all concepts of God are gone along with the human vehicle for experiencing.

The indescribable reality to which the word "God" points is so much greater than the word and thus, must be used carefully. The word God has become stuffed with mental constructs, therefore limiting its potential to unveil its core. To restore the power of the word God, you must hollow it out and allow it to point beyond thought. Typically, when it comes to God, you are either a believer or non-believer, which creates automatic separation or conditional connection. This is why Eckhart said in the beginning of his book *The Power of Now*, "Neither God nor Being nor any other word can define or explain the ineffable reality behind the word, so the only important question is whether the word is a help or a hindrance in enabling you to experience That toward which it points. Does it point beyond itself to that transcendental reality, or does it lend itself too easily to becoming no more than an idea in your head that you believe in, a mental idol? The word Being explains nothing, but nor does God. Being, however, has the advantage that it is an open concept. It does not reduce the infinite invisible to a finite entity. It is impossible to form a mental image of it. Nobody can claim exclusive possession of Being. It is your very essence, and it is immediately accessible to you as the feeling of your own presence, the realization I am that is prior to I am this or I am that. So it is only a small step from the word Being to the experience of Being."

Raised in the Greek Orthodox Church, I was told from a young age who God is. It all seemed completely figured out. Respectfully and curiously questioning what I was told was deemed inappropriate. I never denied what I was told nor thought it impossible, but was always curious how we can know all this for sure? I questioned, "Is it really possible that good people who don't believe will go to hell? Does this really explain everything between and beyond birth and death? Is this really responsible for the infinite expanse of the universe? Does an all-powerful God really care what people do in their bedrooms?" I knew I believed in something beyond the physical, I just couldn't define this belief absolutely. I felt deeply there must be more to life than meets the eye, but never thought it could be found on the level of the eye. Intuitively, I had reservations in trusting fully that a book or something someone says can explain it all. I always wondered, "How can something of the universe fully explain something beyond the universe?" Intuitively, I felt I had to experience something deeper than thoughts, feelings and emotions. Otherwise, God would literally be no more than fleeting thoughts, feelings and emotions, which change and eventually, would all disappear. *God,* I thought, *doesn't change or disappear, which meant I had to find That which doesn't change or disappear. If not now, then when? At death? If the ego, which is born of a dying mind, seeks God, then who is left to find God at death? The lacking seeker perishes with the mind and body. What was always here and now, changeless and deathless, remains. God remains.* Eckhart explains this by saying, "Death is a stripping away of all that is not you. The secret of life is to 'die before you die' – and find that there is no death." In this stripping of all that is not you, God is unveiled and you can only "find" God now.

Despite the comfort of not gambling with my soul, fear was not enough to solidify my complete surrender to defining the undefinable. I always had a nagging sincerity whispering, "I don't know. I really, honestly and whole-heartedly just don't know. I can't pretend that I do." These whispers kept me curious and open to possibility. Into adulthood, I occasionally went to church and enjoyed the experience, but the feeling that something was missing never left me. This "something" was a deeper realization of God beyond thoughts, feelings and emotions. Despite feeling good amongst other good people in an energized church, God dwindled to mere words, sounds, ink, thoughts and emotions, which didn't seem like God.

Jesus said, "I am the way and the truth and the life. No one comes to the Father except through me." Did he mean a personal "me," which is no more than passing thoughts and perishable flesh? Did Jesus refer to his personal self when he said, "Split wood, I am there. Lift up a rock, you will find me there." Surely, he didn't mean you can only find him within wood or beneath rocks. This means there's no separate "him" to find or personal "him" to go through when he said, "No one comes to the Father except through me." Otherwise, he would not be all-pervasive in wood and under rocks. What do you find within wood and beneath rocks? Space, of course. Lift a rock and there is space. Split wood and there is space. Look within and there is space. This is why Jesus said, "The kingdom of God does not come with observation; nor will they say, 'See here!' or 'See there!' For indeed, the kingdom of God is within you." Do not start believing in what I say. Close your eyes and gaze through silence and stillness the kingdom of God within you. Everything appears at birth through the mind and body and disappears at death without the mind and body. You, however, remain as the Father; as you always have been, are and will be. How can you know this beyond reading this? In the absence of thinking, realize your leftover essence untouched by time and form; changeless and deathless; here and now. That which is untouched by time is timeless. That which is untouched by form is formless. What is timeless and formless is eternal. The Father is eternal. God is eternal. You are eternal. Does timeless formlessness vary from Father to God to You? How could it? There's nothing left to differ. There's no form left to vary. There's no time left for change. As Jesus said, "I and the Father are one." All is One.

Within the realm of knowing, there is potential for endless knowledge. For example, while sitting at a customer's home reviewing his solar power system, I excused myself to use the bathroom. I've traveled far and wide, but somehow, have never seen or used a bidet before. I walked into the bathroom, did my business, then glanced for the flush, but didn't see it. For some reason, it was a bit hidden behind the toilet. Before I noticed the actual flush, I looked down toward the toilet seat and saw a small lever with arrows pointing up and down.

I figured, "Okay, this must be some fancy flush." While standing, facing the toilet, I pulled the lever down and got completely soaked. I noticed a little hose in the toilet pointing right at me. In hopes of turning the water off, I then pushed the lever all the way up and continued to get soaked, but this time with more intensity. Finally, I pulled the lever down to the middle and turned the water pressure off. This was my first experience with a bidet. As I walked out of the bathroom dripping, the customer had family over that looked my way and asked with astonishment, "What happened?" Mind you, this was my first time meeting them all. I explained to them, "I thought the bidet was the flush and soaked myself." They burst into laughter, as did I. As I made my way to the kitchen table, my customer spent a good few minutes laughing too. I now know what a bidet looks like and how it works for the most part.

What is the point of this story? Despite my learning what a bidet is, I still ultimately have no idea what a bidet is. On one level, I understand what a bidet is the same way I understand what a tree is. This level of understanding has its place for practical purposes. Like all things, a bidet is a combination of thoughts, matter and space. Does this mean we now know, without question, what a bidet is? Let's see. Can we truly trace the matter that makes up a bidet back to its origin? This investigation would span the universe, ending in inevitable mystery. Can we truly define what a thought is, where it comes from and where it goes? This investigation also ends in mystery. Can we truly explain what space is? There is nothing there to explain. The human mind is a powerful and useful tool, but it cannot ultimately explain the unexplainable. To allow an undying sense of aliveness and vibrancy, you must be at peace with not knowing anything, truly. This does not mean you become unintelligent. This means mental labels no longer completely replace and dismiss everything. Although this undying aliveness alternates in intensity, it remains ever-present when nothing is deemed completely understood. On one level, you can say, "I fully understand this," but on a deeper level, accept and hold on to the inherent mystery of thoughts, matter and space. This keeps the appearance of the present moment fresh with aliveness and keeps open the portal of possibility within you. This portal ripens the possibility of realizing who you are since you are now at peace with not knowing who you are. For wisdom beyond worldly knowledge, unlearning is more important than learning. This is why Mooji said, "In the land of 'I know,' there is always competitiveness, jealousy, pretense, pride and arrogance. It is an aggressive realm – the realm of the ego. I say refuse citizenship. In the land of 'I don't know,' the inhabitants move without conflict and are naturally quiet, happy, and peaceful. The wise stay here."

There are countless theories on the divine nature of reality that try to explain the unexplainable. These theories serve as disposable tools that can point in a helpful direction, but must eventually be let go. More important than the theory is whether you are testing it, not just believing in it, with utmost sincerity and honesty. This "testing" is focusing on where the theory points more than the theory itself. You can pick up whichever theory you like and claim it right above all others. Ultimately, what is deemed right and wrong is irrelevant. This is an endless play of words, thoughts, sounds and ego, all of which are incapable of truly explaining what is deep within, yet beyond this play. What's important is whether the theory is a useful pointer that can help carry you beyond mere belief in the theory. Nothing manifested can truly explain the unmanifested; however, useful pointers can help carry your awareness to the kingdom of God within. You must test a theory until it fades and the eternal essence to which it points remains. This is why Thich Nhat Hanh said, "The kingdom of God is available to you in the here and now. But the question is whether you are available to the kingdom."

When you have a thought about God, all you need to do is polish that thought with feelings, emotions and social conditioning to make it shine. This shining ideology becomes God and varies from culture to culture. Beyond the idea of God, there is the fact of God. You are this fact. Rather than play with ideas, take a good look at this moment and ask, "What can I always know for sure?" Don't derive an answer from memory or expectation. Nothing around you is sure because it is all subject to time. Thoughts will come, go and change according to what happens. You will start to feel like Jon Snow from the television show *Game of Thrones*, who "knows nothing." Eventually, all you'll find is "I am" not as a thought, but as an eternal aliveness. The destiny of the pointer "I am" is to point to its own absence where eternity awaits your awareness. Hence, theory becomes silent fact. As Eckhart says, "Through the present moment, you have access to the power of life itself, that which has traditionally been called 'God.' As soon as you turn away from it, God ceases to be a reality in your life, and all you are left with is the mental concept of God, which some people believe in and others deny. Even belief in God is only a poor substitute for the living reality of God manifesting every moment of your life."

The urge to comprehend the incomprehensible arises from miscomprehension that God is comprehensible. My words are neither theory nor fact. They are subtle signposts pointing inward. The silent excess within you is fact. This fact is neither yours nor communicable; neither perishable nor special. Everything shares this fact because everything arises from it, in it and of it. This sounds like a theory because in the mind, it can only be a theory or pointer. The passing content of the mind can never claim the lasting reality of who you are. There is only one absolute truth, but it cannot be put to words. It is neither thing nor thought. It is formless, timeless and indigestible by the mind. You are this truth. The absolute knowing of who you are derives from beyond the mind; from a deeper, universal intelligence that you consciously connect with in the absence of desire, fear and thought. Here and now, silence whispers your essence. Eventually, due to its felt-omnipresence, this conscious connection persists with or without mind activity and remains strong no matter what appearance this moment takes. You no longer have to sit to know who you are when you are always aware of who you are. This can be referred to as a "current of awareness," which is a term Ramana Maharshi liked to use.

How do you maintain this current of awareness? A one-word summary of how to remember who you are, which Nisargadatta used frequently, is earnestness. Earnestness means sincere and intense conviction. This is a silent, peaceful intensity, not a strong-minded desire, where you constantly "die" to all you are not while holding on to who you are. This is why Eckhart said, "Die to the past every moment. You don't need it. Only refer to it when it is absolutely relevant to the present." You must maintain at least a portion of your focus on who you are until it takes effortless, continuous precedence over who you are not. Remember, the ego has great momentum in reducing, hypnotizing and imprisoning you. Do not resist this momentum. As you see it for what it is, flow with and accept it. Only with, not against, the ego can you diminish the ego. Resisting the ego only empowers it. Work with and accept whatever appearance this moment takes, within and without, and you'll see the egoic momentum begin to slow and reverse direction inward as earnest momentum to who you are.

While on a photography expedition to Antelope Canyon in Arizona, I was looking to get the perfect shot of light beams shining through the canyon. A group of amateur photographers and I were guided by a professional photographer and local tour guide that narrated the history of the area. As soon as we arrived and began walking through this canyon, I kept looking for the light beams, but could not find them. I wondered what the problem was. I thought, *Perhaps there is too much moisture in the air, too many clouds or it isn't the right time of day?* I began to lose hope as we ventured deeper into the canyon. Finally, the guides told us all to stop, take out our tripods and prepare for shooting. As I prepared my gear, I looked around and still saw no light beams. I was confused. Then, one of the guides bent his knee and used his hands to scoop up sand from the ground. He threw the sand in front of him toward what seemed like nothing. To my amazement, the sand revealed the most beautiful light beams. The colorless light of God requires a different tool of revelation. This tool can't be scooped up and thrown. This tool can't be traveled to or observed. This tool accelerates the process of inner revelation the moment you say, "I don't know" and ease into the unknown. This tool is allowing a deep peace with the unknown.

For comfort, security and a deep yearning for absolute knowing, the mind will use whatever means is necessary to explain the unexplainable and seek any reinforcement to validate itself. The fact that so many people do this invites more reason to do it. We try to squeeze the unsqueezable into bits of knowledge and create an organization of That which cannot be organized. Theists and atheists, in this regard, aren't so different. They both seem to know what cannot be known. "Yes, there is a God." "No, there is not a God." Both are just beliefs, not the whole truth. By letting go of knowing the unknown, the peace of God, which Saint Paul said, "surpasses all understanding," meaning it arises from beyond the mind, is now a greater possibility for your awareness. By letting go of keeping up with knowing who you are, which is constantly shaped by the instability of what happens, you can finally be at peace with not knowing who you are.

As the *Tao Te Ching* points out, "Not-knowing is true knowledge. Presuming to know is a disease. First realize that you are sick; then you can move toward health. The master is her own physician. She has healed herself of all knowing. Thus she is truly whole." Belief implies not knowing, yet choosing to believe; however, many of us forget or deny that we do not know and treat beliefs as rigid expectations or absolute truths in themselves. Beliefs are meant to be practical tools, but for many, they have replaced reality and the essence of who we truly are. Whether you express not knowing isn't as important as holding it dear within. At peace with the unknown, the conceptualized you can now be seen for the myth it is, which ripens your potential to reveal the leftover heart of who you truly are. This is not something you achieve or gain, it is a realignment with your innermost natural state; your eternal homecoming.

No one really fears the unknown because there's nothing there to fear. Fear needs something to manifest from and attach to. The unknown has no content for fear to cling to. A "fear of the unknown" is really a fear of letting go of the known. It is a fear of losing what you know. You don't have to let your knowledge go, only your habit of identifying with, relying on and attaching to it. You let this fear go by realizing living within the confines of conceptual knowledge has not served you well. It is not liberating. It provides seeming comfort that isn't really comfort because it's not comfortable living in a conceptualized reality that you know can bend you to its unstable will at any moment. You are safer in stable peace with the unknown than unstable peace with the known. Be safe now.

Chapter 17
Escaping Reality

I used to be an addict. Not to drugs or alcohol, but to a video game called World of Warcraft. This game, also known as WoW, is the world's most successful MMORPG, which means massively multiplayer online roleplaying game. WoW has held this title for well over a decade and continues to draw millions of people. I was always a gamer, but no game consumed me the way WoW did. It can be very difficult to find a balance while playing WoW because it draws you into its great depth and demands a lot of time and effort for even trivial accomplishments. It is hard to jump on the computer and play for a quick half hour. That can easily turn to two or three hours. The game works if you can find a balance, which I failed at for many years. I deleted and reinstalled the game more times than I can remember. Each deletion carried with it a newfound motivation to do something with my life. I would seek adventure in the real world only to start imagining myself flying atop a dragon and landing on real-time players to battle. I would seek love in the real world only to fail and start thinking about my love for the game. I even began to treat myself as a character to level up and wrote down different attributes that I tracked through a real-world leveling system I created. Of course, I couldn't transform into a lion or defeat large monsters. I was the most boring character I ever leveled up! Time and time again, I went right back to WoW.

I played this game throughout my eight years in college while also working full time. I would rush home after work or school just to jump on my computer. This hindered my social life tremendously, but I considered myself one of the most skilled players in the game and that meant a lot to me. Whether on the computer or not, I began to see myself through the game. Being unhappy with my studies and work, this game became my escape from reality. I knew this game was an impediment to living the life I wanted, I just couldn't stop. I was highly addicted and sought no one to help me. I remember the powerful urge I had to play rather than call my friends or family to get together. I remember thinking, "I know I can't keep working in the restaurants. I have to figure out what I will do with my life. Not now though, let me just play and forget about all that." Over and over again, these whispers had full control over me. For years, I kept kicking the can of responsibility down the road. What was it within me that felt so compelled to pursue something so intensely with such little sense and willpower to stop?

This compulsive urge was no more than a powerful energy field that became trapped within me. This trapped energy generated forceful whispers of the addiction. The addiction became its own energetic entity, created as a byproduct of the ego. If you look up the neuroscience on how meditation helps with addictions, you'll be amazed to see what happens to your brain. However, no matter what you read, always remember to sit for nothing. Do not sit with an expectation for new neural pathways in your brain to form or to experience an increase in blood flow to an area of the brain that regulates self-control. Just sit for nothing. This is key. I remember feeling the energy of the addiction within my body. I would close my eyes and feel the surges of temptation. From time to time, I was completely consumed by the whispers of this addiction. Logic was replaced with compulsion. I found my logical mind struggling to convince itself with sound reasons why I shouldn't play, but before I knew it, the computer was starting up and my hand was on the mouse waiting to click, click, click. This compulsion completely shrouded my inner aliveness and would always reveal its falsehood in providing me true joy. I tried to overcome it, but its presence was too strong for my untamed mind. I gave in time and time again. I felt hopeless and weak in the real world, but in the game, I felt incredibly powerful and like I was someone worthy of a name. I tried to forget the failure I was in this world by identifying strictly through the game. The game became a substitute for all the joy, love and peace I failed finding in the world. Since I couldn't find fulfillment out there or unveil it in here, I began desperately seeking it wherever and however possible.

How does such a captivating energy get trapped in the body? Your body is like a valve where energy from what happens passes through. If this energy cannot pass through, it remains stuck and builds up within you. Most of us don't keep this energetic passage open to remain clear. Rather, we leave it up to the instability of what happens to determine when we open or close. If you don't enjoy what happens, you will likely close your passage by resisting the event. If you do enjoy what happens, you will still likely close your passage by clinging to the event. If you accept the impermanence of what happens and allow the event to be, you will keep your passage open and allow the passing energy to pass. This maintains an inner openness. Clinging to what we want while resisting what we don't want traps within us the unnatural energy of samsara, which is the endless cycle of suffering. When your body, which acts as a valve for what happens, closes so frequently, there is a continuous buildup of samsaric energy. Like clogged arteries, this energy builds up over time harming and limiting its host. Through resisting what is, your body physically contracts. To overcome this, you must allow a clear passage for the energetic stream of all that happens to pass through this moment without leaving an impression on who you are. How to do this? You must reject every compulsion to let an event imprint on who you are by realizing who you are and staying with this realization. It always comes back to who you are. You cannot avoid this. This is essential.

When you feel an addiction, allow it to be here because it is already here. Let the addiction be as it is. Allow it to come forth and show its face. Be kind to it. If the addiction were knocking on your door, greet it and let it in. If you shut your door in its face, it will strengthen and find a back window. Let there be no self-judgment. This doesn't mean you have to listen to its whispers. Instead, accept its presence. The addiction presents itself not only as a challenge, but as a means for freedom. You must use the addiction to go beyond the addiction. Addictions are there for their own acceptance and transcendence. They are portals to freedom. This is the divine purpose of all suffering. First, try not calling it an addiction or hollow out the word and use it strictly as a communication tool. The word addiction screams negativity. Let it be as it is, neither good nor bad, but neutral and impersonal as all things are until you think them otherwise. So long as it is a bad thing, you will carry a victim mentality. You, as the subject, are a victim of the addiction, which is the object, that has invaded your life. This is a silly story. Addictions have nothing to do with who you are. The best way to be free of addiction is by bringing attention to the egoic structure on which all addiction is built. Even if you free yourself of one particular addiction, more will come and others will remain, such as the common addiction to overthinking. To "have an addiction" means someone is there to claim the addiction. "I am addicted to so and so," says the ego. No, you are not addicted to anything nor can you be. There may be addiction arising in this moment, but contrary to how it seems, it belongs to no one. No addiction is your addiction. It is just addiction, coming and going. You are the Witness of this happening.

Rather than thinking, "I am addicted to such and such," you can think, "A lot of such and such tends to happen." This is neutral and belongs to no one. Or with even greater presence, you can think, "Such and such is happening now." This uninvites all the times such and such has happened, which tends to carry a heavy weight of shame and false reality. There is no need for this. Use the addiction to find out who is addicted. When you say, "I am addicted," who is the "I" that is addicted? Only the "I" built of memories, anticipation, fear and desire can say such a thing. This "I" is your mind, not you. You can still use this "I" to communicate, but in the depths of your heart, you must know the truth. The real "I" is the observer of the mind, not the changing "I" within it. With one full sweep of truth, the structure on which all addictive clinging is built can greatly diminish when you realize you are neither addicted nor can be. Why? Because a space begins to form between who you are and the passing addiction. Without inner spaciousness, you will feel there is a little, addicted me. You will feel a sense of lack, which breeds addiction. Only the voice of an addiction says, "I can't." This voice is not your voice. "Hunny, you have to stop drinking!" "I can't!" Who can't? The addiction or you? In spaciously seeing the addiction speaking, your sense of self begins disentangling from the memories that weave together the "I am addicted" story. You must stay the seer of this voice to remain free of its whispers.

All addiction stems from a sense of lack. How can you know this? Try sitting and doing nothing in the midst of a strong desire to satisfy your addiction. You will come face to face with this deep-rooted lack. The good news is your primal completion is endlessly deeper than this. You must realize the boundless completeness left in the absence of there being someone to claim, "I am addicted." When you realize you are already complete, you have no more deceptive holes that need filling through an addiction. This is a powerful medicine. Use the mind and this medicine will be indigestible. Only through silence can you ingest this medicine. Keep in mind, even if you stop the engine of an addiction, the wheels will likely continue spinning for a while, especially the physical component.

As is evident throughout this book, there seems to be many teachings. In reality, the only teaching is that there is no teaching. Ultimately, there is no teaching, teacher or student. The highest teaching is to reject all teachings. The Buddha went from teacher to teacher until he realized this. His very search for enlightenment was hiding it all along. I point to Being, not doing. Everything you encounter is about doing. This is about non-doing. The doing takes care of itself once you root in Being. You must remain quiet. It is easier than easy. It only seems hard because you apply effort. It requires absolutely nothing, yet you chase something because this is all you know. Do not make this into some task. Simply, be as you are right here, right now. As spiritual teacher Rajneesh, also known as Osho, once said, "Don't seek, don't search, don't ask, don't knock, don't demand – relax. If you relax, it comes. If you relax, it is there. If you relax, you start vibrating with it." Stop trying to accomplish all that I point to. All my pointing always comes back to effortlessness, not effort. Stay quiet, even as you speak, think and read. There is always quietude and solitude. Do not be afraid of being alone, you are always alone. Eternity has no companions. There are no others. Your aloneness is the eternal fountain for all that comes and goes. You are this fountain. Stay as the fountain. Stay as the ocean. You are not the waves, yet the ocean is inseparable from the waves. You are no particular wave, yet you are all the waves. You must stop seeing yourself as a single wave wanting to reunite with the ocean. How can a wave reunite with the ocean? It is your time-bound quest for reunion that creates the illusion of separation. You must realize the ocean you already are by realizing what is left in the absence of all you think you are. You can be alone as a wave or alone as the ocean.

You may be wondering what I mean by, "Simply, be as you are." This doesn't mean to be as your memories tell you to be. This doesn't mean to be as your desires tell you to be. This doesn't mean to be anything in particular. Rather, unite with the passing appearance and underlying awareness of this moment. When you let go of being this or that, what is left to be? Being itself. Whatever appearance this moment takes, within and without, remain united with it. Be the space containing the appearance of this moment. To be what you already are requires no effort, time or distance. If you feel sadness, do not resist it. Acknowledge and accept the sadness as it passes. There is no right or wrong way to be. Self-concepts, such as being enlightened or spiritual, are common traps which build up images to chase. As Mooji said,

"Don't be a spiritual person, just be free." Be wary not to let your ego convince you it's okay to start harming others and excuse it as, "Being as I am." Always remember the ego reads this book alongside you and may dig up these memories at any time for its own defending and strengthening. Even this you must accept in order to diminish. You cannot use resistance, which is the ego, to ward off the ego. Anytime you resist what is, you are living in a fantasy land of imagining an alternative reality which doesn't exist.

During my years in high school, I was known as the crazy kid. "Crazy George," they would call me. All I really cared about was having fun and making others laugh. I was dubbed, "The craziest kid in New Jersey." I would go to nightclubs in a speedo, jump naked into neighbor's swimming pools, throw wild house parties, get kicked out of class, sneak into underground ancient tombs for an overnight stay and plenty more. When my parents left for the weekend, it felt like divine purpose to throw a house party. I would invite a few friends at school and say, "Spread the word!" That same night, around a hundred teenagers would arrive at my house. I often drank socially and acted very wild. When the house parties were over, I would scan my home for stolen or damaged items. The house was rarely in good condition. Glasses were broken, small items were missing, water was left running, the floors were a mess and some bedrooms were in disarray. I remember the last house party I had ended with the police coming to break it up. I thought that would be the last major gathering of instability to my home. I was wrong. You see, we all have an open house party every day when we allow words to possess us, events to hypnotize us, thoughts to define us and things to consume us. The condition of our inner home is determined by what happens and everyone is invited. What makes this any different than me screaming in the hallways, "Party at my house tonight!" For most of us, the open house parties last a lifetime and thoroughly shape our thought-made realities.

We try to escape reality because we allow thoughts to create reality. Whether through regret, addiction or distress, we all attempt escape from our thought-made realities. The more we try to escape, the more we'll have to escape. We get more of what we focus on. We create our own, ever-changing prison, then spend a lifetime trying to break out of it. This is not your personal madness, it's a universal conditioning of the mind. You never chose this path, it was passed down to you with great momentum. When thoughts are your bedrock for reality, you have tied a lasso around your freedom. Remove this lasso by removing time. As you chase desires and enjoy their fleeting returns, this lasso can pull you right back into the depths of unconsciousness at any time. Like dust pulled into a vacuum, you get pulled into a story. Instead of endlessly trying to dodge incoming lassos, let there be no one there to get caught to begin with. Only conceptual identities can get caught in lassos of storytelling. Without a false you, the theatrics are over. This is why Jesus said, "If anyone would come after me, let him deny himself." You don't need to live this life with a rope around your belly. This rope disguises itself as a snake. It is fear and lack that conjure the snake and keep it coiled around you. How do you free yourself from this slithering lasso? Simply realize the snake is really a rope. You keep fearing things that at present do not exist. You keep imagining lack that at present does not exist. See the false as false and the snake will reveal itself to be a harmless rope and disappear altogether. You must see the stories behind your fear and lack for the illusions they are. In this seeing, you are free. This is a vantage point for your conditioning wherein you must gain foothold by holding onto the wisdom of real versus unreal.

We try to escape reality because we rarely question reality. What is real? What is unreal? Think of the most memorable appearances this moment took. Think of how you fell in love, chased love and lost love. Think of how determined you were to achieve a goal. Think of how much pain you've been through. Remember someone you had to let go. Remember how you were raised. Close your eyes and remember what it felt like to see the ocean for the first time. Think of your first kiss. Recollect how you first drove a car, rode a bike, played a sport, lived on your own, the places you worked and travelled to. Remember the longest hike you went on, the most dangerous situation you've been in, the most beautiful sight you've laid eyes on, the competitions you participated in and the one time you felt most alone. Go down memory lane to the one event that really shaped who you have taken yourself to be all these years. Think of the scariest, happiest and most inspirational appearance this moment took. This moment has offered the passing of many faces.

What do all of your experiences have in common? They once stood before you. Where are they now? They are ghosts of a previous appearance of this moment in this moment. What reality do these memories have? Only that they, too, are passing through this moment. These thoughts are part of reality in the sense that you can only have these thoughts now, which means they are part of this passing appearance, but they are not reality in themselves. Treating memory as actual reality is the trap humanity has fallen into. What comes and goes has relative reality. It is perishable. Anything perishable is not ultimately real. Do you think that what is happening or will happen will face a fate other than instant memory? Everything faces the fate of mere memory until the mind fades taking your memories with it. This disappearance is the fate of all that happens. This is why Nisargadatta Maharaj said, "Experience is of change – it comes and goes. Reality is not an event; it cannot be experienced. It is not perceivable in the same way an event is perceivable. If you wait for an event to take place, for the coming of reality, you will wait forever, for reality neither comes nor goes." He continues, "All you can do is grasp the central point that reality is not an event and does not happen, and that whatever happens, whatever comes and goes, is not reality. See events as events only, the transient as transient, experience as mere experience and you have done all you can. Then you are vulnerable to reality, no longer armored against it as you were when you gave reality to events and experiences."

All of life is an ever-changing instant, which *A Course in Miracles* calls the "holy instant." In this instant, everything comes. Then, poof! In this same instant, everything is gone. Our minds, bodies and this book are all part of this poof. All the stars, suns and moons are part of this poof. Nothing can escape it. Poof is the inescapable destiny for all that happens. Like a cosmic joke, this ever-changing instant creates the paradox of time. Eckhart explains this by saying, "Whatever you do takes time, and yet it is always now." There has been, is and always will be one Constant which doesn't face a time-bound fate. You are this Constant. The appearance of this moment is a vanishing act played out in the timeless space of who you are. Everything instantly becomes memory. The dying appearance of this moment is ever-vanishing into memory. If all you knew was memory, then it would seem more reasonable that memory is the only reality you have. However, we all have an underlying awareness that we are remembering. There is not just memory, there is the awareness of memory. How often are you aware of this awareness in comparison to the memories that arise from it? This awareness doesn't fade with time. Do you consider passing memory to be as real as the lasting awareness? Can both be absolutely real? Which one contains the other? Which one allows the other?

Memory arises in awareness, exists only in relation to something else and inevitably dissolves in awareness. Awareness has no opposite or "otherness" to relate to, has no divisions or borders, doesn't sway with what happens and never dissolves because it has no form that was assembled in the first place. Even when you say, "I am not aware," you are aware that you are seemingly not aware. Whether there is something to be aware of or not makes no difference to the imperishable presence of awareness. Question is: can you turn this awareness onto itself and be aware of being aware? Yes, you can – now. Rupert Spira often encourages his students to ask themselves this powerful question: "Am I aware?" The moment this question arises, there is a pause. In this pause, you realize your mind can't help and so you let it go and become aware of awareness which is the only way to generate an answer that forever fits. Your attention falls further back to its directionless source as you answer, "Yes." I would encourage you to pose this question as often as you can.

The appearance of this moment is like the passing tip of an endless iceberg. Exposed to time and nature, this tip constantly changes according to its surrounding climate. Someday, this tip will disappear altogether, but the rest of the iceberg remains as it is. This Remainder is consciously accessible only through its own tip, which is the appearance of this moment. You must peacefully deny mental constructs from constructing a time-bound reality. Then, the appearance of this moment, no matter how it looks, can serve its purpose and allow you conscious access to eternity. Again, as complicated as all this seems, there is great simplicity here. All it takes is a moment of consciousness turning its gaze upon itself. You must reroot in this moment by coming face to face with who you are. You must uproot from your mental identity back to your spiritual divinity. Remember, although words present a subject and object, there is no duality when consciousness meets consciousness. Despite "consciousness" being a noun, it is not a person, place, thing or idea. This is beyond the play of words and thought.

To be free of endless attempts to escape your thought-made realities, you must face the heart of a story, not run from it. This is why Buddhist Ajahn Chah said, "Trying to run away from suffering is actually to run toward it." No matter where you run, your mind follows. What is the heart of a story? The fact that it is a story. We are so caught up on the content of a story, we forget that it is a story. Seeing fiction as fiction can dissolve stories from the inside out. You can still talk about a story without becoming entangled in it. You can still agree and disagree without becoming entangled in it. How to do this? Listen while keeping your heart grounded in reality, which has nothing to do with time-bound stories. When stories lose their density, you can participate in the world without becoming a slave to it. Stories have their place. Without them, there is not much functioning in this world. Stories are not bad or wrong; however, when they are all you know and take to be actual reality, then you have forsaken the present moment, which is the only reality there is. Emotions, which correspond to thoughts, can empower the apparent reality of past and future because the body cannot tell the difference between the reality of this moment and a thought projecting away from this moment. Emotions can make the past and future feel real when in reality, they have no reality. People will try to suck you out of this moment and into their stories. Do not let anything present itself as more important than this moment. There is nothing more important than this moment because this moment is all there ever is.

Like poison ivy entangling a tree, psychological suffering is built on stories that entangle our sense of reality and who we are. One can climb a tree and slowly start untangling the ivy only to find it popping up in other areas or one can cut it by its root removing the foundation on which it is built. How to cut suffering by the root? Realize who you are beyond who you think you are. This realization requires no thought, takes no time and has no distance. This way, your sense of self is no longer entangled by the instability of time-bound storylines. You can still listen to, take action on and use such stories, but you are free from their seductive nature and gravitational pull and you can only be free now.

Whatever feeling arises, stay with it. Do not try to keep it. Do not try to avoid it. Just be there with the feeling no matter how uncomfortable. Do not deny its discomfort. What arises always belongs. Internally accept what is no matter how unacceptable it seems. Feel the raw feeling, but don't become it. Ease into the space which allows this feeling to arise and pass and you will discover comfort within the discomfort. The Roman Emperor Marcus Aurelius explained this by saying, "What stands in the way becomes the way." By wishing this moment any different than it already is, you build up desire and emotion. Once these feelings reach a certain momentum, they weigh heavy on your heart and cast a full shade over the appearance of this moment. The heavier the emotion, the heavier the felt-realization of the leftover space beneath the emotion. Bring neutral awareness to feelings the same way you bring neutral awareness to certain perceptions. See a feeling the same way you see birds flying across the sky, feel raindrops falling on your skin, hear crickets singing into the night, etc. No feeling is your feeling. Do not claim it as your own. Do not become it. You must allow your awareness of the feeling to devour the story attached to it. First allow, then choose. The serenity of allowing what is to be is very powerful. In doing so, the feeling dwindles to a physical sensation more so than a conceptual frustration and passes quickly. Otherwise, the story will continue fueling the feelings and the feelings will continue affirming the story. This is the hamster wheel of samsara. Do not just read these words and nod your head. Directly experience what I point to. Next time life takes you out of your comfort zone, which won't take long, experiment with accepting what already is and see what happens.

If you experience unhappiness, do not be unhappy about your unhappiness. That only adds an extra layer of unhappiness. There are enough layers. Do not try to be happy about your unhappiness either. That won't work very well! Just allow what is to be. Rather than solely try to chip at the story from the outside and mold it into what you want or escape it altogether, go directly into it. Physically locate and feel the raw emotion. You must be like the Greeks who sent their Trojan horse into the heart of Sparta filled with soldiers; but instead of soldiers, be filled with acceptance. Like a butcher's blade slicing warm butter, allow your acceptance to cut through the story. Surrender to this moment as it is, not as you conceptualize it to be. Herein, the unwanted emotional charge, along with the story, passes. Eckhart explained this well when he said, "The ego says, 'I shouldn't have to suffer,' and that thought makes you suffer so much more. It is a distortion of the truth, which is always paradoxical. The truth is you need to say yes to suffering before you can transcend it." Neither Eckhart nor anyone is as great a teacher as suffering itself. Is such a teacher necessary? Suffering is necessary until you realize it is no longer necessary. If life always happened the way you would like it to, there would be no enlightenment. Imagine you lived in a beautiful home on your own island without any danger, bills to pay, bad weather, lack of food or water, human drama or anything that didn't match your expectations and desires. If you could "have it all" and never experience any suffering, you would miss your birthright potential to coalesce with an incomparable, reasonless, ever-available peace that emanates from beyond the reach of time. Siddhartha Gautama would never have become the Buddha if he didn't leave his perfect palace life. Everything that has ever gone "wrong" has been a blessing in disguise. To a large extent, you are here to experience problems – until you no longer need to. When will you no longer need to? Now. All problems crash here and now. Suffering is meant to drive you inward toward the light of this moment, which is normally obscured by the mind. All darkness, if you allow it to be, becomes an opening for the light. In allowing darkness to be, it is transmuted to lightness, which points your way home. Michael A. Singer reiterates this point in his book *The Untethered Soul: The Journey Beyond Yourself*, by explaining, "Pain is the price of freedom."

When suffering becomes so intense, it has the power to burn itself out and dispel your pseudo-self. Like a raging candle that burns through all of its wax, the ego can dissolve through its own stories. No matter how powerful an emotion you experience, the space in which you experience it always has the power to devour the emotion. No matter what comes and goes, nothing is greater than the space in which it comes and goes. In other words, there is nothing greater than no-thing. There is always more space than things in space. There is always more space than sadness, anger, jealousy, resentment, hatred, etc. To allow what comes to be and go, you must ease into the space in which everything happens. Easing into this space can swallow up any emotion or thought. Be here, but not as a "little me" stuck in a story called "my life." Be here as the space, not its content. You must be like an empty Pac-Man gobbling up all that happens. Again, do not just read these words and store this in your memory bank. You must resurrect these pointers, then dispose of them and experience the emptiness and fullness of what I speak of. You must directly experience the power of spacious easing. What was once intense energy trapped in the body becomes intense aliveness flowing through the body. This transformational shift is pure freedom.

The ego splits reality into many pieces. There is what was, what could have been, what should have been, what is elsewhere, what could be, what should be and what will be. These realities share a time-bound, thought-made, little existence. When these mind-dominated realities align in your favor, you are happy. When they misalign, you are not happy. It all depends on the instability of what happened, happens or is expected to happen. The most popular reality is your story of what is and your belief of what should be. Reality has diminished to a back and forth play of thought. These realities are of absolute importance to the ego. Why? To the ego, this is what life is. You can't blame the ego for doing all it knows to do. What you can do is watch all that happens from the eternal watchtower of who you are. Sounds complicated and fancy, but it's really the simplest and easiest thing to do. Why? Because there is absolutely nothing to actually do. You might find that difficult, but that's only because you are turning nothing into something. This, too, is not your fault. This is how the mind has been conditioned. The mind isn't used to nothing, it is only used to something. When faced with nothing, the mind doesn't understand and so it creates something, which makes all this seem so difficult. You can't try to stop your mind from doing this because that revs up the engine even more. Just see what it does and be okay with it. Do this long enough and a space begins to arise between who is watching the mind and what is happening in the mind. Your identity starts to pull away from the content of the mind to the watcher of the mind.

Be empty beyond the concept of being empty. As you get used to this emptiness, you may find your sense of self being drawn back into the mind to do what it has always done: attach to something. Accept and see this for what it is to be free of it. Your identity may go back and forth between the seer and what is seen, but eventually, you will remain the seer. When I use the word "eventually," I mean now. "Eventually" means you may have to wait for "now" to change its face a bit more. Nothing happens eventually. Everything happens now.

I can't help but pause and smile at the silly perspective of how many pages I've written thus far on absolutely nothing. This book points to the very space from which it is read. Engulfed in paradox and limited language, just look at the ending of the last paragraph: "When I use the word 'eventually,' I mean now." This seems reserved for late-night comedy. Sometimes, I hear my ego, "What the hell are you talking about George!" None of this seems to make any sense, yet I know it is the only sense there is. Onwards to nowhere we go!

The mind is like a pendulum hammer that can destruct old walls, then swing the opposite direction and construct new walls. You cannot rely on the mind for true freedom, which is an effortless emergence from the continued realization of your intrinsic nature. In the realm of the mind, what lifts you up today can knock you down tomorrow. Seeing the mind-made walls you build for yourself by yourself allows you to tear them down. You can only truly enjoy things if you are not dependent on them. You must feel the presence that allows the animation of your mind, body and moment. This aliveness frees you from the storytelling of the mind. As Eckhart says, "To be unable to feel the life that animates the physical body, the very life that you are, is the greatest deprivation that can happen to you." From all deprivation arises a need for replenishment, but where do you turn for it? Your family? Your career? Your new car? You must turn inward beyond thought and instability. This is the only true replenishment.

Since childhood, you've set out on countless journeys. Unveiling the presence that you are is the final journey. Unlike all other journeys which need time, this renounces time. Negate time and it is here. Negate who you think you are and it is here. Once your inward gaze touches the timeless dimension, there are no more journeys. There is only this moment and what is currently passing through. Journeys do not truly exist, only the step you are taking at this moment does. Only the breath you are taking in this moment does. You may envision the mountaintop you are journeying toward, but this thought has no separate reality outside of this moment. Everything is contained here and now. You can't get to the top of Mt. Everest in the future! The future always appears as this moment. Only now can you arrive anywhere, except now will look different as it always does. If your mind still denies this, then try arriving somewhere and saying it is not now. In truth, you never arrive anywhere. You are everywhere and nowhere. As everything and nothing, you are the untouched Watcher of this changing moment, not a separate body traveling from point A to B. Ultimately, even saying this moment changes isn't entirely accurate since all you have is the precise appearance of this moment now – and now – and now. Only memory claims with relative truth that this moment changes, not reality. The thought of a changing moment is just another story. Time aside, there is only now. Even if time obscures this moment, this obscuration happens now. No matter the intensity of thought, there is always only now. Reality asserts itself as the appearance and formless essence of now. Do not try and grasp this intellectually. This is beyond logical reach. Simply sit for nothing and all will come to you.

The difference between what this moment looks like and what you think it should look like is a reality trap many of us fall into. What you wish was versus what actually is has become a lifelong blur between fiction and non-fiction. All fictitious realities are created by channeling your attention away from this moment. The moment you turn away from this moment, what is left? Thoughts, of course. Only thoughts can make it seem like there is another reality outside of the appearance of this moment. Like a double-edge sword, thoughts carry great potential to serve and deceive. The thoughts you impose on this moment carry an apparent reality of their own by covering up this moment. When this moment is obscured entirely by thinking, it seems your thoughts are the only reality there is. The human mind is incredibly powerful, yet seductively misleading. To overcome mental seduction, heed the words of Nisargadatta Maharaj who said, "Let go of your attachment to the unreal and the real will swiftly and smoothly step into its own. Stop imagining yourself being or doing this or that and the realization that you are the source and heart of all will dawn upon you." He continues, "However long a life may be, it is but a moment and a dream."

During the movie *Creed*, Rocky Balboa said to his trainee Adonis while pointing to the mirror, "You see this guy here? That's the toughest opponent you're ever going to have to face. I believe that's true in the ring, and I think that's true in life." The first step in defeating this opponent is by not considering your ego an opponent. That's just more ego. You have no otherness. There are no pieces of you. There is no me and my ego. Fantasizing multiplicity where there is none does, indeed, create the toughest opponent you can face: the sexy trickery of the mind. Rocky's words echo throughout all of human history. Everyone carries the inherited weeds of multiplicity. Only through realizing your primal oneness can you pull the weeds of illusion by the roots and realize the freedom that always was.

Most humans see themselves as separate actors and actresses on a stage playing roles in a grand drama. We are fooled through sole fixation on what we see, ignorant of the seer. We only know the lights, camera and action. We mostly know to rewind and fast forward. We have been rehearsing over and over the conditioned scripts in our heads. This is what we have come to call reality. You must show up as the audience of the play, not a character in it. If your girlfriend, for example, leaves you as you bend your knee to propose, all she is doing is walking away in a certain direction. Your resistance to her footsteps causes you to suffer. The stories you impose on her footsteps is not actual reality. Actual reality belongs to no one, but you think there is someone there to claim it. If you don't remember it is just a thought, then the thought becomes your reality. As she walks away, all that is happening in the moment is she is walking. To be in this moment fully, you must allow this moment to be. Here and now, you are perfect just the way you are and everything is perfect just the way it is because it already is. Once your roots leave this moment, there is imperfection everywhere. This imperfect reality is not a result of what is, but your fixed interpretation of what is, which needs time. This is why Eckhart said, "The ego cannot distinguish between a situation and its interpretation of and reaction to that situation. You might say, 'What a dreadful day,' without realizing that the cold, the wind, and the rain or whatever condition you react to are not dreadful. They are as they are. What is dreadful is your reaction, your inner resistance to it, and the emotion that is created by that resistance."

Once you worry about a life without her, you suffer in the future. Once you regret what you didn't do with her, you suffer in the past. Even the future you cannot think of without the past. All thoughts of the future necessarily involve the past. Rather than create a false reality to escape, take a few conscious breaths and realize the neutrality of what is actually happening in this moment. See it all happening within you, not to you. Accept this passing appearance unconditionally by realizing the unconditioned space in which it appears. Use your senses to stay grounded here and now. Step out of the mind for just a moment and redirect your focus to the underlying awareness of what is happening, not just what is happening. Without effort, you must continuously carry a felt-realization of this awareness by easing into it until it no longer fully disappears beneath the veil of thought. Like a root making its way through a dense jungle, there must always remain a conscious connection to who you are. Even as the jungle burns and turns to barren land, beneath all that happens, this root must remain.

You can lose things, but you can never lose who you are. You can gain things, but you can never gain who you are. You always have been, are and will be who you are. You have no beginning or end. The same divinity that writes this, reads this. There is only what is and what allows what is to be. This means there is only this moment and what allows this moment to be. What allows this moment to be? You do. You are like a canvas realizing through the painting that you are the canvas. You must give up trying to analyze this. This, too, is a trap. Everything faces our analytical minds, which has great usefulness, but what I speak of eludes all methods, practices and analysis. No number of books, thoughts or conversations can explain the unexplainable. To be free of attempting escape from your thought-made realities, you must realize the One Reality that doesn't come or go. You are this Reality.

Chapter 18
Unborn

I was born on August 6, 1985, or so I was told. Every year, my birth is celebrated. Of course, there is nothing wrong with this. My mother especially loves this day. Growing up, she would do everything in her power to make my birthdays memorable. Little did I know, in the mind-identified state, we are reborn every day, hundreds, if not thousands of times. Should we have hundreds of birthdays or rather birth-moments a day? My mother would be very exhausted if she knew this! How is it we are born and die every day throughout the day? Well, if you asked me years ago who I was, I would say, "George." Although my name doesn't change, what the name means changes all day, which means who I am changes all day. George the happy. George the sad. George the confused. George the thought about that. George the feeling about this. George the whatever he said. George the whatever she said. George the memory about that. George the expectation about this. George the short, smelly, hairy, Greek guy and so on. When there is no space between the thoughts you have and who you are, you experientially become the thoughts you have. They are all you know and take to be you. You can't blame yourself for being the only reality you know. This is normal, but rarely observed, understood and questioned.

When your entire reality is made of thoughts, your entire identity is made of thoughts too. Identity and reality are the same thing. Both identity and reality merge with each passing thought. From nothing, a thought arises. This is your reality and identity until it passes. Then, woof, another thought arises and passes. If you are happy about the beautiful day at the beach, your identity is the feeling of happiness. You are happy. Happiness is what you are. Additionally, your reality is happiness. If someone walks by you on the beach and calls you fat, then your identity is sadness. From happiness to sadness, who you are changed within a few seconds. Every thought you identify with, you are reborn into. You are constantly taking the form of whatever thought pops up. For most, this continuous death and rebirth occurs from the moment you wake to the moment you sleep in the relentless torrent of thinking. When you first wake up, your mind is like an old car that needs a few seconds to start. The engine chokes for a bit before getting into full gear. Then, until you sleep, it runs all day carrying your identity with it in an ever-changing road trip.

The movement of psychological death and rebirth perpetuates your karmic structure. What is karma? Karma is the unconscious conditioning of your mind. It is the weight the past has over who you are. Part of your karma is inherited through many millennia of collective human unconsciousness. The rest is your past impressions flowing through what you feel, think and do. To be free of karma is to be free from the psychic weight of experience. Remember, do not fall into the trap of, "One day, I'll be free from the karma that binds me." Time cannot free you from karma. Relying on time is the exact reason you have karma. Only by delving deep into this moment through the shell of the world to its formless essence can you be free of karma.

In the mind-identified state, life is a dream of what was and what will be, which means life is a continuous stream of imagination. Who is dreaming this dream? Consciousness is. The goal is for consciousness to awaken from its own dream. Otherwise, the dream is who you are. In deep sleep, when you dream, you usually don't know that you are dreaming until you wake up and think, "Oh, it was just a dream." On more rare occasions, you do know that you are dreaming. We call these lucid dreams. To know that you are dreaming within a dream is to know that nothing about the dream is ultimately real, correct? Without the understanding that you are dreaming, all you know is the dream. There is no other reality but the dream. In lucid dreams, you step outside the dream and see the dream. To maintain lucidity while dreaming during your sleeping hours is akin to maintaining lucidity while dreaming during your waking hours. Both dreams are similar in the sense of not being ultimately real, but you can't know this until you step outside the dream and see the dream. What is a dream? All which comes and goes. What doesn't come and go? You, the Watcher of the dream. You are the timeless Reality that allows all passing reality. How can you know this? Feel and sense the very Presence which allows the mind to read this word. This Presence is always here and now, untouched by all that happens; neither coming nor going; neither living nor dying. What is this Presence? You are.

In his book *A New Earth*, Eckhart explained dreams by saying, "There is the dream, and there is the dreamer of the dream. The dream is a short-lived play of forms. It is the world – relatively real but not absolutely real. Then there is the dreamer, the absolute reality in which the forms come and go. The dreamer is not the person. The person is part of the dream. The dreamer is the substratum in which the dream appears, that which makes the dream possible. It is the absolute behind the relative, the timeless behind time, the consciousness in and behind form. The dreamer is consciousness itself – who you are. To awaken within the dream is our purpose now."

There is an African proverb that says, "When death finds you, may it find you alive." You must die to who you think you are to unveil who you really are. This requires a beating heart. This is what it means for death to find you alive. You can't force this death with a willful mind. This is a silent baptism that washes away all that you are not. This doesn't mean you no longer use your name and memories, but that they no longer use you. Give up the future. Give up the past. Let concepts of death go. Be fully present, immune to ideas of death. Find death first. Find death now. This is why Nisargadatta Maharaj said, "The jnani has died before his death; he saw that there was nothing to be afraid of. The moment you know your real being, you are afraid of nothing. To be free in the world, you must die to the world. Then the universe is your own; it becomes your body, an expression and a tool. The happiness of being absolutely free is beyond description." What happens if death doesn't find you alive? Well, my heart still beats, so I couldn't tell you exactly what happens and after my heart stops beating, I still won't be able to tell you exactly what happens. There is a Zen story of a monk who asked, "What happens when you die?" The Zen master replied, "I don't know." The monk said, "What do you mean. Aren't you a Zen master?" And the Zen master replied, "Yes, but I'm not a dead one."

What we do know is birth cannot be without death and death cannot be without birth. What sparks birth? Desire, which is another word for attachment and identification. So long as there is desire, there is birth. So long as there is birth, there is death. Without desire, there can be no birth. Once you embody desirelessness with every cell in your body, you will no longer be reborn into every passing thought. You will use thoughts, not be them. Thoughts will no longer touch who you are. This means your thought-rebirths are over. How to do this? Breathe life into the words of Thich Nhat Hanh who said, "Water is free from the birth and death of a wave." You are the water and what happens are the waves.

While alive and full of desire, you are reborn into every passing thought. When your body goes poof, the desire carried into the poof will create something or desirelessness will allow nothing. This is no different than what is happening now with the relationship between desire and thought. With desire, you are reborn. Without desire, you are unborn. This applies now and always. This is why Nisargadatta said, "It is the satisfaction of desire that breeds misery. Freedom from desire is bliss." This, too, is why Swami Sri Yukteswar, the guru of Paramahansa Yogananda, said, "So long as the soul of man is encased in one, two, or three body-containers, sealed tightly with the corks of ignorance and desires, he cannot merge with the sea of Spirit. When the gross physical receptacle is destroyed by the hammer of death, the other two coverings – astral and causal – still remain to prevent the soul from consciously joining the Omnipresent Life. When desirelessness is attained through wisdom, its power disintegrates the two remaining vessels. The tiny human soul emerges, free at last; it is one with the Measureless Amplitude."

Desirelessness doesn't mean you can't like something or have an opinion. You can have your preferences, likes and dislikes, but the only sane way to have all this is after first fully accepting what is. I also have political opinions and don't like when I see a person or animal suffering, but there is space surrounding these opinions and preferences. Don't try and be a certain way, just be as you are. What does it mean to be as you are? Be here and now as the space containing the appearance of this moment. Then, use memory, anticipation, imagination, likes and dislikes. Who you are must consciously precede what you do.

When a desire is fulfilled, you are happy. It seems the fulfillment of that desire has brought you happiness. Truth is, you are not happy because you fulfilled a desire. You are happy because the desire is absent. Your happiness is there because the desire is not. You do not need to fulfill a desire to experience the happiness you hope to attain from it. You need only be here now. It is not the fulfillment of desire that brings happiness, it is the lack of desire which allows happiness to shine because it is no longer trapped beneath the endless stream of desire poking its head out when circumstances allow. To attribute happiness to fulfilling a desire means you must endlessly chase desires to stay happy. This chase stems from a deep-rooted, inherited sense of insufficiency and fear. No matter if desires are fulfilled or failed, they only bring more desire and more suffering. Happiness arising from the fulfillment of desire is not wrong, it's normal. With that said, this happiness contains deep within its seed of opposite, which is suffering. Such happiness is short-lived, conditional and carries a fear of loss. Anything gained can be lost. Everything gained will be lost, hence the subtle undercurrent of fear. True happiness is not personally gained from anything in particular and therefore cannot be lost by anything in particular. It is a deep, uncaused joy arising from presence. It seems to come and go because the mind, which can be like a cloud to the sun, keeps covering it up. Despite the clouds, it is unconditional, self-sustaining, ever-present and complete in itself – awaiting your attention now.

Rebirth can only be understood now. Do not turn it into an abstract idea about the future. To truly understand the cycle of rebirth, you must see how you become what you think, feel and do. The mind is always looking for the next thing to be born into. Notice in yourself and others the tendency to be habitually reborn into passing thoughts, feelings and emotions. Notice how what happens endlessly constructs and deconstructs your conceptualized sense of reality and who you are. Remember, a conceptualized reality and identity go hand in hand. If something takes away from the story of your conceptualized reality and identity, no matter how subtle or apparent, you die to the previous mental version of "me and my life" as you are reborn into a new version. If something adds to the story of your conceptualized reality and identity, no matter how subtle or apparent, you are born into a new mental version of "me and my life" as you die to the previous version. The residue of each death seeps into the next birth and the residue of each birth seeps into the next death. Your thought-made self exists within the confines of a relentless birth and death mental cycle. The exception here would be if you remain unattached and spaciously observant of conceptual realities and identities to use them rather than become them.

Rebirth is a direct experience, not a concept to carry around. Reincarnation means to be reborn into a form. Whether this form is a thought, sensation or body, all incarnations are built on desire. Desire breeds form. Desirelessness breeds nothing. As Nisargadatta said, "With desirelessness comes timelessness." After your body takes its final breath, the compulsion to incarnate may survive and another body and universe may pop up. Humans call this change death. Nature calls it recycling. Whatever you call it, what matters is what you know deep in your heart. Desire has incredible momentum, which is why it is said to survive the death of a body and carry over into another body. This process, it seems, has been going on for eons. In the book *Wake Up and Roar*, Papaji explained that spiritual awakening is, "Emancipation from the process one has been passing through for millions of years." So long as you believe you were born, then you are subject to death. Birth leads to death and death leads to birth. They go hand in hand. Only the unborn are free from the cycle of womb to tomb.

The Buddha explained, "As long as there is a doer, you are stuck on the wheel of life and death." As a doer, you carry the residue of illusion which expands when events inflate your sense of self and contracts when events deflate your sense of self steadily building up momentum over a lifetime. The energetic expansion and contraction of egoic residue can be observed in thoughts, emotions and experiences. Each expansion seeps into the next contraction and each contraction seeps into the next expansion. This cycle continues until there is no more residue or doer, as the Buddha said. If you carry a strong sense of fear and anxiety, these energies will likely manifest as a dream and comprise its environment. The same goes for peace, joy and so on. Similarly, the quality of energy you carry throughout and into the ending of a human lifespan determines the type of manifestation that ensues or unmanifested lack thereof. By energy, I don't just mean what you feel with regards to the spectrum of feelings, but also your degree of presence, deep insight that you know with every cell in your body and felt-sense of reality and who you are. As the human body dissolves, these energies are released into the vastness of consciousness as residual leftover remnants of what once was that flow with the capacity to manifest once again as building blocks for a new dawn. Without force or time, face what you feel now, then face the Facer that faces it.

How exactly does all this happen? Who knows! What you can know is the leftover revelation when you die to the idea of death. Such revelations show clearly the tendencies of form as a continual play within the formless realm of who you are. I believe it was Jiddu Krishnamurti who said, "Can you look at death without the image of death?" A human birth is most unique due to our potential to, as the ancient Greeks said, "Know thyself." Human beings are the only known species capable of ending the cycle of birth and death. This ending does not happen at death, it happens now.

For many years, when I would hear of reincarnation, I immediately dismissed the "unfounded nonsense." If science couldn't prove it, then I didn't want to be bothered. This was my stance for virtually everything. Scientific evidence is the best we have on the level of form. With that said, no form can explain the formless. What is science? The understanding of form. What does this book point to? The formless dimension that you are. Can science help here? It can only point, but never truly explain because there is literally nothing to explain. The second an explanation arises, you've turned nothing into something and it becomes a pointer like everything else said, done or thought. Science has its place, but do not look to it for understanding rebirth or who you are. Do not look to me either. You must look to your own depths. In his book *The Power of Now*, Eckhart explained rebirth with these words: "There are countless accounts by people who had a visual impression of this portal as radiant light and then returned from what is commonly known as a near-death experience. Many of them also spoke of a sense of blissful serenity and deep peace. In the Tibetan Book of the Dead, it is described as 'the luminous splendor of the colorless light of Emptiness,' which it says is 'your own true self.' This portal opens up only very briefly, and unless you have already encountered the dimension of the Unmanifested in your lifetime, you will likely miss it. Most people carry too much residual resistance, too much fear, too much attachment to sensory experience, too much identification with the manifested world. So they see the portal, turn away in fear, and then lose consciousness. Most of what happens after that is involuntary and automatic. Eventually, there will be another round of birth and death. Their presence wasn't strong enough yet for conscious immortality."

When a version of your thought-made self dies, there is a brief pause before being reborn into the next thought. Pay attention to the thoughts you are having. Watch them come and go. In between coming and going, between birth and death, there is a momentary void of no-thought. This is very subtle, yet necessary for thoughts to arise. Without this void, not only would there be no thoughts, there would be no form whatsoever. The same way no painting can be without a canvas to be, no form can be without space to be. All objects require the prerequisite of space. All motion requires the prerequisite of stillness. All sound requires the prerequisite of silence. You are the changeless prerequisite for the changing appearance of this moment. I recently saw the movie *Black Panther* and found the sand table technology to be fascinating. In the beginning of the movie, a table made of sand took the form of moving jeeps. Without the sand table, there would be no form. The moving jeeps are akin to everything that happens. You are a formless sand – a necessary undertone – from which everything can take form and happen. This is why Nisargadatta said, "You are nothing perceivable, or imaginable. Yet, without you there can be neither perception nor imagination."

To incarnate into a form means you are lost in that form which means you have mistaken the form for who you are. How do you mistake a form for who you are? All experience consists of thoughts, feelings, emotions and perceptions. When all you know is the experience, then you become the experience. You must carry a deeper knowing of who you are beyond the experience. Otherwise, your identity is lost in the experience as you mistake what comes and goes for sheer reality. What passes through this moment is like a ghost appearing and disappearing, except you can see, touch, taste, smell and hear the ghost. This makes for a very deceptive and seductive ghost that presents itself as ultimately real. Humanity has fallen for this deception and seduction. We have been fooled by this ghost. Despite its tangibility, the ghost still does what ghosts are meant to do – disappear. Imagine sitting on a chair for a lifetime while ghosts called "what happens" come and go changing the appearance of this moment. You never go anywhere, but everything around you changes. Another way to look at this is by visiting a theatre, such as a Broadway show. There may be scenes where an actor or actress is sitting in the middle of a stage and the entire scenery around them changes, but they don't. You can see these changes taking place, but you are so engulfed in the changes that you totally miss the changeless Being at the center of it all. Author and meditation instructor Mark Van Buren said it well when he said, "Death doesn't happen at the end of our lives, but moment-to-moment. When you sit on your cushion in meditation, allow whatever arises to die. If a sad self arises, let it die; an angry self, allow it to die. Let any version of the self-arise and cease. Grasp nothing and see that death always leads to rebirth. Remain still in the center of it all."

The ancient Hindu scripture *The Bhagavad Gita* states, "We behold what we are, and we are what we behold." The Gita continues, "Man is made by his belief. As he believes, so he is." The same way man is made by his belief, dreams are made by belief, especially those we carry into sleep. Each night, our final waking hours largely determine what happens during our sleeping hours. Either something happens, meaning dreams, or nothing happens, meaning dreamless sleep. This is similar to the state of consciousness you carry into the ending of a human lifespan. Dreams are echoes of what you carry in your body and heart. It is as though the mind is trying to make sense of the body. When you fall asleep, before entering dreamless sleep, your mind is left only with the feelings and emotions you carry deep within. Because it no longer has any sense perceptions to analyze due to a suspended body, it is left with the bewildering task of trying to construct a conceptual reality based on your feelings and emotions which are energetic bodily remnants. It goes on and on using these remnants to piece together images and form a mental story until you finally fall into deep sleep. Whether joy or fear, your mind will reflect, in one way or another, these bodily energies. The human body is akin to being a mind-receptor, meaning it responds to your beliefs with utmost honesty and even stores these responses, especially the most dominant ones, for the mind to potentially play with before you enter dreamless sleep. The dream doesn't create the feeling or emotion. The entrenched feeling or emotion attracts the dream and energizes itself through it.

Of course, there is nothing wrong with dreams, but you will find the more conscious and present you become, the less dreams, especially nightmarish dreams, you will have. This is due to a diminishment of incessant mind activity throughout the day and consequently, throughout your sleep. Eckhart teaches, "You take a journey into the Unmanifested every night when you enter the phase of deep dreamless sleep. You merge with the Source. You draw from it the vital energy that sustains you for a while when you return to the manifested, the world of separate forms." Similarly, Paramahansa Yogananda wrote in *Autobiography of a Yogi*, "Unknowingly, the sleeper is thus recharged by the cosmic energy that sustains all life." In dreamless sleep, your ego dies. All your worries, fears, anxieties, thoughts, memories, goals, dreams and identities die. The world and universe die. There is no more time because time is only in the mind. You have no memory of this because there is nothing to remember. This lack of remembrance doesn't mean there is a lack of consciousness. You can lose your mind, such as in deep sleep or conscious presence, but you cannot lose what you are. Rupert Spira explained this by saying, "Deep sleep is not the absence of awareness; it is awareness of absence." In deep sleep, there is only consciousness with nothing to be conscious of. There is simply contentless consciousness. Nisargadatta Maharaj reiterated this point when he said, "A gap in memory is not necessarily a gap in consciousness." Consciousness has no gaps; it is the gap. To the mind, it seems pointless to pay attention to the gap between breaths, words, sounds and thoughts. In reality, "the gap" is akin to being a canvas that allows the painting of life to be drawn and contains all the peace, love, joy and unity humanity needs and yearns for. The gap between breaths, words, sounds and thoughts is always the same gap. Don't just see the gap, be the gap. The ego's daily death of deep sleep is vital for human beings. Sleep is so revitalizing because you rest as consciousness, but you do so unconsciously. How to die to the ego during your waking hours? Try to find it. The next step in human evolution is to consciously rest as consciousness. There is no greater replenishment than this.

"The gap" is analogous to the number zero. When someone asks you to count to ten, from where do you start? One or zero? We overlook zero because it seems to have no value; but without zero, would there be one or two or three and so on? No matter how complicated the equation, all numbers stem from zero. Zero is the prerequisite for the infinite string of numbers just as you are the prerequisite for the infinite expanse of the universe. Don't be fooled into thinking you are just a tiny human roaming a tiny rock in space. You are infinitely vaster than that. You are zero. Start from zero.

The dream of form is a dream of unimaginable proportions. From the innumerable life forms on the planet to the countless stars in the universe, the dream of form is a remarkable dream indeed. Sitting here looking outside the window to my front yard, I see deer, squirrels and birds. I see trees, grass and plants. There is also so much I cannot see. There is an entire micro-world of epic proportions on top of and below the soil. Beyond the blue sky, there is an endless universe with endless mystery. Humans are specks of dust in an infinite universe, but all it takes is a speck to open a void for consciousness to wake up from its own dream. I am speaking to you from within your own dream, whispering, "Wake up now." For most forms, the gaze of consciousness is almost entirely on the world of form. Once a form evolves as an opening for consciousness to turn its gaze upon itself, then such a form becomes what Eckhart calls an "isolated flower." These isolated flowers are like a new species living in a radically new way. The human being serves as a focal point for consciousness – through this moment – to become conscious of itself. The "poofs" of various forms can go on forever in the cycle of samsara, but when you wake up to the reality of who you are, you experience the final poof.

There is nothing special or memorable about this final poof. Be wary not to carry fancy expectations of something because you will then be stuck with something when you are really searching for no-thing. This search requires no time and has no distance. The ego may whisper that it will be an addition to who you think you are when in reality, it is the elimination of who you think you are and leftover realization of who you really are. Once you realize this, it is not something you can run to your friends and family and say, "Hey, guess what!? I found out! I know!" When they ask what you know, you won't be able to give a concrete answer and realize you turned nothing into something as the realization becomes obscured by the mind looking to inflate itself. The mind will try and congratulate you as though you accomplished something memorable that can be shared proudly. You cannot recollect or share the timeless formlessness of eternity. You can only be it and point to it. Remember, only the ego can be added to and taken away from, never the wholeness of consciousness. All you can do is point and know deep in your heart the unspeakable, indescribable truth.

My wife and I took our daughter bowling recently with her friends from her class as a going away party since we are moving. One of the little girls dropped the ball gently on the pathway and it rolled slowly toward the bowling pins. The ball hit directly in the middle and had just enough force to knock down all the pins. I found the last pin to fall, which was swerving left and right before collapsing, symbolic of the final desire. As you begin awakening to the truth of who you are, desires will bear less weight over you. Desires will carry less and less weight until they have no weight as they are transmuted to light intentions and preferences. All desires disappear into emptiness. Although it is ultimately unnecessary, it can be useful to carry the desire for freedom and hold onto it as your final desire. Similar to suffering, desire is necessary until you realize it is no longer necessary. Desire creates suffering and suffering creates the possibility for awakening. Everything has its place. Carrying this final desire as your sole desire is especially useful if you already embarked "on a path" toward enlightenment. The moment you make it into a journey, your freedom is overcast with the illusion that more time will lead to enlightenment. If you are waiting for something, a thousand years of meditation will still not wake you from this dream. Only through this moment can you wake to the truth of who you are. Remain fully devoted to freedom until there is no devotee left. This doesn't mean to disregard responsibilities and others. This means to hold this one devotion deepest in your heart and allow all that happens to deepen the devotion until the devotee and devoted merge into One. Freedom remains when there is no one left to be free or not free. Let go of the concept of freedom, the character in your head that is or isn't free and freedom remains with no one to claim it. Thus, your final desire naturally fades as you rest in its silent completion. This is why Ramana Maharshi said, "The question 'Who am I?' is not really meant to get an answer, the question 'Who am I?' is meant to dissolve the questioner."

Everyone has a deep-rooted desire to be free from suffering, but to carry this disposable desire as your primary purpose in life is rare and helpful. Beyond carrying the useful paradox of desiring to be free of desire, another possibility is spontaneous initiation. I never cared for spiritual truths, mystics, Indian men with large beards, etc. I only wanted to live a good life – whatever that meant at the time. Yet, spontaneously, spiritual truths, mystics and Indian men with large beards came to me in the form of spiritual sledgehammers shattering the outer crust of my ego. As Eckhart said, "Life will give you whatever experience is most helpful for the evolution of your consciousness. How do you know this is the experience you need? Because this is the experience you are having at the moment." Everything is meant to drive you inward beyond desire, form and time to the leftover essence of who you are. Whether this happens through spontaneous initiation, carrying the final desire for freedom, intense suffering or in deep meditation, there is no right or wrong way. Everything that happens is the way. Don't get stuck on any one way because everything is the way. Right now, this book is the way because it is what is happening at this moment. Soon, this book will fade as the appearance of this moment changes. Whatever appearance it takes will then be the way. Whatever appearance this moment takes is always the way. You never need anything other than what is happening right now. This is it. Nowhere to go. Nothing to do. Just be here, now. Through stillness of mind, root behind or rather deep within this changing moment to its changeless essence. Then, as Mooji says, "When the person moves out, the universe moves in." You disappear into everything and nothing. You are home.

Chapter 19
The Experience of Experience

If you pay close attention to your experience of experience, you'll find three overarching elements: perceptions, thoughts and sensations. Perceptions include all the senses i.e., touch, taste, sight, sound and smell. Thoughts are energetic pulsations of time-bound projections. Sensations include your feelings and emotions. All human experience falls under these three umbrellas. Let's separate each element and take a closer look at their essence.

We'll begin with the first element of experience: perceptions. Although you can substitute any sense perception, take a few moments and fixate your attention on something you see. Focus completely on what is seen, without mixing in thoughts or sensations. If you isolate what is seen from what you think and feel, what is left? Without imposing thought onto the object, what constitutes the object? Without allowing thoughts to define the object and sensations to seemingly affirm such definitions, what is it you see? If you look without thinking about what you are looking at, what is left? In other words, if you don't mix in the other two experiential elements of thinking and feeling to what is perceived, what is left of the perception? A simple Knowing of it.

This Knowing is ever-present, immutable, indivisible, timeless and formless. Sense the Knowing that knows what you see. Once you reintroduce thoughts to the object of perception, you have combined two elements of experience – thoughts and perceptions. If these thoughts about the perception generate an emotional response, we have now reunited all three elements of experience and the Knowing is easily obscured unless you are firmly established in the omniscient Knowing that knows all this to be.

Let's say you are walking through the open plains of Africa and you see a large lion in the distance. Your experience, which unfolds instantly, is threefold, meaning it's based on all three elements. The first element is the perception of the lion. Immediately after seeing the lion, the thought "lion" appears in your mind. This thought is the second element and is in response to the first. Immediately after the thought "lion" appears in your mind, fear arises. This sensation of fear is the third element. Once combined, this trilogy of experience can quickly become very dense and bend you to its will. Of course, there's nothing wrong with the commingling of perceptions, thoughts and sensations, but without a deeper realization of who you are beyond this play, your sense of self and reality gets swept away by the seductive, gravitational pull of this lightspeed mixture. This is what we call suffering.

Next, let's focus on the second element of experience: thoughts. Close your eyes and whatever your first name is, hold that thought in your mind without an image of what you look like, how you see yourself or how others see you. For example, if your name is Angela, hold the thought "Angela" in your mind without any personal history. Because your eyes are closed, you cannot see anything and because you aren't attaching any memories to the thought of your first name, there is only the thought of your first name. Now, what comprises this thought? If there is no personal history or further definition to add to this thought, what is left of the thought? If you can't see your reflection in a mirror or a photo of yourself, what is left of this thought? A simple Knowing of it.

Finally, let's focus on the third element of experience: sensations. With your attention, isolate your current sensation from perception and thought. Close your eyes and feel any feeling or emotion. Whether it's hunger, irritation, peace or pain, feel what you feel without imposing any thought whatsoever onto that feeling. Keep your eyes closed so you don't invite any sights. Without mental definition or physical appearance, what is left of this feeling you have? A simple Knowing of it.

When I use the word "Knowing," we can substitute it for Awareness, Consciousness or Presence. We can say the Knowing that knows all experience. We can say the Awareness that is aware of all experience. We can say the Consciousness that is conscious of all experience. We can say the Presence that is present with all experience. When we take a close look at each element in itself, all we find is a Knowing of that element. When you strip one element from the others and focus on its essence, all you find is a Knowing of it. Rupert Spira summarized the importance of this very well when he said, "All that is known of a mind, body or world are thoughts, sensations and perceptions. All that is known of thoughts, sensations and perceptions are thinking, sensing and perceiving. All that is known of thinking, sensing and perceiving is the knowing of them. Thus, all that is ever known is Knowing, and it is Knowing that knows itself alone." Remember, these are just words and pointers. You must realize this directly and know this deeply.

All that is experienced arises in the field-like space of Knowing. All that is experienced is seen by the field-like space of Knowing. All that is experienced is ultimately made of the field-like space of Knowing. Put another way: all of life arises in, is known by and is ultimately made of the field-like space of Knowing. This is not an abstract philosophy, but a readily available realization for you. Don't get caught on these words by trying to rationalize this. This realization is beyond mental understanding. This realization can only be known by the Knowing, not by the person or intellect. This Knowing is not separate from who you are. Although "space" and "field-like" are good attempts at describing this Knowing, they ultimately fail because they add a dimension to what ultimately has no dimension. The word "dimension" is a pointer too. You cannot add or take away from eternity. We can say it is a changeless, formless, timeless or spiritual dimension for communication purposes; but ultimately, the Knowing that knows these words has absolutely no dimension to it. It is neither space nor silence nor stillness. These are useful words and concepts pointing to a dimensionless reality in their absence.

The purpose of isolating one of the three elements of experience is it becomes easier to discover the unchanging essence hidden within each element whereas when two or three elements begin blending, the Knowing of it all can more easily be veiled. Each element is a layer of veiling. When you have one element, there is one veil. When you have two elements, there is a thicker double veil. When you have three elements, there is an even thicker triple veil. Despite this, at any moment all veils can collapse into transparency or disappearance as a spontaneous awakening of truth beyond the veils takes place unforced. This is not your doing nor is it done on behalf of a doer. This is an effortless revelation in the absence of there being anything to do, any doer to do it or any future to attain something. Simply, be here now as the Knowing that knows your current experience.

Although thought is the most important veil to fall away, the veils don't necessarily need to "go" anywhere. They can stay as you unveil your capacity to see the veils and at the same time see the Seer of such veils. Such a capacity means the elements of experience are no longer veils. To know your essence as Knowing and all perceptions, thoughts and sensations as Knowing is to know your Self as everywhere and nowhere at the same time. You are disentangled from the trickery of experience. You no longer carry around the belief that you have borders. Where are your borders? Where do you begin and end? Where is your center? This is freedom from living in a so-called world as an isolated bundle of flesh, bone and thought.

This doesn't mean that you are, in fact, any particular perception, thought or sensation, but that the essence of all that passes is That which doesn't pass and That is the Knowing of all that passes. In other words, you are not the fleeting object of attention, but the One who knows it. A useful way to grasp this is by taking on the identity of light in a movie theatre. The light portrays characters on a screen, but the light is no particular character, yet it is the untouched essence of all characters. In the same way, you are no particular perception, thought or sensation, yet all objects of experience arise in, are seen by and derive their temporary existence from consciousness. All characters and objects in a movie arise in, are seen by and derive their temporary existence from the light. The light is not born alongside a character in a movie. Although light is not an object in a movie, it can be realized through the movie. Consciousness or "the light" is the eternal essence of all that passes. Be the light, not a character made of light. This is why Rupert Spira said, "Don't be an inside self, listening to an outside sound; just be the hearing. Don't be an inside self, seeing an outside world; just be the seeing." You can substitute hearing for knowing and seeing for knowing as mental divisions of inside and outside fade away. There is only an outside world when there is an inside you. Without thought carving such divisions, you are neither inside nor outside and no longer feel like a little person in a big world.

Only the mind concludes consciousness is personal, trapped inside the body and has somehow been split into countless pieces inhabiting countless bodies. However, the mind, which is another word for thinking, appears in the untouched consciousness it tries to touch and assign definition, division and borders. The mind is like a universal construction company capable of building anything it imagines. Thoughts are the construction workers, machines, tools, building materials, foundation, design plans, etc. All constructions can be built in an instant and bulldozed in an instant. Those with a heavy ego have a thought-constructed metropolis as their mental citadel, but even these mammoth strongholds can be deconstructed with the light of your attention and exist at the mercy of other constructions no matter how stable they appear. Consciousness is the essential, timeless, formless, boundless, inconceivable, indestructible, indescribable, indivisible ground for all that is. It allows, watches and contains all that happens. Thoughts cannot objectify the non-objective field in which they appear, from which they are seen and because of which they are. The same way fish can't give borders to the ocean and birds can't give borders to the sky, thoughts can't give borders to awareness. Rupert Spira once said in a talk, "If we ask thought about the nature of awareness, it would tell us that every single body has its own package of awareness, but if we ask the one who knows – that is if we ask awareness itself, 'What do you know about yourself? What is your experience of yourself?' Awareness would reply, if it could speak, 'I have no knowledge of any border or distinction or form in myself. I am a single, open, empty, indivisible, intimate field.'"

With this understanding, does anything truly exist? To exist is to stand out as "other than," meaning to have a seemingly independent existence. No matter the appearance, the essence is always the same. This is why the Buddha said, "Things are not what they seem; nor are they otherwise." What conceptually seems to have its own existence is really just you masquerading as another. Instead of being with another, always be with yourself. This means when you meet another human being, or any object of experience, don't be one object with another object – be with yourself. Remember, despite language making it seem so, there is no separation, distance or time when you are with your non-conceptual self. In other words, this "meeting" is beyond duality. You are always with yourself, no matter how it seems through a divisive thought-filter. Before assigning definition to an object of experience, first neutralize it. Before you see a "person," see a perception. Before you hear a "bird," hear a sound. Before you feel "anger," feel a sensation. Remember the essence is all the same. Then freely assign necessary, practical definition, such as person, bird and anger, to use skillfully and creatively without mistaking it for the absolute truth of what someone or something is.

Many people travel great distances to sit with a guru or master, but really, they are looking to sit with themselves. The guru or master make it easier for you to be with your maskless self. They are helpful signposts. Let the guru help, but don't become reliant on or attached to their reflecting your own reality. Put distance and time aside. Let the journey go and silently unmask your fanciful self now to allow the natural unmasking of all "others." This way, you are never "with" someone else; you are always only meeting yourself. This is why poet and Sufi master Rumi said, "I come to you without me, come to me without you." Don't be a wave meeting another wave. Be the ocean meeting the ocean while acknowledging the waves. Don't be a piece of knowledge meeting another piece of knowledge. Be the Knowing meeting the Knowing while acknowledging the pieces of knowledge.

Now, the mind always has questions and many of them, in relation to paradoxical topics such as this, start with, "Yes, but..." or "Well, how come..." When one question is answered, it usually leads to more questions. The mind can go on endlessly, never fully satisfied for long. Such questions have their importance and it can help to have them answered if possible, but no question is absolutely important. Why? For starters, you aren't the one asking. Only the mind conjures questions and seeks answers. All questions and answers belong to time. You are timeless. What is being pointed to here is timeless. The mind can intellectually agree, disagree or become curious, but in the end – it's still the time-bound mind. There are many accounts of people – most famously Paul Brunton – who visited Ramana Maharshi with a list of questions and upon seeing the silent sage, their questions began vanishing in his presence. Like this, your own questions can vanish in your silent presence which is no different than that of a silent sage. The difference is not in presence, but to the extent presence can shine through the form. Eckhart Tolle said in one of his talks that, "No one is closer to God than you." This can be said to anyone because it stands true with everyone. This means you are one thought away from realizing who you are beyond name and form. Just one thought away and no one is closer than you.

Chapter 20
Use Thinking

Human beings are a species of thinking and knowing. This is what we do. Sometimes knowledge uses us and sometimes we use it. It is an endless dance between master and slave. All of life has become concepts. This is that and that is this. What is missing is intuition; a deeper knowing beyond concepts. Intuition is a ready-made knowing or realization arrived at non-conceptually. Without intuitive knowledge, we get lost in conceptual knowledge and fall victim to the machinery of overthinking. Without the deeper understanding of who we are, which is intuitive knowledge, all we know is who we think we are, which is conceptual knowledge. In a conceptualized reality, thinking is primary because it constitutes absolutely everything. Thinking must become secondary. Thoughts need to go on a diet and shed some weight! Why? Because they paint your entire world dragging you along wherever they go as you fall victim to their seductive nature. To become powerful tools, thoughts need to be seen as secondary to your sense perceptions. What you see, touch, taste, hear and smell always has to do with this moment because physical senses cannot generate their own false reality based on past or future. Only thoughts can do that. Only thoughts can fabricate the reality around you and cloak your primal completeness.

Although primary to thoughts, your senses must remain secondary to the transcendental reality of who you are, which is the field in which thoughts and senses arise. This is the order of freedom. No matter what happens or who you are with, you must always be here and now primarily as consciousness and secondarily as a human. If someone is speaking to you, always keep part of your attention on the field in which listening happens. Once you are locked into that field, which you can only be locked in now, you can freely and fully listen without becoming entangled in what is heard and thought. You can listen and respond more effectively because your sense of self isn't seized by what is said or done. A fresh, creative and wise response can more easily flow through you because you aren't concerned with self-loss or self-gain. For over three decades, my thinking was as primary as primary gets. Even my senses I could barely experience without imposing past or future on them. Trapped on the level of thinking, we are trapped in a perpetual state of waiting. This is hard to notice because it has become so normal. Whether subtle or apparent, this state of mind we call "waiting," which you are free to give up now, consumes almost all humans. For most, life is all about the next apparent moment with brief interludes of presence. What does the next moment consist of? The past. Future thoughts are always about past thoughts. Sadhguru reiterates this point by saying, "Thinking is just recycling of the data you have already gathered." He continues, "Because we are trapped in thought we have to glorify thought so we don't look like fools." We spend almost every waking minute thinking about how absolutely important the past and future are when they do not exist and cannot be experienced. What a joke! What can you do but laugh? Do not take this joke too serious. After all, the cosmic joke of past and future has incredible momentum and gravity. Moreover, it has its necessary place of usefulness on the level of form. It only becomes a joke when we grant skeletons and ghosts a reality they do not and cannot have.

What are thoughts? They are short-lived, energetic forms of time-bound projections. Where do they come from? Where everything ultimately comes from, dances in and fades into: consciousness. Is anything I just wrote important? No, not really. These questions never end and have no definitive answer. What is most important about the mind is to let it go where it goes and do what it does. This doesn't mean if you have a thought about shooting your neighbor's dog that you should. Rather, you accept the thought, then let the choice of what to do with that thought happen from a space of presence. Do not resist what passes in the mind. Do not judge what passes in the mind. Simply, let it be and watch its content pass. Do not resist or cling to any thought. That is all. Even this is not something to do. It is natural non-doing wherein you are allowed the choice for doing to happen more powerfully and spontaneously because you are aligned with reality. Internally resisting the fact of now, no matter what appearance this fact takes, isn't necessary for reflecting, learning or taking action. Cultivate an unconditional inner acceptance of what is because it already is and everything has led up to it.

At first, it may seem totally pointless, boring and unproductive to "watch the mind." This new, subtle energy-field is unlike the old, pronounced energy-field of a mind-dominated reality. It can certainly throw you off and thwart you at first. You may feel like life is being reduced and you are being reduced. Your mind may fool you into thinking you are "less than you were," but in reality, there is no limit, shape or size to who you are. What is actually being reduced is your personalized sense of self. Your friends and family may look at you with bored, frustrated eyes. Your phone may get less rings. Or perhaps the opposite will happen. Who knows! Do not carry any expectations, just remain aligned with the appearance of this moment and trust that all is well. This deep trust is intuitive knowledge of the truth spoken in *A Course of Miracles*: "Nothing real can be threatened. Nothing unreal exists. Herein lies the peace of God." All the passing pleasures offered by the mind and body will begin to pale in comparison to the lasting pleasure of being as you are; of spacious presence. All passing pleasures and beliefs will crash somewhere. Only the lasting reality of who you are will sustain itself. Stay with this sustenance and let it fill your body and mind with undying aliveness. Even the smallest thing, such as putting on your shoes or washing your hands, will then be quite enjoyable. As a matter of fact, you may find the "small things" will be as or more enjoyable than the "big things."

In the mind-identified state, wherever you go follows a story that is always trying to sort itself out or keep itself together. This story is what we call "my life" and is what the mind considers most important. It follows you everywhere and is written by what happened, what happens, what may happen, what you would prefer happened, what you couldn't believe happened etc. This story chit chats itself together and apart endlessly trying to maintain a favorable plot based completely on the instability of what happens. This is why all stories of "my life" are ultimately dysfunctional. No matter how good "your life" is at the moment, you are trying to keep it good and if it's not good, you are striving for the elusive goodness. Suffering is always there to some degree. Until you realize there is no such thing as "my life," suffering always lurks within all you do and think. Why? Because you need to keep "your life" together! It is a full-time and lifelong job trying to keep things together so you can stay happy. You must hold onto what makes you happy and keep away from what doesn't. What makes you happy, you know you'll have to let go someday. What makes you happy, you know you'll have to try and keep that apparent source of happiness.

Surely, it doesn't help that everything is completely unstable no matter how stable things may appear. The story of "my life" demands endless engineering for happiness with inevitable failure time and time again. You are either working for it or trying to keep it. Searching for happiness is similar to sticking cheese on the belly of a mouse and watching it run around a maze searching for food. The moment your roots leave this moment, you are that mouse.

I recently read *Sapiens: A Brief History of Humankind* by Yuval Noah Harari. In it, he said, "According to Buddhism, the root of suffering is neither the feeling of pain nor of sadness nor even of meaninglessness. Rather, the real root of suffering is this never-ending and pointless pursuit of ephemeral feelings, which causes us to be in a constant state of tension, restlessness, and dissatisfaction. Due to this pursuit, the mind is never satisfied. Even when experiencing pleasure, it is not content, because it fears this feeling might soon disappear, and craves that this feeling should stay and intensify. People are liberated from suffering not when they experience this or that fleeting pleasure, but rather when they understand the impermanent nature of all their feelings, and stop craving them. This is the aim of Buddhist meditation practices. In meditation, you are supposed to closely observe your mind and body, witness the ceaseless arising and passing of all your feelings, and realize how pointless it is to pursue them. When the pursuit stops, the mind becomes very relaxed, clear, and satisfied. All kinds of feelings go on arising and passing – joy, anger, boredom, lust – but once you stop craving particular feelings, you can just accept them for what they are. You live in the present moment instead of fantasizing about what might have been. The resulting serenity is so profound that those who spend their lives in the frenzied pursuit of pleasant feelings can hardly imagine it. It is like a man standing for decades on the seashore, embracing certain 'good' waves, and trying to prevent them from disintegrating, while simultaneously pushing back 'bad' waves to prevent them from getting near him. Day in, day out, the man stands on the beach, driving himself crazy with this fruitless exercise. Eventually, he sits down on the sand and just allows the waves to come and go as they please. How peaceful!"

All of this is mental gymnastics, as Papaji put it in his satsangs described in the book *Wake Up and Roar*, which requires continuous effort. You may not mind this effort, but that's only because you haven't realized the effortless joy of Being. Then, you'll know there is no need for effort when it comes to joy, peace and love. It is always here and now as your natural background state.

You just need to stop covering it up with your story of "my life." How can you have what you are? Can you really have yourself? "This is my life and that is your life," says the ego. This is like a wave in the ocean saying to another wave, "You stick to your life and I'll stick to mine. As a matter of fact, I'm going to gather other waves and create a boundary called 'my country' while you and your band of waves can stick to your slice of the ocean. Even better, I'm going to build a wall to block all 'other' waves from coming into my territory." Imagine waves of the same ocean, of the same water and essence, having this conversation. This is no different with humans. In order for the wave to "wake up," it must realize it is a manifestation of the same ocean; that it is inseparable from all other waves. Thus, the shenanigans of "me and you" stop as such words and concepts become tools to communicate rather than entire realities to identify with. The wave can then return home, so to speak, and identify as the ocean from which all waves arise and cease. This is analogous to the awakening of a human being.

If only humans knew they were sitting on a pot of gold, as Eckhart put it in the beginning of his book *The Power of Now*. Even this metaphor doesn't suffice. All the gold in the world can't compare to the joy of being fundamentally free and complete. Why? Because with all that gold comes a mansion, lots of cars, lots of attention, lots of bills and bigger problems. If you look at a gossip magazine, the ones that "have it all" have the same problems, if not more, than most "normal" human beings. The only difference is they have a larger spotlight on their drama. No matter how much wealth or things you accumulate, the inherent dysfunction to being unaware of who you are will persist and it's not long until that becomes clear time and time again. Of course, there's nothing wrong with money, but who runs who? Is the money in your pocket or in your head? Surely, you have had enough of this game. If not, that's fine too. The game of "I am this and you are that" is always here for you to play.

Freedom from the thinking mind comes with learning to use the mind. This is not something you learn in school. There's no class, to my knowledge, called *Using the Mind 101*. Such a class would require a focus on silence, which is considered close to useless in schools and society. Without inner silence, the mind runs amok dragging you along for the ride. With inner silence, the mind may still run amok, but won't drag you along so easily. Perhaps, there won't even be a rope tied from you to your mind that can drag you. If there is no one there to get caught, the mind loses its power over you as you unveil your power over it. Notice the silence between thoughts, not just the thoughts. The moment you notice the spacious silence, you are free from keeping up with your life story; free from the thinking mind.

Scientists say humans have as much as 70,000 thoughts a day where up to 98% are repetitive and 80% are negative. We really don't need to think so much. It is counterproductive and destructive both within and without. Do not let your mind convince you that it is necessary to think every waking moment. The vast majority of thoughts are not conducive to well-being. Most of these tens of thousands of thoughts you have in a day are about your life story. Why? Because this story seems to be the most significant story in the universe. It really isn't. It's actually quite insignificant. This story is your prison. When it's polished, you are striving to keep it shining. This striving is suffering because it all stems from a deeply rooted sense of lack and fear for what may happen to your story. When your story inevitably falls apart, you have to try and put it back together and you know it never stays together for long. Whether it's small parts of the story or vital components, it is always falling apart because it is born of instability, lives among instability and dies of instability. The mind creates a mental model of reality because it has some control over this creation and seeks comfort in it. It is an illusion created and perpetuated by the egoic mind to keep you entangled in what happens and unaware of who you truly are. Why? So the ego, or who you think you are, can live another day. All thoughts want to proliferate, expand and survive. They want to stand out and prolong their existence. Everything that happens – happens within you, not to you. So long as you think life happens to you, the false mind-made you will become entangled in what happens.

Overthinking has become the common addiction of humanity. What happens with addictions once you start to release their power over you? Withdrawal symptoms, of course. With the powerful momentum of the human mind, spiritual awakening may not be all that pleasant at first. It may require a lot of effort for effortlessness to prevail. What is simple may have to go through the withdrawal effects of pure complication and difficulty. I know a few people that smoked their entire lives and stopped abruptly without much effort. Most people, however, need patches, e-cigs or some type of aid. This is the same with enlightenment, except most people turn to gurus and books as their aid. Of course, there is nothing wrong with this. The spark of transparency for this human body called George was Eckhart Tolle's audiobook *The Power of Now*. That was the initial spark. After that, it was a gradual deepening with direct experience and the aid of books. Although books helped make relative sense of it all, they must remain secondary. Your experience is primary. Without direct experience, words and thoughts are of little use. They can only help the mind add to its one-dimensional understanding. Not in, but through a silent mind you have access to a deeper, universal intelligence. This is the primal intelligence of Life, which is beyond all concepts. Terms like "Oneness" and "I Am" would mean close to nothing without your attention reversing to its source. As you read any spiritual book, pay close attention to the arising stillness within, which is more important than the words you read and thoughts they generate. Thoughts can, at best, only give a dose of the truth. No thought is the whole truth. They are tiny perspectives and angles filtered through the past, useful in their own right, but never capable of encapsulating the totality of reality. Only thoughtless awareness allows direct contact with who you are beyond name and form.

Whatever happens is only a ripple in the vast ocean of consciousness. Jesus knew this when he said, "I have overcome the world." He knew all events are mere ripples in an ocean with no beginning or end. Only this deep knowing overcomes the world. Such knowledge allowed him the power to forgive those who carried him to the cross. He was fully surrendered to what is and thus, the power of Life flowed through him and into the world. You don't think. Thinking happens. You don't perceive. Perception happens. You don't feel. Feelings happen. You don't act. Action happens. Spiritual teacher Rupert Spira explained this well in his book *The Light of Pure Knowing* when he said, "Meditation has nothing to do with what is or what is not taking place in the mind. Give the mind total freedom to do whatever it has been conditioned to do. There is nobody personally responsible for the activity of the mind. In fact, the entire universe conspires to make every event take place. That is, every thought, every feeling, every action, every wind that flutters, every butterfly that moves, everything in the entire universe, is involved in the slightest thought or feeling. So the universe is responsible for our thoughts. If we're going to take on our thoughts, we will have to take on the entire universe. Leave thoughts alone. Be effortlessly and knowingly that which is aware of our thoughts. Notice that we are that, and simply be that knowingly. Know yourself as that. And don't restrict Awareness to thoughts; include feelings.

There may be no feelings present or there may be feelings of sadness, shame, guilt, fear, inadequacy, lack, etc. Let whatever feelings are present simply be as they are." No thought is your thought. Know this beyond reading this and you can relinquish thoughts of their immense power over you and begin using them. It is only when we take thoughts to be personal and fully reflective of reality that we fall victim to their energetic force.

Ultimately, there is no independent, personal agency responsible for your thoughts, feelings, emotions and actions. If there is, where is it, who is it and what is it? There are about seven octillion atoms that comprise your body. Is it all of these atoms that are responsible, or just a select few? Do these atoms have seven octillion names or one name to cover them all? Do they come inherently bundled with a name or are they anonymous? Should we include all the atoms in the air, water, food and environment that flow in and out of your body as well? At what point and with what boundaries do we decide who or what is responsible? Can we really disconnect seven octillion atoms from the rest and say, "This bundle of separated seven octillion atoms is responsible." Can the word "me" really summarize the immensity and mystery of seven octillion atoms working alongside countless other atoms to formulate thoughts, feelings, emotions and actions? Of course, this doesn't mean you are relinquished of relative responsibilities with a free pass to shoot your neighbor's dog again and blame it on all the atoms in the universe! Always be aware of the cunning ego taking advantage of and misusing pointers. The purpose here is to give up being anti-life, meaning anti-fact-of-now, and relinquish your self-judgment and judgment of others by no longer taking anything personally.

Are you a thought or prior to the thought? The famous saying, "I think, therefore I am," should really go, "I am, therefore I think." Before anything, you are. For anything to be, you must be. Before something, there must be nothing for something to appear in. Hm, how else to word this? Try looking to the last sentence before and after the word "else." If there was no space before and after this word and also between the letters, would it be possible for the word to be written? Of course not! Without space, the word could not manifest. There would be no canvas, so to speak. You see, you are the space that allows all form to rise; all paintings to be drawn. Who is drawing? Life is. Yes, it seems that you are drawing. It seems that people are doing this and thinking that. Contrary to appearances, you are the awareness that is aware of all doing and thinking, not the doer or thinker. If you were the doer or thinker, there would be no underlying awareness, which is the subject, of the doer or thinker, which is the object. An object cannot be both subject and object. You would only be what is done or thought, incapable of realizing the Watcher of what is done or thought. The fact that you can observe your thoughts is evidence that you are not your thoughts. Otherwise, there would only be thought with no spacious awareness of the thought. As Rupert said, the universe is responsible for all that happens. There is only this moment and what arises in it. The appearance of this moment is a manifestation of the consciousness that underlies this moment. You are that consciousness, or as Rupert, Nisargadatta, Papaji and virtually all who have realized this commonly say, "You are That." "That" is Consciousness; Being; God; the Divine. One of the greatest spiritual books that Nisargadatta spoke is called *I Am That* for this reason. The mind, however, will try to convince you that thoughtless awareness is unimportant because there is nothing happening there. Do not believe this thought. Rather, dive in and find out for yourself.

Philosopher Alan Watts once said, "I'm not saying that thinking is bad. Like everything else, it's useful in moderation. A good servant, but a bad master." How do you allow thinking to be a good servant? Simply notice the space, silence and stillness between thoughts. This noticing is easier than breathing. It requires no effort to "notice" stillness. Effort arises when you apply force. This is forceless and actionless. This is "action in inaction and inaction in action," as explained in the Bhagavad Gita. The more you notice, the less you think. The less you think, the more rooted in stillness you become. The more rooted in stillness you are, the more effective thinking will be when it happens. As a particular thought stream or task at hand ends, return all your conscious focus back to stillness, spaciousness and silence. Let there be no thought until thought is once again required. Be like a boomerang rooted in Being. What do boomerangs do? They return back to the source from which they were flung. This doesn't mean you should lose grounding in who you are as you do this or think that and then return to being grounded when doing and thinking is no longer necessary. No. Once you are rooted in Being, all action and inaction stems from there. Your new base is spacious possibility, not limited personhood, and never fully leaves you.

Ask yourself frequently, "What am I here as?" Are you here as one thought in your mind at the mercy of other thoughts in your mind? Are you here as a separate self in a conceptualized reality? Are you here as a time-bound "drifter" drifting from past to future with little to no attention on the reality of this moment? Or are you here as a non-judgmental, unconditionally-accepting presence of spacious possibility undefined by the past? Are you here without a center? Are you here without borders? Are you here using thoughts rather than existing in their captivating whispers? What are you here as?

Do not mind the mind. This is key. Do not take your mind all too seriously and remember that nothing about it is ultimately real or absolutely important. The more serious you take your mind, the more power it has over you. This doesn't mean to treat it poorly because it is a wonderful instrument and biological marvel. This doesn't mean to disregard it completely. This means to take a few deep, conscious breaths every time you notice being pulled into its stories unwillingly. Such breaths generate conscious awareness that helps free you from the story so you can better handle the story by remembering it is just a story the mind is whispering to you. As a child, my mother used to read me bedtime stories. As I grew up, my mind continued reading me bedtime stories and it was always bedtime! All thoughts are stories because they require the past. The past is just a story that arises in the present. All of humanity is listening to the buzz of bedtime stories. The torrent of thinking is the story and we are lying in bed, so to speak, in a dream-like state, totally immersed in thinking. In such a dream, there is no space between "I" and thinking. How to wake up? You must realize this is all just a story and pay attention to the subtle divinity within and beyond the story. What is the subtle divinity? Space. Silence. Stillness. Emptiness. You. Again, no word truly fits here so don't get caught on words.

This reminds me of a quote from the Bhagavad Gita which goes, "What is night for all beings is the time of awakening for the self-controlled; and the time of awakening for all beings is night for the introspective sage." In other words, what is sleep for the person is waking for the sage and what is waking for the person is sleep for the sage. When people are awake, they are really asleep. When people are in deep sleep, they are really awake. The goal, which really isn't a goal because goals need time, but we only have limited language to work with, is to spiritually awaken during your waking hours. This is a conscious awakening whereas in deep sleep, it is an unconscious "awakening."

As clouds come and go, the sky never says, "Okay, that cloud is mine, but this cloud is not mine." This is no different with consciousness and thoughts.

The sky allows clouds to come and go the same way consciousness allows thoughts to come and go, but neither sky nor consciousness claims, "This is mine." Only the mind-made you can claim thoughts, emotions, things and people. The more you claim something, the more you empower your ego. In other words, the more reality you breathe into words like "my" and "mine," the more power you grant your seeming possessions over you and deeper you fall into illusion. No thought is your thought. Yes, only you can hear the thoughts in your mind so it is easy to assume possession, but once you disassociate your identity from your mind, you realize nothing was ever yours. In its own detachment, the mind will be very happy. For something to be yours, there must be a subject and object. To own something, there must be an owner and owned. To claim something, there must be the claimant and claimed. All that comes and goes are dual echoes in eternity. You need duality to feel something is yours. As a reminder, duality is the tendency of the mind to divide life into bits and pieces with each fragment attached to its opposite like the heads and tails of a coin. Thoughts are like knives that cut up reality and you are the ultimate carving. Duality is me and you; this and that, with no sense of deeper unity. It is the lock for your mental prison cell. Duality has its temporary, necessary place, especially with language, but if it's all you know, then your entire sense of reality and selfhood is trapped in it. You cannot use your mind to convince yourself that no thought is your thought. This is like trying to climb Mt. Everest with only a bottle of water. The mind can work wonders on the level of form, but you cannot turn to it for truths beyond form because all it knows is form. Only the universal language of silence can unveil such truths. This is the most powerful language. Silence, in the way I use the word, means thoughtless awareness. Your senses still function, of course, and you are still aware of your surroundings, but your mind is quiet and it is this effortless quietude that reveals the Self.

Ramana Maharshi, who was completely entrenched in the Self, sat still for many years not speaking and barely eating, even while insects gnawed away at him. His devotees had to put food in his mouth. It took years for him to return to speaking and eating. He barely spoke because he knew how limited language was. There are books on the few words he did speak. His main teaching was silence. He knew the power of silence and was only focused on being and transmitting it. To be more precise, he did nothing, yet through him, something was happening to those around him. When I look at a picture of

Ramana Maharshi, I don't see Ramana Maharshi. I see myself or, put more accurately, the Self. I see a stainless window to Being. Now, this doesn't mean you need to stop eating, never speak, hire people to feed you and gather flesh-eating insects for company! Again, there is no checklist to go through. Get rid of your checklist! For Ramana, that was the spontaneous will of the universe; however, it is not a requirement for enlightenment.

What is the purpose of realizing no thought is your thought? You are able to use thoughts better because they lose their heaviness over you once you stop believing they are yours. The moment you see thoughts as universal comings and goings and realize yourself as the Watcher of thoughts, you are able to use thinking without self-entanglement in it. Again, this doesn't mean you will become perfect. The projection of a perfect version of you at some point in the future is one of the most common blockages to liberation. There is no perfect personality anywhere so do not wait for it. Do not postpone your freedom. In truth, you are already free. You just need to stop fooling yourself that you aren't. You are always free to be free. Enlightenment doesn't mean you are mistake-free, it means you are illusion-free. It doesn't mean you will always be perfectly effective at whatever challenge this moment takes. With that said, you are certainly more effective because you are clear-minded to take on the challenge or, put in other words, spaciously watch the challenge and allow spontaneous action or inaction to arise. Remember, this moment can be challenging, but never problematic. Without past or future in the space of now, what problem do you have? Only the "other moments" you visit in memory or anticipation can have problems unless, of course, you visit them without attachment or identification.

Although thoughts vary, they all have the same pulling force that whispers, "I am important, give me all your attention. Find yourself in me. I am reality. I am capable of fulfilling you." Of course, you don't hear these whispers directly, but it surrounds virtually all thoughts as a continuous gravitational pull. Aside from basic physical necessities, it seems thoughts are capable of giving us everything we need to thrive. When you look at Maslow's hierarchy of needs, some of the psychological needs of a human being are self-fulfillment, esteem, belongingness and love. Although Maslow doesn't suggest it directly, it is assumed and implied that humans will turn to their own thoughts for these needs. After all, where else would one turn? Thoughts are the only avenue we know. Most humans haven't yet realized "The Power of

Now," as Eckhart puts it. Can thoughts truly grant us fulfillment, esteem, belongingness and love? No, not truly. They only grant fleeting glimpses of crumbling feelings amongst the unstable dimension of form. Even the fleeting glimpses contain subtle traces and doses of suffering because we know they cannot be held onto for long and exist at the mercy of what happens. This means deep down, we are worried about losing our apparent source of happiness because we know it is conditional and can be lost. These feelings can still be wonderful, but are not true in themselves because they are seemingly derived outside of themselves. True fulfillment, esteem, belongingness and love derive from your eternal abode, which is unconditioned and ever-present. It cannot be lost or contaminated. Even if your attention fully sways from it, this doesn't mean it has left you, only that your thoughts have dragged your full attention elsewhere and covered it up. This is like clouds covering up the sun or the planet rotating away from the sun. Despite the clouds and rotation, the sun hasn't gone anywhere. It is always shining just as You are always shining. Ramana pointed to this when he said, "Thoughts come and go. Feelings come and go. Find out what it is that remains."

When asked to summarize his teachings in one word, Ramana said, "Attention." He didn't mean attention on thoughts. He meant attention on the Source of all phenomena. He meant attention on the Self. Attention, itself, is the Self. Pay attention to attention. The moment you do this, your mind stops and all that is left is a directionless field of attention. This field is consciousness. All you sense and feel is the field itself. When your attention deepens into this field, you can clear the field of all thoughts at will or rather, no-will. It is a forceless choice with no willpower or effort. When you need to think, thoughts will be there. When you don't need to think, no thoughts will be there because no thoughts are needed. Not thinking is far more useful than thinking because it allows you to realize you are not the thinker and be free of thinking. Not thinking dissolves your attachment to thinking allowing you to truly use thinking because you are no longer entangled in thinking.

Ultimately, you aren't doing anything. You are simply aware of what is happening now, not a person doing this or thinking that. The person you've taken yourself to be, which is just a thought attached to a reflection in the mirror, is seen by something. What is this "something?" Who sees the person? Who sees the thought? Who sees the reflection? Can you be both the person and the one who sees the person? Does the seer share the same qualities as what is seen? What is seen comes, goes, lives and dies. Does the seer come, go, live or die? Can you see the seer like any object of experience? Is the seer bound by time, vulnerable to what happens, have any definition or visible in any way, shape or form? You must give up the notion that you are a person, which is one thought in your mind, in control of a life story, which is another thought in your mind. Outside of those fleeting, misleading thoughts, who are you and what life do you have? Stripped of time, who are you and what life do you have?

You must surrender to the divine will of the universe, which is whatever appearance this moment takes, and watch it unfold without personal involvement because no such involvement exists. There is nothing personal about being conscious or unconscious; sad or happy; jealous or envious etc. The totality of all that has ever happened is responsible for what is happening. Whatever appearance this moment takes, envelop it in thoughtless awareness. The body and mind will then take care of its needs through surrendered action or inaction in a state of presence. Do not concern yourself with it. Do not identify with being enlightened or not enlightened. You must reject both ideas and be free of being free and being found. Do not make enlightenment into a serious business. There is no business to attend to. No meetings. No conference calls. No checklist. No agenda. Nothing to do. Nowhere to go. Nothing to achieve. "Just keep quiet," as Papaji always said in his satsangs. Unless the mind intervenes, it's really that simple. With that said, one can extrapolate that in order to use thinking, you must not concern yourself with it. Or, in other words, to use thinking, don't identify as the thinker. Or, in other words, to use thinking, surrender fully to the divine will of the universe. Then, thinking uses itself. You don't use it. This is true "use" of thinking. It is all the same pointer, only from different angles. This entire book is the same pointer, from different angles. All it takes is one angle, sentence or phrase to fulfill its purpose and point your attention onto Itself.

Chapter 21
Why Are We Here

Why are we here?

We are not here.

We are here to realize we are not here.

We are not here, there or anywhere in particular.

The question of why we are here contains an underlying assumption that we are here. There are two parts to the question: We are here. Why? The first part is an illusion. The second part is to realize that the first part is an illusion. Only the body, mind and all else that appears in this moment is here. You are not that. We are not here to change the world. Changing the world is a byproduct of enlightenment, not the goal. We are not here to fall in love. Love is your leftover quality in the absence of inequality. We are not here to help others. "There are no others," as Ramana Maharshi said. That, too, is a byproduct of enlightenment. We are not here to collect a few things that will be lost. We are here to recollect That which cannot be lost. Nisargadatta Maharaj said it well: "Forgetting your Self is the greatest injury; all the calamities flow from it. Take care of the most important, the lesser will take care of itself. You do not tidy up a dark room. You open the windows first. Letting in the light makes everything easy. So, let us wait with improving others until we see ourselves as we are – and have changed. There is no need to turn round and round in endless questioning; find yourself and everything will fall into its proper place."

I used to feel with every ounce of who I took myself to be that my ultimate purpose here was to take action on climate change. It took me 25 years or so to figure that out. Once I discovered the extent of the issue, I knew deep in my heart, "This is why I'm here." I studied the science, built a website dedicated to it, volunteered, marched, gave passionate speeches, rallied everyone I knew, made social media posts, etc. In one sense, that certainly is one of the most pressing challenges to society because it underlies all other challenges. Although there is a great movement to reverse the manmade effects of climate change, positive feedback loops have begun and if they haven't already, will soon become irreversible by taking on a momentum of their own. The necessary changes in how societies function is happening, but not fast enough it seems. All this doom and gloom used to be quite depressing. Why is climate change happening? I used to point with utter disgust at the fossil fuel executives and politicians that took money from them. Now, I point inward. Climate change, along with all other manmade calamities, stems from a deep-rooted sense of lack and fear. This is the hidden driving force, like an earthquake on the bottom of the ocean causing tsunamis. This is why Eckhart said, "There is only one perpetrator of evil on the planet: human unconsciousness." With that said, all the surface-level solutions to climate change and other challenges do matter and have their place; however, what matters most is addressing the nuts and bolts of the problem-making machinery itself, which is fear, lack, a sense of separation, misidentification with the body and mind, etc.

Alongside climate change, my other "ultimate life goal" was to find love. Instead of finding love, I disappeared into it. No matter the peace you exude, this can be very difficult for partners who haven't disappeared into it. My wife sometimes asks why I no longer say, "I miss you." She enjoys when I say it just so she can smile, even though she knows it's not true. She misses me saying it. We sometimes have the conversation about the "George" she married not being the same "George" she's with now. It's not easy wanting someone and getting no one. It's not easy losing the personality she fell in love with. She asks why I'm with her and I say, "I'm not with you." It breaks her heart, but she's learned to accept it. She asks, "Why don't you miss me?" I tell her, "Because no matter where I go, you are there," and then I laugh saying, "How can I miss you if you are always with me?" She shrugs my responses as silly nonsense. She worries I'm only with her because I can "be with anyone," as she puts it, and married her before "the shift." She asks, "Would you have married me if you were already this way?" I tell her, "I can't predict what I will do." I explain, "Don't look to me for love, look within." Although I'm not pushy, I'm "brutally honest," as she puts it. I tell her, "This is not personal.

The same consciousness that speaks, listens. You are listening to yourself." She once said, "I feel like I'm married to a walking void." I responded, "One thought in your mind called 'Alexis' is relating to another thought in your mind called 'George'. Both thoughts interact with a memory-filled 'I' as their center." She responded, "So, are you telling me I'm married to a thought?" I responded with a chuckle, "Yes." In the beginning, when I had very little balance, these statements understandably frustrated and hurt her very much, but she's inevitably grown more receptive. She sarcastically asks, "Why are you always so honest, can't you just lie and tell me you miss me and sound like you mean it or pretend you want something from me just to make me happy?" It's a rather humorous dynamic at times. My daughter Adriell calls me weird when I "get in Zen mode," which she loves to call it, but expresses her love for Zen mode and wants to get in Zen mode herself. When one person in a family becomes more conscious, it has unpredictable repercussions that can swing wildly in any direction. Sometimes it works, sometimes it doesn't. Sometimes it doesn't work initially, then works eventually and vice versa. Whatever the case, never assume it easy or desirable for others, especially those close to you.

None of the life purposes I carried were capable of allowing true joy, peace, love and unity. Not finding love out there, building a family, being successful in the eyes of society, taking action on climate change or whatever would have come next. Of course, there is nothing wrong with pursuing such endeavors. What do all of these purposes have in common? They are typically sought after in the future as some misleading source of identity and lasting fulfillment. Many people only stop living for the future once they are on their death beds and have no more "future" to live for. They are either forced into the past and become so-called grumpy old people or forced into presence and portray strong elements of lightness, peace, transparency, possibility, joy, inner acceptance, love and wisdom. Those who are forced into presence, especially those who are on death row or whose days are officially numbered by the doctor, realize deeply the words of Sensei Carl Genjo Bachmann who said, "This is it. No matter how much the mind wishes it were otherwise." You don't need to wait to "lose your future" to be present. You have the power to abide in a state of presence now.

Trying to figure out the meaning of life is a distraction. This is why I said, "This book is not meant for philosophical discussion." As Nisargadatta said,

"There is no need to turn round and round in endless questioning; find yourself and everything will fall into its proper place." When you are fully present, all questions disappear as you realize the end result of what you hope to attain through such questions already presents itself in the absence of such questions. Sure, we can say the meaning of life is to be here now primarily as consciousness and secondarily as a human. We can say the meaning of life is to realize there is no meaning and be at peace with the unknown. We can say the meaning of life is to disidentify from the body and mind and disappear into love. We can say the meaning of life is to realize who we are beyond who we think we are. There are many "meanings" we can assign as an answer. Ultimately, these are just more thoughts for the monkey mind, as they call it in the East, to process and play with. We are nearing the end of this book and therefore the end of the need for words and thoughts. They've been fun to play with, but it is time to let them go. It has always been time to let them go, meaning lose our attachment to words and thoughts, and ease back into the Aware Watcher of it all. Rather than look for meaning, simply stay with this moment and all that appears in it. Instead of chasing temporary meaning, it is time to unveil your permanent Being. Watch and watch and watch it all until you realize you are that alert, watchful Presence. As the Bhagavad Gita said, "The goal of evolution is to return to unity: that is, to still the mind." This cannot happen in the future because nothing happens in the future. This can only happen now.

If there wasn't already a spaciousness arising within you, the first chapter would have likely been your last chapter. The egoic mind would have found it quite intolerable to keep reading a book that makes it feel diminished and threatened. With nothing to grasp onto, your ego, if it were totally in control, would have stopped you many chapters ago by whispering, "What's the point of reading this when I can actually learn something useful elsewhere?" This book is not meant to give you anything. It points to your own removal of what seemingly stands in the way of enlightenment. I say "seemingly" because, as Marcus Aurelius said, "What stands in the way becomes the way." This means nothing stands in the way when everything is the way. Let go of your reliance on practices, methods and meditations. Do not rely on time-bound quests with time-bound instructions for a timeless realization. All that has its disposable place, but we are not looking for things that have their place. We are not looking for things or places. No methods. No practices. No meditations. These can be useful, but are never absolutely necessary. Do not mistake anything in this book as necessary. Nothing is necessary to be what you already are. Your belief that you need more method, practice and meditation is in itself the impediment to freedom. They are like rocket boosters that can help propel a space shuttle to the vastness of space, but must eventually be let go or they will turn into a hindrance. Use them until you no longer need them beyond enjoyment. Upon realizing who you are, you realize it was not because of the method, practice or meditation, but the absence of it. All activity requires time whereas the realization of who you are does not. You are timeless and require nothing.

As you transition from someone to no one in particular, you will feel what it means to be the space for what happens. I cannot ultimately explain what this means. Do not look for understanding. Just ease deeply into this moment and allow what is to be. You can only know it by being it. Being it is being transparent to all that happens. Being it is being who you are beyond name and form. If there is physical pain, be the space for it. If there is mental suffering, be the space for it. If a meteorite is heading toward the Earth, be the space for it. Then, you may choose to take action while remaining spaciously present. Your presence is always primary. The action that arises from presence is secondary. Yes, the action matters, but only relatively and temporarily. What is most important is holding the space of presence. Hold this frequency. Be this frequency. Know it is always here and now. Know it requires no effort. If you cannot be the space for what happens, then be the space for your attachment to what happens. Be the space for your reaction to what happens. You always have that next chance; however, do not purposely seek out challenges to be the space for them. It won't be long until life presents a challenge. Do not wait for it either. Just be here now. Instead of being in the here and now as some isolated fragment, be the here and now. Feel the innermost Being of all that appears in this moment by feeling your innermost Being. Once you feel it within yourself, you sense it everywhere because it is the very essence of all that is. This is how an alive sense of Oneness is born.

For the universe to be, you must need it to be. Otherwise, it serves no further purpose. This lifetime will be its final sunset. This lifetime will be your final birth. The universe only manifests because the unmanifest eludes you. Realize your true nature – the unmanifested – and you no longer need the universe. The divine purpose of all creation is the destruction of your assumption that you are one of its creations. Everything in the universe exists for this purpose. All the stars for you. All the creatures for you. All the inconceivable mysteries and vastness of space came into being for you to realize who you truly are. This is the magnitude of your importance. In the bottomless depths of inner stillness, you realize the truth of who you are. In doing so, you will no longer seek to understand these insights with the limitations of a conditioned mind. Consciously connected to the universal intelligence responsible for all that is, you will already know.

Forget enlightenment. Forget this book. Forget the next book. You need nothing and need to do nothing. Be still. Be here. Awaken now.

Chapter 22
Who You Are